Praise for *Traffic Secr*

"Controlling traffic is the holy grail for any profitable business. This book is the online formula to create the attention every product needs to thrive."
— Steve J Larsen

"If you have an existing business, then Traffic Secrets *is like throwing gasoline on the fire!"*
— Daniel Rosen, founder and CEO of Credit Repair Cloud

"What's cool about Traffic Secrets *is that the principles are universal. They will help you to build your social media platforms and learn the psychology of sales!"*
— Natalie Hodson, owner and president of NAH, Inc.

"This is the step-by-step playbook for how Russell grew ClickFunnels. If you are doing any type of marketing, you need to get this book!"
— Joe Marfoglio, creator of DIY Entrepreneur

"Traffic Secrets inspired me to try alternative forms of traffic to build a stronger foundation for my business."
— Rachel Pedersen, author of *Unfiltered,*
founder and CEO of The Viral Touch

ALSO BY
RUSSELL BRUNSON

DotCom Secrets

Expert Secrets

All of the above are available at your local bookstore,
or may be ordered by visiting:

Hay House USA: www.hayhouse.com®
Hay House Australia: www.hayhouse.com.au
Hay House UK: www.hayhouse.co.uk
Hay House India: www.hayhouse.co.in

TRAFFIC
SECRETS

THE UNDERGROUND PLAYBOOK
FOR FILLING YOUR WEBSITES AND FUNNELS
WITH YOUR DREAM CUSTOMERS

RUSSELL BRUNSON

HAY HOUSE, INC.
Carlsbad, California • New York City
London • Sydney • New Delhi

Copyright © 2020 by Russell Brunson

Published in the United States by: Hay House, Inc.: www.hayhouse.com®
• **Published in Australia by:** Hay House Australia Pty. Ltd.: www.hayhouse
.com.au • **Published in the United Kingdom by:** Hay House UK, Ltd.: www
.hayhouse.co.uk • **Published in India by:** Hay House Publishers India: www
.hayhouse.co.in

Cover design: Jake Leslie
Interior design: Julie Davison
Interior illustrations: Arturo Alcazar
Cover photography: Brandan Fisher and Erin Blackwell

Cataloging-in-Publication Data is on file with the Library of Congress

Hardcover ISBN: 978-1-4019-5790-2
Tradepaper ISBN: 978-1-4019-7373-5
e-book ISBN: 978-1-4019-5791-9
Audiobook ISBN: 978-1-4019-5792-6

10 9 8 7 6 5 4 3 2
1st edition, May 2020
2nd edition, July 2023

Printed in the United States of America

This book is dedicated to the entrepreneurs whom I have been called to serve: my "Funnel Hackers." You've made it possible for me to do a work that interests me and that I feel is meaningful and worthwhile. This final book in the Secrets trilogy was created to help you find more of the people who are waiting to hear your message. If this book helps you to reach even just one more person and change their life with your God-given gifts, then this work will have been a success.

CONTENTS

FOREWORD

"Twenty-five thousand dollars. Do I hear thirty?"

The voice of the auctioneer was fast, and the suspense built as the bidding got higher and higher.

"Yes," I said.

"Thirty thousand dollars from the black-haired gentlemen in the front."

"Forty," a voice behind me said.

"Forty thousand dollars from the man in the back."

"Forty-five," I said.

"Forty-five thousand dollars!"

I couldn't see who was bidding against me, but when the auctioneer finally arrived at $50,000, I decided to stop bidding.

To my surprise, so did the person behind me. The auctioneer yelled out, "Number 27, you win the bid!"

I was Number 27. I won. I was bidding to name a commercial Virgin Atlantic plane. Yes, I know that may sound pretentious, but it was for a great cause.

About 12 years before writing this, I was at one of Richard Branson's charity events. I had met Richard several years earlier when a friend and I raised a lot of money for his charity Virgin Unite.

At this charity event, I had decided I'd go all in. Richard was paying all the bills for the charity, and 100 percent of the money we donated was going to help those who needed it most.

Well, the gentleman three tables behind me had come to the same conclusion—which is why it was going to cost me $50,000 to name a plane.

After I won the bid, Richard stood up and proclaimed, "Why fight over it, boys? I'll give it to both of you for fifty thousand dollars each! It's all going to charity!"

The person who walked up on stage with me (and who was bidding against me) was a young man who looked 10 years younger than he actually was.

His name was Russell Brunson.

It was the first time I had actually met him in person. What a charming guy he was, there for the same reason as I was: to help people in need.

There were people in the room that day who were super famous, a lot richer, and way more well known than both Russell and me. But he was the guy who left a mark on me.

I didn't really get to know Russell until a few years later, but when I did, I realized he was one of the most humble, smart, ambitious, energetic, and authentic human beings I'd ever met.

What most impressed me was how he talked about helping entrepreneurs grow faster. He talked about them as if they were his children, and with an authentic excitement.

That's very rare in our world today.

Russell's focus was never on how much money he was going to make or how big his business was going to be. He always looked through the lens of how to help people go faster.

He took that energy and passion and cofounded a company called ClickFunnels, which has revolutionized the way people use the internet to turn their ideas into sellable products and services. Russell has truly given people a faster way to make an impact and profit from their ideas.

Russell's passion drove ClickFunnels to become one of the fastest-growing software as a service (SaaS) companies of all time, creating massive impact on tens of thousands of lives around the world.

The overwhelming success people have gotten from using Russell's software and trainings is unprecedented.

But that's not the only reason you need to read this book.

The global economy and how we consume products and information has already changed drastically and will continue to evolve. Those who don't have the necessary skills and capabilities—to sell their products and services, to market their brick-and-mortar company, or to create funnels that brings customers to their doors—will be left behind.

I'm not saying that to scare you.

But understand, I'm not just taking a wild guess.

I see it coming, and I have the same passion Russell does. I've been blessed to be in the self-education industry for over 22 years. I'm a multiple *New York Times* best-selling author, and I've been able to start 13 companies that have generated over a billion dollars in sales.

These opportunities have positioned me at the edge of this world, and I can see the change coming.

Is there any worse feeling than being left behind? Russell Brunson's passion for helping you avoid that feeling is why he wrote this book, and my shared passion is why I wrote this Foreword.

This book reveals the most cutting-edge way to drive eyeballs to your product or service **to help people find you.**

There's a classic movie with Kevin Costner called *Field of Dreams.*[1] It's about building a baseball stadium in the middle of nowhere. The movie is great, but it sends a bad message that people will come simply by something being built.

Unfortunately, too many people in business have taken the concept literally and have decided to run their businesses that way. They think if they build the best product or service, invent the best widget, create the best mastermind, or write the best book, the world will just find it. They think that as long as they build the best product or service, people will just show up to buy it.

The reality is they won't just come.

Unless people know that you exist and you give them a compelling reason to come find you, they aren't coming.

Without good marketing, your ideas will just be that: good ideas. Imagine looking back when you're 80 years old and feeling like you just dabbled with 20 different great ideas but never really made the impact you desired.

It doesn't have to be that way.

Russell's expertise is massive, and he uses all of it in this book to expose the "new" way to drive the right people to your product, service, idea, company, mastermind, or book. He's giving you secrets that no one has revealed in this way before, and he does it in a simplistic manner that makes his lessons easy to absorb and understand.

He reveals exactly how to drive traffic to your business, product, or website.

This is one of those books that, if consumed and applied properly, could be a game changer for your life.

By the time you're done reading this book, you will understand so much more clearly why certain online companies are thriving and why others are struggling.

You will understand why the business you started in the past didn't get the results you had hoped for.

You might also realize the reason why you're already doing so well and learn how you can do even better.

The world has changed. And for those who don't know how to pivot, a life of struggle may lie ahead. Or—less dramatic but equally sad—yours could be a life, a purpose, unrealized. A life in which you don't tap into your next level and you never reach your full potential.

In this powerful book, Russell Brunson opens his heart and shares the tactics and strategies necessary to make sure you reach your full potential.

Hold on tight and discover what it's like to profit, make an impact, and create a company with momentum that thrives in today's world.

—Dean Graziosi

PREFACE

YOU BRING THE FIRE . . .
I'LL GIVE YOU THE FRAMEWORK

On September 23, 2014, Todd Dickerson, Dylan Jones, and I launched a new software company that we naively believed would change the world. The goal was to create a product that would free all entrepreneurs and give them the ability to get their message out to the market, faster and easier than ever before, so they could change the lives of the customers they were called to serve. The company we launched was called ClickFunnels.

A few short months after we launched ClickFunnels, I released a book that I had been working on for almost a decade. I was a first-time author, and because my book was about sales funnels (something that was *extremely* exciting to me, but pretty boring to most others), I was nervous about how people would respond to it. That book was called *DotCom Secrets*, and little did I know that book would become *the* playbook for how to build sales funnels online and was the key to the initial growth of our company. When people understood *how* they could use funnels to grow their companies . . . well, they started using funnels to grow their companies.

A few of the core concepts that I first revealed in *DotCom Secrets* were:

- **The secret of the value ladder,** and how you can use it to provide more value to your customers and make more money from every customer in the process.

- **How to attract your dream customers** that you want to work with and repel the types of customers you don't want to work with so you only spend time serving the people that you enjoy being around.

- **The exact funnels and sales scripts** you can use to convert website and funnel visitors into customers and move them through your value ladder so you can serve them at your highest level.

- **And a whole bunch more . . .**

As Garrett J. White told me after reading the book and applying it to his company: "I already had the fire, but you gave me the framework I needed to grow." Over the next two years, that book became the underground playbook used by over 100,000 marketers to build their sales funnels online.

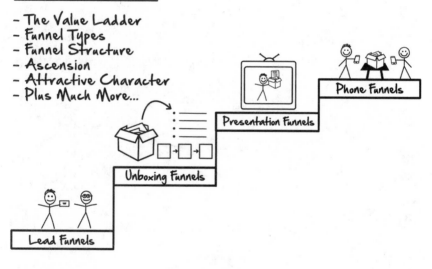

Figure 0.1:

DotCom Secrets helps marketers to build their sales funnels online.

(If you don't have the *DotCom Secrets* book yet, go to DotComSecrets.com to get a free copy.)

But as ClickFunnels grew, I started to see a big division between those who were making money with their funnels and those who made funnels but weren't making any money. People had mastered funnel structure and framework because of *DotCom Secrets* (and they could quickly build those funnels inside of ClickFunnels), but some people weren't making any money because they lacked the basic understanding of how to convert their funnel's visitors into customers. They didn't understand the fundamentals of persuasion, storytelling, building a tribe, becoming a leader, and communicating with the people who entered into their funnels.

And so I began my second book with the goal of helping readers to learn and master the persuasion secrets that are necessary to convert people at each stage of their funnels. While *DotCom Secrets* was the "science" of funnel building, *Expert Secrets* became the "art" behind successful funnels, helping people to move through your funnels and become your dream customers.

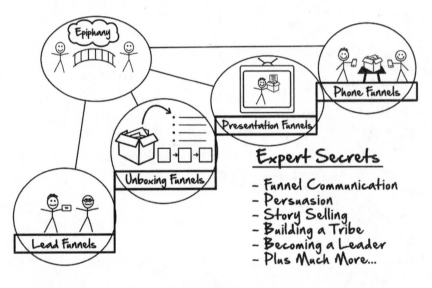

Figure 0.2:

Expert Secrets helps marketers master the art of converting leads into dream customers. (If you don't have the *Expert Secrets* book yet, go to ExpertSecrets.com to get a free copy.)

That brings us to this book, the third and final volume in the trilogy, *Traffic Secrets*. Traffic is the fuel for every successful business. It is the people who are coming into your funnels. The more people you can get in front of, the bigger impact you and your company can have, which, in turn, usually creates more money for your company.

As we watched members of ClickFunnels growing their companies with funnels using the structure from *DotCom Secrets* and the persuasion skills they learned from *Expert Secrets*, many people were still struggling because they didn't know how to get consistent traffic or people into their funnels. On the flip side, those who were getting traffic from Facebook or Google were nervous that if either of their sources dried up, they could lose their company overnight.

Traffic Secrets approaches traffic from a completely different direction than anyone has discussed before: less from the tactical, fly-by-night operations and more from the strategic, long-term model that will ensure a consistent flow of people into your funnels. The strategies inside of this book are evergreen and will never change as long as there are humans on this planet to sell to.

Traffic Secrets

- The Dream 100
- How to Work Your Way In
- How to Buy Your Way In
- Building Your Platform
- Growth Hacking
- Plus Much More...

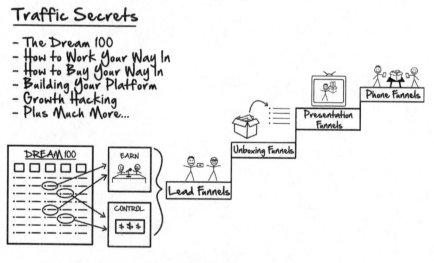

Figure 0.3:

Traffic Secrets helps marketers learn the strategies to drive consistent traffic to their funnels.

Each book in the Secrets trilogy was written as a stand-alone playbook, but mastering the skills from all three books is essential for the long-term growth of your company. Because of that, each book refers to and ties in important concepts from the others.

If you are interested in the most up-to-date information, I invite you to go to MarketingSecrets.com to listen in on my podcast, *Marketing Secrets*. It's published twice a week and covers everything we're learning and discovering in real time. I share new secrets every week for free that build on the evergreen topics and frameworks that you're mastering in these books.

I hope that you can use this trilogy of books to change the lives of the customers you have been called to serve. Everything written in these three books is evergreen and focuses on concepts that have worked yesterday, are working today, and will continue to work tomorrow and forever.

INTRODUCTION

THERE'S A STORM COMING . . .

April 27, 2018, was a day that my kids and I had looked forward to for a long time. It was the opening night of the movie *Avengers: Infinity War*.[2] I've been a superhero fan ever since the first *Iron Man* movie came out, but not long enough to know the entire history from the original comic books, so everything that was happening in the movie was a huge surprise to me. This was the 19th movie in the Marvel Cinematic Universe, and all of the prior movies had culminated into this epic standoff between Thanos and the Avengers.

In the movie, you see Thanos as the ultimate bad guy, but he actually thinks he is doing good. He's concerned that the universe is overpopulated, and he believes it's his mission to save it. His goal is to gather all the infinity stones, put them into his gauntlet (like a big glove), and, when he snaps his fingers, restore balance to the universe by killing half its population.

The movie ended (spoiler alert) with a huge cliffhanger after Thanos collected all the infinity stones and snapped his fingers. In an instant, half the people in the universe disappeared. The next day after watching the movie, I was talking to my friend and fellow online marketer Peng Joon about the movie and he said something that sparked an idea. That idea later became an event and has since resulted in me writing this book.

Talking about the founder of Facebook, Peng Joon said, "Do you ever feel that Mark Zuckerberg is like Thanos, and his whole goal is to wipe out half the entrepreneurs who are advertising on

Facebook? He could literally snap his fingers and half the online entrepreneurs would lose their businesses overnight."

That statement quickly got my mind racing back to 2003, the year I bought my very first Google ad. I had just purchased a book from Chris Carpenter: *Google Cash*. It showed how easy it was to set up Google ads and drive them to any website you wanted! It was simple arbitrage. I would spend $0.25 to get someone to click on my ad, they would go to my website, and I would (hopefully) make $2–3 dollars in sales for each click I received.

At first, it seemed too good to be true, but I decided to set up my first ad in Google selling a DVD on how to make potato guns. When someone would search for "potato guns" or "spud guns" in Google, my ad would show up. If they clicked on my ad (charging me $0.25), they would end up on my website HowToMakeAPotatoGun.com. A percentage of the people who landed on that page would buy the DVD, and I became an instant "DotCom thousandaire." (I wasn't quite a millionaire yet, but if everything kept working the way it was those early days, I would have been in just a few short months!)

But then it happened . . .

People called it the "Google slap," but for me it looked like it was the end to my online career. My costs went from $0.25 a click to $3 per click or more! Instantly, half the online entrepreneurs who were buying ads on Google (including myself) lost their businesses overnight.

Most of the people I knew at that time who were making a killing on Google never recovered from that first Google slap. Most of us were confused about why Google would charge 10 times the prices of our ads overnight. Soon, though, after the dust settled, it started to make sense.

Google only wanted the big brands: the companies who would spend a million dollars a month in ads, not the small guys like me who were just spending a few thousand dollars a month. The small entrepreneurs like myself only made up a tiny percentage of their overall revenue, and we were likely the ones who caused 90 percent or more of their headaches. They didn't care about us; they only cared about the really big advertisers. And what started as the best way for the little guys to have success quickly disappeared when Larry Page and Sergey Brin (the founders of Google) decided to give us small entrepreneurs the slap.

In *DotCom Secrets*, I share that the way I saved myself (and my tiny little company) from this Google slap was by learning how to use funnels. I changed my little potato gun website into a funnel where I could make more money from each visitor who clicked on my ads. Google's costs didn't go down, so I found a way to pay for those costs. I would spend the $3 per click that Google wanted to charge me, and then I would make $5–$6 from everyone who came into my funnel. That strategy is outside of the context of this book, but I write about it extensively in both *DotCom Secrets* and *Expert Secrets*.

After that initial Google slap, the entrepreneurs who survived started looking for other ways to save their companies. Some turned to email marketing and others turned to paid ads on other blogs and websites, but the majority of marketers started getting the bulk of their traffic from Google's free search platform.

We all started to learn how to play that game. We'd get ranked really high for the core keywords that we used to pay Google for, and traffic started coming back to our funnels for free! Again, this seemed like it was too good to be true, but for years this was the secret!

Then one day, just like before, Google decided it was time to change things up once again. The next few years were known for dozens of new Google slaps that affected people who were ranking high in the free search results.

Each morning we would wake up, hoping and praying that we were still ranking for the keywords we had worked so hard to earn, but we were at Google's mercy. Our future was outside of our own control. Each slap would take out another huge percentage of entrepreneurs. Soon, they started giving each of these slaps cute little names like "Panda," "Penguin," and "Hummingbird," but each new slap meant another group of entrepreneurs had to wake up to a reality where their companies had dried up overnight. They had lost all their traffic, and because traffic equaled customers, they had no business.

The decade from the early 2000s to 2010 was a constant fight for most entrepreneurs to stay alive. Then, in 2007, the dawn of a new era of online advertising started when Mark Zuckerberg introduced his new Facebook Ads platform. Just as Google did when they first opened up their platform, Facebook made it easy and affordable for entrepreneurs to buy ads. The costs were low, and arbitrage was simple. Facebook's goal was adoption: to get as many people as possible (and as fast as possible) to use their ads service. And that's exactly what happened.

For people like me, it was like the good ol' days of Google where I could spend $0.25 in ads and make $2–$3 back for each click! Many of the entrepreneurs whom I now coach started their companies around this time and have leveraged Facebook to grow their companies quickly.

But for the marketers who have been around long enough to remember the earlier blood baths that Google and other platforms had put us through, the patterns of Facebook have almost identically matched what Google did when it started.

Step #1) The Adoption: Make the barrier of entry easy to get everyone in and using the platform.

Step #2) The Price Hike: Slowly raise the prices to squeeze out the margins, killing off any entrepreneurs who don't understand how to use funnels.

Step #3) The Slap: Kill off the 50 percent of advertisers who cause 90 percent of their headaches. (If you spend less than $1 million per month on ads, you're considered a small advertiser. You only make up a tiny percentage of their revenue, yet you're 100 times harder to support than a big brand who cares less about ROI and more about just seeing their brand everywhere.)

That day after the movie, Peng Joon and I joked that instead of a Google slap, we were going to see a Zuckerberg/Thanos (we've now nicknamed him "Zanos") *snap*, where 50 percent of all entrepreneur businesses would disappear overnight.

If you rely 100 percent on Facebook for your traffic, then this is your warning that a storm is coming. You should implement everything you read in this book so you can protect your company and thrive during that storm. On the other hand, if the Zanos snap has already happened and you woke up one morning to a dead (or quickly dying) business, then this book is your answer on how to save your company and get it to thrive again.

Over the past decade and a half that I've been playing this game, I've survived (and even thrived) during dozens of Google slaps, the "death" of email marketing, algorithm changes, the rise and fall of tons of social networks, and the fragmentation of online media. The question begs to be asked: Why did we survive when so many other companies have failed?

TWO REASONS WE SURVIVED WHEN OTHERS FAILED

- **We understand how to use funnels.** With funnels, we can make 5–10 times as much money for each visitor who clicks on our ads, so we survive and thrive when costs go up.

- **We have mastered the *strategy*** (not just the tactics) behind getting traffic, and these strategies work on *all* advertising platforms in the past, present, and future. If you master these strategies, then no slap or snap can affect the lifeblood of your company.

There will be another storm soon, just like there was with Google. It's happened time and time again, and we know that the greatest predictor of the future is the past. This storm is headed our way, and thousands of entrepreneurs are unaware.

I feel like I have a moral responsibility to the 100,000-plus members of our ClickFunnels community and to the 1,000,000-plus entrepreneurs who follow me, and to anyone else who will listen to prepare them for this storm. Those who master these strategies will absorb the traffic, customers, and sales of those who were not prepared. Master these principles and you and your company will thrive.

AN EVERGREEN BOOK ABOUT THE FASTEST CHANGING TOPIC OF ALL TIME?

My biggest fear when I decided to take on writing this book was figuring out how to create a book about traffic that was evergreen. After all, how do you teach concepts that will last forever on a topic that changes almost daily? Every book that I've read about traffic in the past 10 years has focused on trendy tactics, which usually became irrelevant within months of being published. Oftentimes they became obsolete before they even got to print.

The tactics behind how to get someone to click on an ad and come to your website literally change daily. In fact, I know people whose full-time jobs are solely dedicated to keeping up to speed with the changes that Facebook makes to its algorithm and Ads Manager. If I try to give you the latest tactic or hack that works today, by the time you read this paragraph, it will likely be *wildly* out of date.

How many of us would have known five or six years ago that Instagram would be the powerhouse it is today? Who could have foreseen that Messenger bots would turn into a really cool thing, then be almost dead in the water for a few months because of Facebook legal troubles, and shortly thereafter come back to life? What social platforms and technologies are still waiting to be discovered that we haven't even yet conceived?

I then started to think about the wake of dead businesses I had seen in the past 15 years. So many entrepreneurs found temporary success because they figured out one way to get traffic or they mastered one tactic (e.g., Google ads or SEO), but then in one quick slap, they lost everything.

I started thinking about why I'd been able not to just survive during each of the slaps, but actually thrive. The more I thought about why we've done so well, despite the constant changes, the more I realized that I didn't learn traffic the way most other entrepreneurs learned traffic.

Normally, most people learn how to get traffic in the following manner. A new website will become popular and quickly grow a big user base where entrepreneurs will see an opportunity where they can buy or earn traffic on this new platform—for example, Twitter or Facebook. A group of early adopters start using it, and they figure out the tricks to leverage the platform to get traffic. For the next few months or years, they use these concepts to mine out tons of traffic at very low costs.

Eventually, more people find out about it and start using these channels. With more demand for this new traffic, the supply goes down, and the platforms start charging more money for each click. An entrepreneur may see the opportunity that this new tactic has created and try to capitalize on it by teaching others how to do it. After learning how to exploit this new traffic, tens of thousands of new people start using the platform. Demand goes up, supply goes down, and prices quickly increase.

Others see the success of this new course teaching this new tactic, and they want in. A few dozen copycat courses come out, and now there's a small army of people selling courses on how to leverage this new type of traffic. Demand goes up, supply goes down, and prices keep going up.

Somewhere in this process, you (or the marketing person on your team) see the ad for the course, so you buy it, study it, and start leveraging this new loophole. How much you are paying for these ads will depend on how early you got in, which also determines how much success you'll have using this tactic. Eventually, the costs will get high enough that most businesses will no longer be able to profitably use these tactics. Those who understand funnels will last much longer because they will make more money from each visitor who clicks on their ads, but this tactic will soon become obsolete.

This process is how most people learn to get traffic to their websites and into their funnels, and that's where the problem comes from. How are you supposed to build your foundation for your company on a slippery slope like that?

The reason I am still here today is because when I started playing this game 15 years ago, there weren't any traffic courses teaching the latest tactics. The people I studied with didn't have the internet when they were growing their companies. The people I learned from were some of the old-school, direct response marketing greats like Dan Kennedy, Bill Glazer, Gary Halbert, Jay Abraham, Joe Sugarman, Chet Holmes, Fred Catona, Don Lapre, Eugene Schwartz, David Ogilvy, and Robert Collier. These guys didn't have the luxury of Facebook or Google; they learned the strategies of driving traffic before there even was an internet! Instead, they drove traffic with direct mail, radio ads, TV, and newspapers.

These direct response marketers forced me to look at marketing and sales in a completely different way than people do today. They trained me on the core strategies of what makes a direct mail campaign work: how to get radio, magazines, or classified ads to profitably drive customers to you. The strategies I mastered during a decade of studying direct response marketing gave me a very different lens which has given my companies the ability to be at the front of the new trends, master the emerging tactics before most people even know they exist, see opportunities that are invisible to most everyone else, and laugh every time there is a Google slap or Zanos snap.

Moving forward, you have to understand that traffic is people, and people are extremely predictable. The core strategies that I'm going to teach you will outlast and supersede any particular platform, so you can apply them anywhere.

THE BIG CHALLENGE

Some of you may be shocked or offended that nowhere in this book—a book entirely about traffic—will you see a single image of the Facebook Ads editor or a detailed explanation showing you how to set up your Google Ads campaign. I didn't put any platform-specific screenshots inside of this book because I wanted this work to remain evergreen for you. The backends of each system are constantly changing, and any snapshot I take today would be out of date before you even started reading.

Instead, we will be focusing on strategies that don't change, including:

- Identifying your dream customers
- Finding out where they are already congregating online
- Learning how to "work" your way in
- Understanding how to "buy" your way in
- Creating your own publishing platform
- Building your own distribution lists

All these strategies have one big thing in common: when the storms come, the user interface changes, or the traffic moves, they will still work! They leverage the big media properties (such as Google, YouTube, Facebook, and Instagram) when they are hot, but also when these platforms change, you can easily move to where the eyeballs go. It worked for me when I was forced to move from Friendster (most of you don't even remember Friendster, do you?) to Myspace to Facebook . . . and it will work when we have to move from Facebook and Google to the next big networks too!

This book will give you the safety and security you need to know that your business, traffic, and leads are all on stable ground. In Section One, you will learn how to identify exactly who your dream customers are, where you can find them, and how to get access to them. In Section Two, I will show you the simple pattern that you can use to drive traffic into your funnels from any advertising network, including Facebook, Instagram, Google, and YouTube. I'll also demonstrate how mastering this simple pattern will unlock the doors to a consistent stream of traffic on any of these networks. Finally, Section Three will reveal powerful growth hacking techniques that will help you to increase your traffic even if you don't have access to Facebook or Google or any other advertising networks.

Mastering these growth hacks will give you the ability to build your traffic foundation on solid ground. I've spent over 15 years learning and mastering these concepts and strategies, and I'm so excited to be able to give them to you right now!

SECTION ONE

YOUR DREAM CUSTOMER

The phone rang. It was Chad. Well, he was Chad to me, but to his patients, his name was Dr. Woolner.

"Hello?" I answered.

"Hey, man. I know it's late, but do you have some time to talk? I'm in a really bad place right now."

"Sure," I quickly responded. "I'll be right over."

Just five years earlier, Dr. Woolner had graduated with his Doctorate of Chiropractic (DC) degree. Shortly thereafter, he moved his family to Boise, Idaho, to work as an associate chiropractor for a new clinic in town. His goal wasn't to work for someone else, though. While Chad is an amazing chiropractor, he's an even better entrepreneur, and he wanted to start his own practice. He went through the process of writing a business plan, getting a small business loan, remodeling a new office, getting logos designed, and everything else that goes into starting your own business.

I knew that business had been slow ever since he had opened his doors, but I didn't know how slow until I got to his office that night.

"I'm not gonna make it," he said. "We're out of money and we have no way to get more patients in the door."

I spent some time talking to him about the situation and gave him some possible ideas to get more business. Then he said something that hit me like a ton of bricks.

"I went to college for four years to get my degree, then I spent an additional four years at chiropractic college to become a chiropractor. In all that time, *not once did they ever talk about how to actually get patients to come to my clinic."*

Isn't that unbelievable? They could lock up an entrepreneur for eight years to teach them a skill, but not even spend 10 minutes showing them how to market that skill. To me, it's the biggest problem with our education system, and it's one of the biggest issues that plague new entrepreneurs in any market. They believe that if they build a great product, or create an amazing company, the customers will automatically follow.

I see entrepreneurs who will invest every last penny they have to create the products and services they think will change the world without ever considering who their dream customers are or how they're going to reach them.

They'll happily invest in coaching, product creation, design, education—almost everything—but when you then tell them to buy ads on Facebook or Google, they freeze. Or when you tell them that they're going to have to put in their own time and sweat equity to get visitors organically, they often think they're above it.

Some think, *My product is so good, I don't need to pay for traffic.*

Still others believe they're entitled to customers because they feel they built a better product than their competitors. So they wait, all the while thinking, *I built it. Why aren't they coming?*

Yet after coaching hundreds of thousands of entrepreneurs, I can tell you that the people who put all their focus on creating something amazing (instead of also focusing on getting people to actually see what they created) are the people that fail. The biggest problem they have is getting their future customers to discover that they even exist. Every year, tens of thousands of businesses start and fail because the entrepreneurs don't understand this one essential skill: **the art and science of getting traffic (or people) to find you.**

And that is a tragedy.

I feel like I have been called and placed on this earth with a mission to help entrepreneurs get their messages out to the world about their products and services. I strongly believe that entrepreneurs are the only people on earth who can actually change the world. It won't happen in government, and I don't think it will happen in schools.

It'll happen because of entrepreneurs like you who are willing to risk everything to try and make that dream become a reality.

For all the entrepreneurs who fail in their first year of business, it is a tragedy when the one thing they risked everything for never gets to see the light of day.

Waiting for people to come to you is not a strategy.

But understanding exactly *who* your dream customer is, discovering where they're congregating, and throwing out hooks that will grab their attention to pull them into your funnels (where you can tell them a story and make them an offer) *is* the strategy. That's the big secret.

The good news for Dr. Wooler is that after that night, he started geeking out on funnels. He built a client acquisition funnel and learned how to buy ads on Facebook and Google. His funnel now generates new patients for him 24 hours a day, 7 days a week, and to this day he has a thriving practice.

I'm assuming that if you're reading this book now, you have a product, service, or a skill that you've focused countless hours mastering. This book will become your education on getting people to actually see your art.

This section of the book will be focusing on answering two very important questions:

- **Question #1: Who is your dream customer?**
- **Question #2: Where are they congregating?**

When you have a *perfect* vision of who your dream customer is, it becomes easy to find where they are congregating. On the contrary, if you don't have perfect clarity on *who* that person is, it's really hard to find them. When you have completed this section, you'll know exactly who your dream customer is and where they are hiding so you can get their attention long enough to tell them your story.

WHO IS YOUR DREAM CUSTOMER?

Figure 1.1:

Each business needs to understand their dream customer avatars better than the customers know themselves.

"I don't know if Alexis will like this," said an executive at Sally Beauty Supply.

Confused, my friend Perry Belcher asked, "What?" He set down his new scented hand sanitizer that he had brought in to pitch at the meeting.

He picked up his new UV nail polish and handed it to the group. "Okay, well, how about this product?" he asked.

They looked at it, opened it up, and smelled it. "Yeah, I'm pretty sure that Alexis won't like this either," they replied.

More confused than ever, and now a little frustrated, Perry brought out his third and final product to pitch to them.

In a similar fashion, they looked at the product, gave it a quick once-over, and then said, "Sorry, Alexis *definitely* wouldn't be interested in this one either."

More frustrated, Perry looked at the two execs he was talking to and finally blurted, "*Who is Alexis?!* Is she the decision maker? Why isn't she in this meeting instead of you two? Is she here? Can I just talk directly to her? I know that I can convince her that your company needs to sell these products!"

There was a moment of silence, and then both of the execs burst out in laughter.

"Alexis isn't a person. She's our customer avatar!" one replied.

"What?" Perry asked. He had never heard of a customer avatar before. "I'm sorry, I don't understand. Alexis isn't a real person?"

The execs just smiled at each other and asked Perry to follow them into another room.

When they entered the new room, he saw a wall full of pictures of "Alexis," a fictitious character who represented Sally Beauty Supply's dream customer. The wall also featured a full bio about who she was, how many kids she had, where she lived, how much money she made, and the type of home she lived in.

The execs then went on to explain that everyone in the company was trained that when they make *any* decision about what products to purchase, what colors to use in the stores or their branding, what ads to run, what promotions to create, what their websites looked like, and what music to play in their locations, *everything* was run through the lens of Alexis's eyes.

If it was something that Alexis would love, then the answer was yes. If it wasn't something she would love, then the answer was always no.

They didn't run a product-centric company; they ran a *customer-centric* company.

Their customer avatar is what drove everything from the products they created to the ads that they ran.

When Perry first told me this story, I had my big "aha"!

Most entrepreneurs mistakenly think that their business is about them, but it's not. On the contrary, your business is about your customer.

If you want customers (traffic) to come into your funnels, then you have to be able to find them online. And if you want to find them online, then you have to start to understand them at a much deeper level.

BECOMING OBSESSED WITH YOUR DREAM CUSTOMERS

The first step in this process is to become obsessed with your dream customer. Companies that become obsessed with their products will eventually fail.

As we've grown ClickFunnels, I've seen this happen time and time again. Every company we competed against—even though some of them had hundreds of millions of dollars in funding behind them—eventually lost to us because they were busy focusing on their product while we became obsessed with our customers.

What do I mean when I say obsessed? Being obsessed with your customer means understanding them just as well, if not better, than they understand themselves.

For many, this is the most difficult part of the process, even though you may have actually been your "dream customer" not too long ago. Often, just remembering how you felt when you were trying to solve the very problem you're now solving for people is usually hard.

I was recently talking to my friend Nicholas Bayerle about the fact that most businesses are created from a problem that an entrepreneur had, and their product or service was the result of them figuring out the solution to that problem. "Our mess becomes our message," Nicholas said.

When you're frustrated about a problem you're having, you look for a solution. If you're not able to find a solution that gives you the result you want, then you'll likely go on a journey to find or create your own solution. In that way, your problem becomes your business; in other words, your mess becomes your message.

If that's true, then you need to look back in time to find the point where you were struggling with the same problem your dream customer has now. Then you need to remember what you were feeling when you were in that pain.

In our community, we have so many amazing examples of leaders who have made their mess their message, and one of my favorite power couples is Stacey and Paul Martino. Years ago, they found themselves at a crossroads. Their relationship was broken. Paul had tried for months to stay, but eventually, he felt so much pain that he decided to leave. As he broke the news to Stacey late one night, she broke down and cried. Her relationship was over, and the pain she felt was too much to bear.

I won't tell their full story here, but the short version is that because of this experience, Stacey knew that to save her relationship, she needed to change first. She put in the work to transform herself, and in the process of her changing, Paul changed as well. After saving their own marriage, they developed a unique process to heal marriages that doesn't require "couples work." Instead, they believe that it takes just one person in a relationship to change it for the good.

Their mess became their message and now they have dedicated their lives to helping others find relief from the same pain that they felt years earlier. With their unique system and tools, they've helped to save thousands of marriages. In a society where more than 50 percent of all marriages end in divorce, the students who go through their program only have a 1 percent divorce rate.

Stacey and Paul are successful at finding and helping their dream customers because just a few years ago, they were their dream customers. Because they really, deeply understood the pain, they could identify their dream customers' goals and aspirations and could identify where they were congregating to help move them toward those goals. They are a product of their product.

In the early 20th century, Robert Collier published one of the great books on copywriting, *The Robert Collier Letter Book*. In this book, he shares how to really understand your customers. If you're going to find them, persuade them to follow you, and hopefully change their lives with the products and services you sell, you need to know and understand them better than they understand themselves.

Collier believed that we as marketers should not be trying to figure out how to create the next amazing ad campaign, but instead we need to learn how to *"enter the conversation already taking place in the customer's mind."*[3]

If you want to really understand who your dream customers are and where they are congregating online, you need to be able to enter the conversation that is already taking place inside of their mind and see the world the way that they see it.

When you truly understand the core pains they are trying to move away from and the core desires and passions they are trying to move toward, it becomes very easy to identify exactly where they exist online. As soon as you know where they are online, then you can hook them and bring them into your funnels where you can serve them. We will go into greater detail on how to do that throughout the rest of the book.

Now that we have the foundation covered, let's dive into identifying your dream customer with the 3 Core Markets, sometimes known as the 3 Core Desires.

THE 3 CORE MARKETS/DESIRES

Figure 1.2:

People purchase products hoping to get a certain result from one of these 3 core desires/markets.

In *Expert Secrets*, I introduced the concept of the 3 Core Markets, or the 3 Core Desires. The three desires (in no particular order) are health, wealth, and relationships. When people purchase any product from anyone, they're hoping to get a certain result in one of these three areas of their lives. So the first question you need to answer is this:

> Which of these three desires is my future dream customer
> trying to receive when they buy my product or service?

This is the first layer to getting inside the mind of your dream customer, and for most people the answer is pretty simple. However, sometimes people get stuck on this question for one of two reasons.

Reason #1 — My product fits into *more* than one of these desires: Many products can be marketed toward getting a result in more than one of these desires, but your marketing message can only focus on *one* of them. Anytime you try to get your potential customer to believe in two things, your conversions will usually cut in half (most times by 90 percent or more). To target two different desires, you need two different ads leading to two different funnels. Only focus on one desire with each message you put into the market.

Reason #2 — My product doesn't fit into any of these desires: This false belief was best resolved at one of our recent events where someone told one of my head coaches, Steve J Larsen, this exact same thing. Steve responded by telling the story of Gillette razors and asking which desire a razor fulfilled.

At first everyone was quiet, and then a few people started guessing. "Health?" Another mumbled, "Or maybe . . . hmmm . . ."

Steve then played one of Gillette's ads. In it, you see how a story develops. First, a man is shown shaving. After the shave, a beautiful woman gets closer to him. Then the two go out for a night on the town. Finally, the ad shows the two together back home in their room.

After showing the ad, Steve asked the question again a little differently, "What desire was this marketing message created for?"

Instantly everyone responded, "Relationships!"

Most products can fit into multiple categories, even if they may look as if they don't fit into any category at all, but no matter what, the key is that your marketing message can and must be focused on only one of the 3 Core Desires. I want you to take a few minutes and decide which of the 3 Core Markets or Desires your product or service currently fits into.

AWAY FROM PAIN/TOWARD PLEASURE

Figure 1.3:

All humans either move away from pain or toward pleasure.

Now that you've identified which core desire your product or service is focused on, the next step to entering the conversation inside your customer's mind is to understand which direction they are moving. Every human being on this planet is always moving in one of two directions when they make a decision: away from pain or toward pleasure.

Moving Away from Pain: The first direction that people can be moving in is away from pain. Let me show you a few examples of moving away from pain for each desire.

Health (moving away from pain)

- I'm overweight and don't feel comfortable in my clothes.

- I don't have energy and feel tired all of the time.
- I hate what I see when I look into the mirror.

Wealth (moving away from pain)

- I hate my job and want to fire my boss.
- I have no money saved, and I'm scared I could lose my job.
- Everyone around me makes more money than I do.

Relationships (moving away from pain)

- I'm in a bad relationship and don't know how to get out.
- I feel alone and want to feel what love feels like.
- I feel awkward when I'm around people I don't know.

Each of those statements above are conversations that people are having inside of their own minds. While these are broad examples, when I actually wrote down the thoughts that my particular dream customer was having, I did three things to try to understand the conversation that they were having with themselves each day.

1. I wrote out hundreds of phrases that I used to say to myself when I was trying to solve the problem for myself initially.

2. I looked online in forums, message boards, and groups to see what others are saying when they are trying to get out of pain.

3. I really tried to put myself in their shoes and wrote out what I believed people were thinking.

EXERCISE

For this exercise, I want you to write down at least a dozen things that your potential future customers are saying or thinking as they're trying to move away from pain. This exercise is something you should be continually doing every day. I'm always looking for the questions and statements that people in my market are saying as they try to move out of their pain.

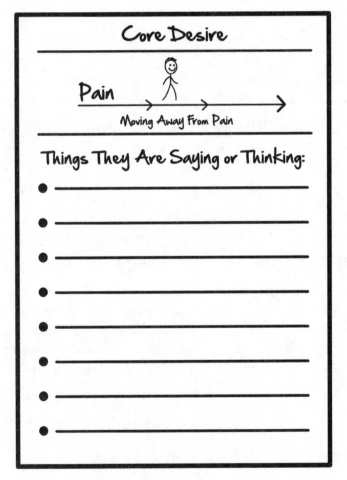

Figure 1.4:

Exercise: Write down all the things your dream customers
are saying or thinking as they move away from pain.

Moving Toward Pleasure: The second direction that people can be moving in is toward pleasure. They don't have a desire for health, wealth, or relationships because they are unhappy; they have a desire because they are happy and looking for more. Let me show you a few examples of moving toward pleasure for each desire.

Health (moving toward pleasure)

- I want to get six-pack abs.
- I want to be able to run a marathon.
- I want to eat healthier so I can get more energy.

Wealth (moving toward pleasure)

- I want to buy my dream house or dream car.
- I want to grow my company so I can have more impact.
- I want to learn leadership so I can grow my team.

Relationships (moving toward pleasure)

- I want more passion in my relationships.
- I want to spend more time with my spouse and kids.
- I want to meet more people through networking.

Do you see how different these phrases are even though they are addressing the same core desire? I wanted to put them together in a chart so you could see them side by side. It's powerful to see that while everyone may be trying to accomplish the same goal, the reasons why they're doing it are almost polar opposites.

MOVING AWAY FROM PAIN   MOVING TOWARD PLEASURE

Health *(moving away from pain)*	Health *(moving toward pleasure)*
• I'm overweight and don't feel comfortable in my clothes. • I don't have energy and feel tired all of the time. • I hate what I see when I look into the mirror.	• I want to get six-pack abs. • I want to be able to run a marathon. • I want to eat healthier so I can get more energy.
Wealth *(moving away from pain)*	**Wealth *(moving toward pleasure)***
• I hate my job and want to fire my boss. • I have no money saved, and I'm scared I could lose my job. • Everyone around me makes more money than I do.	• I want to buy my dream house or dream car. • I want to grow my company so I can have more impact. • I want to learn leadership so I can grow my team.
Relationships *(moving away from pain)*	**Relationships *(moving toward pleasure)***
• I'm in an abusive relationship and don't know how to get out. • I feel alone and want to feel what love looks like. • I feel awkward when I'm around new people.	• I want more passion in my relationships. • I want to spend more time with my spouse and kids. • I want to meet more people through networking.

Figure 1.5:

While two people's goals might be the same, their reasons for accomplishing that goal might be completely different.

EXERCISE

Now I want you to spend a few minutes doing this second exercise. Write down at least a dozen phrases that people in your market who are moving toward pleasure may have running on a loop in their head.

Figure 1.6:

Exercise: Write down all the things your dream customers
are saying or thinking as they move toward pleasure.

The more phrases you can find, the more traffic streams you'll
be able to tap into, so make it a continual process to identify and
write down the conversations happening inside of your customers'
minds. And as you'll see in the next secret, understanding the

phrases that are going on inside of your customers' minds in both directions (moving away from pain or toward pleasure) will guide you to finding them.

THE SEARCHER AND THE SCROLLER

To really understand how to use the conversations that are going on inside of the minds of your dream customers, we need to go back in time a few hundred years before the internet, before TV, and before radio to where traffic began.

Until the early 1800s, people mainly obtained products based on what they needed. They would be in some type of pain, and they would search for a solution to solve it. It started with food. Our ancestors had a desire for health (food), so they would search for food, kill it, and bring it home. In more modern times, we have stores. When you need food or something else at your home, you go to the local store, search for what you need, and buy it.

In 1886, the Yellow Pages directory was created, and it was awesome for consumers because you could find exactly what you needed, and business owners had the luxury of people simply showing up, looking for what they had to sell. It seemed like the perfect solution, except for one thing: as a business owner, if you wanted to make more money or grow your company, you were not in control. You had to wait for people to have a need in order for them to come and find you.

But then, in 1927, the television was invented, and just 15 short years later, on July 1, 1942, during a Brooklyn Dodgers–Philadelphia Phillies game at Ebbets Field, the first-ever TV commercial aired.[4] At the time, there were over 4,000 televisions in New York, and that day, while families gathered around to watch the big game on NBC, it was interrupted by the first-ever TV commercial. That ad, which was just nine seconds long and cost only $9, featured a map of America with a Bulova watch clockface in the middle. At the end of the ad, a voice announced, "America runs on Bulova time." And with those nine seconds, the shift from search advertising to interruption advertising had officially begun.

People watching TV that night were not searching for a new watch, but as they saw the commercial and the picture of the watch, it placed a seed of desire in their hearts and minds. They didn't need this watch, but they wanted it.

This TV commercial gave business owners a window where they could grab their potential customers' attention long enough to plant that seed of desire and show the perceived value of what they were selling. No longer would people only buy when they needed something; now advertisers had the ability to create desire and sell people stuff that they wanted.

This interruption advertising started happening in other types of media such as radio, newspapers, and direct mail. The process was simple: get a captive audience, entertain or educate them, and then, when you have their full attention, interrupt them with your message. You can then grab their attention and create desire for the product or service that you are selling.

Nowadays, this type of interruption advertising happens every day around you, but I'm guessing you don't realize how profound of an impact those advertisements actually make on your buying decisions. To show you how effective interruption advertising is versus traditional search advertising behind the scenes, I will share a story from my friend Trevor Chapman.

Trevor used to run a big sales team of people who sold alarm systems door to door. At the time, if you were to go to Amazon and search for "home security systems," you would quickly find hundreds of options, each one competing on price. If someone had a need for an alarm and went to Amazon to buy it, usually they would buy the cheapest one that still had the highest ratings.

Trevor then compared people searching online for home security systems to what his sales team did every day. He explained, "We would go down the street and knock on people's doors and interrupt them from their day. Minutes earlier, they had no desire for a home security system. Because we interrupted them, though, we had a small window where we could make a presentation and show them the perceived value of our home alarm system. This presentation would create a desire in them to buy the alarms from us. We would then make them a special offer that they could only get from us, right there, right then. In less than an hour, we'd walk away with a monthly monitoring contract that would be worth over $2,999 to us in the next five years as opposed to the $199 version they would get by buying the alarm on Amazon."

It's interesting to note that when the internet started a few decades ago, it followed a very similar pattern. It began with searches. People had some type of need, usually to get out of some type of pain, and they would immediately go to the search engines looking for a solution to their problems. Later we were all introduced to social media through platforms including Myspace, Facebook, and Instagram; and just like the Bulova ad in 1941, in 2007 Facebook announced the first-ever social interruption advertising with Facebook Ads. People would be online talking to their friends, posting pictures, liking images and videos, and then suddenly, your ad would show up in their Facebook feed. You'd have a small window of time to grab their attention, create a desire for your product or service, and make a special offer.

Figure 1.7:

People will either be searching for your product (left), or you will interrupt them (right) to get their attention with your ads as they are scrolling.

Pros and Cons for Search: The pro for search-based traffic is that when they come to you, they're hot buyers who are ready to buy. This is similar to people who walk into your store or find you in the Yellow Pages and give you a call.

The con with search-based traffic is that they're not just searching; they're also comparing options with your competitors. You've got to be the price leader, as well as the quality leader and the niche leader. People who are searching are also researching all those things, so until you become good at funnels and offers, you'll likely be trying to beat your competitors by lowering your prices. Unfortunately, trying to be the cheapest product is never a good strategy.

Pros and Cons for Interruption: As a marketer, you can target people who are interested in certain people, ideas, TV shows, or bands, and then you can interrupt them with your ads. You open a small window of time where you can grab their attention and show them the perceived value of what you're selling. You no longer have to wait around for someone to come looking for you. Now you can create desire in your dream customers.

The pro for social-based interruption traffic is that you can target warm traffic based on people's interests. Therefore, you can sell based on the perceived value of your product or service.

The con for social-based interruption traffic is that because the customer isn't actively looking for you, you have to become good at your "Hook, Story, Offer," where you can grab their attention, tell them a story, and then make them an offer. We will be covering how to do this in more detail in Secret #3.

Now that you've identified who your dream customer avatar is, what their core desires are, and if they are moving away from pain or toward pleasure, the next question we want to ask is "Where are they congregating?" As you will learn in the next chapter, there are congregations where the scrollers are hanging out, and congregations you can target for the searchers.

WHERE ARE THEY HIDING? THE DREAM 100

One day in college, I knew I was supposed to be doing homework, but my ADHD mind couldn't take it anymore. I had to stop writing, even if it was just for a few minutes. I looked around to make sure no one else was looking, then I opened a new tab on my browser.

I started typing *www.TheMat.com* and then, within seconds, I was taken to a new universe: a universe occupied by hundreds of thousands of wrestlers just like me, all around the world. This was our playground where we could talk about wrestling, post pictures and videos, and debate about who was going to win every match happening at the next big tournament.

I read a few articles and watched a video showing a new way to finish a single-leg takedown. Afterward, I went to the forums. Oh, how I loved the forums! *Who is better? Dan Gable in his prime or Cael Sanderson now?* someone had just posted. Of course, I had an opinion, and it took everything I had not to spend the next 90 minutes writing my thoughtful response about how if we shrunk Cael down to Dan's size and took him in a time machine back to the '70s, Cael would have destroyed Dan head to head, but I knew I couldn't. My paper was due the next day, and I was locked away in study hall until it was done. Angrily, I closed down the tab and sat back in my chair to stretch before I made the trip back to reality.

As I was leaning back, I started looking at my other wrestler friends who were locked away in study hall with me because of our bad grades. As I glanced toward our 133-pounder, I noticed a smile on his face. *What? How could he be smiling in study hall?* As I shifted my gaze from his face to his monitor, I saw it. He was also on TheMat.com, and he was writing his comments on why he thought Dan would actually beat Cael!

Then, looking at the other wrestlers in the room, I decided I had to know what they were doing. Faking that I had to go to the bathroom, I stood up and started to walk past their desks. I looked at our 157-pounder's screen. Yup, he was looking at TheMat.com too. The 178-pounder? TheMat.com! *But what about our heavyweight? He* has *to be actually doing his homework, right?* Nope, he was also on TheMat.com, and as I passed his computer, I quickly read his forum reply that Bruce Baumgartner (two-time Olympic heavyweight champ and four-time Olympic medalist) would beat both Dan and Cael at the same time.

WHAT!?! Was he crazy? There was no way that Cael would lose to Bruce . . . That's when it hit me. TheMat.com was our little corner of the internet. All the wrestlers in study hall were congregated on that website talking about wrestling, but we weren't the only ones. Wrestlers in other colleges across the country, along with high school wrestlers and their parents, were on the website too. All around the world, hundreds of thousands of people were all together in this one spot to talk about the topic that we loved most: wrestling.

Honestly, that is the real power of the internet: it has allowed us to connect with like-minded people in a way that wasn't possible before. It's allowed each of us, with our unique and sometimes weird hobbies and interests, to congregate with *our people* to discuss the things that mean the most to us.

It wasn't always like that, though. When I was in high school, we didn't have TheMat.com, so the only people we had to talk to about wrestling were the other few dozen wrestlers in our school. But we weren't the only group. High school was full of different groups, like the basketball players, weightlifters, jocks, band members, and kids who played *Magic: The Gathering*. Before the internet, groups like this were limited in size to how many people they could find that had the same interests and were located geographically near them.

Pre-internet, it was expensive for a marketer to sell products and services to each of these small groups. After all, how do you target just those people in every city who were interested in what you have to sell?

If you had a huge mass market product, like shampoo or pain killers, you could run ads on TV and know that mostly everyone who saw your ads probably had hair or got headaches sometimes, but it was way too expensive to run an ad for wrestling shoes or training DVDs and pray that the dozen wrestlers in each city actually saw the ad.

But the internet changed everything. It took the dozen wrestlers from my high school, and every other school around the world, and put them together in one spot. If wrestlers were my dream customers and I had a product to sell to them, I didn't have to run huge mass media campaigns. Instead, I could go directly to TheMat.com, or wherever they were congregating, and just buy ads there, knowing that 100 percent of the people who actually saw my ads were people interested in wrestling! Instead of wasting money showing my ads to millions of people who would not want or need my product, I could make sure that *only* my dream customers would ever see what I'm selling. This targeting has cut ad costs down to a tiny fraction of what people used to have to spend to get access to their dream customers. This is what has made it possible for smaller businesses like ours to compete against, and oftentimes even dominate, the biggest brands.

This same principle is true no matter *who* your dream customer is. The internet has made it so that when you find those existing congregations of your dream customers, it's like catching fish in a barrel. You simply have to find the barrel of fish with your dream customers and throw in your hooks. If your hook is good, it will pull people from that barrel into your funnels!

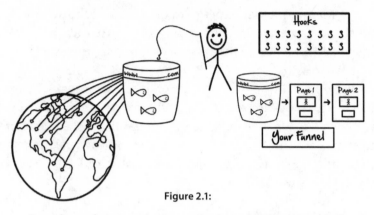

Figure 2.1:

To catch your dream customers, you simply need to throw out enough hooks in an area where your dream customers are congregating.

With Secret #1, you identified your dream customer, and with Secret #2, you can locate where they're hiding or congregating. If I was selling a product to wrestlers, I shouldn't be asking, "How do I get traffic to my funnel?" Instead, I should be asking, "Where are my dream customers (in this case wrestlers) congregating?"

EXERCISE

Here are some questions you should be asking yourself at this point:

- What are the top websites that my dream customers already go to?
- What forums or message boards do they participate in?
- What are the Facebook groups they engage in?
- Who are the influencers they follow on Facebook and Instagram?
- What podcasts do they listen to?
- What are the email newsletters they are subscribed to?
- What blogs do they read?
- What channels are they following on YouTube?

- What keywords are they searching for in Google to find information?

These questions will help you to start identifying *where* your dream customers are hiding. The answers to these questions should be simple, especially if you are your dream customer.

When I launched ClickFunnels, it was easy for me to find startup entrepreneurs (i.e., my dream clients) because I was a startup entrepreneur! I started looking at where I was already congregating (which podcasts I was listening to, which blogs I read, which email lists I was on, etc.), and instantly I knew exactly where my future dream customers were hiding.

If you don't truly understand your dream customers (everything we talked about in Secret #1), then it will be hard to find them. But if you *really* understand them, then you should already know where they're congregating to get out of pain and where they're congregating to move toward pleasure. And when you know where they're congregating, it's pretty easy to put your messages or your hooks in front of them and pull them into your funnels.

One of the common misunderstandings with traffic is that you have to "create" traffic, but, as you can now see, that just isn't true. Traffic (your dream customer) is already there. Your job is to identify where they are, tap into those existing streams of traffic, throw out some hooks, and then get a percentage of your dream customers to start coming to you.

THE DREAM 100 (ONE TO ONE)

Now that you understand that traffic already exists and isn't created, I wanted to share with you a concept I learned from one of my friends, Chet Holmes, called the "Dream 100."[5] He wrote about it in detail in his best-selling book, *The Ultimate Sales Machine*. The way that Chet teaches and uses the Dream 100 is a little different than how I use it, but understanding Chet's model will open up your ability to get unlimited traffic into your funnels.

Early in Chet's career, he worked for Charlie Munger, whom you may know was Warren Buffett's business partner in Berkshire Hathaway. Chet sold advertising for one of the company's legal magazines. At the time, they were really struggling; they were last in sales in their market. Chet was working with a database of over 2,000 advertisers. He made sales calls every day, but they were still dead last at number 15 out of 15 magazines in their industry.

Then one day Chet had an idea. He did some research and discovered that out of those 2,000 advertisers, 167 of them were spending 95 percent of their advertising budgets with his competitors. So he defined those 167 spending all the money in the industry as his best buyers. Then he stopped marketing to everybody else and focused his time and efforts on those 167 advertisers. His strategy included sending out direct mail pieces with lumpy objects in them every two weeks, where he followed up on each package with a phone call. Twice a month he'd mail a package, and twice a month he'd call.

Because these were the biggest buyers, they were the hardest people to reach. After four months of following this strategy, he got zero responses. (Pretty discouraging, right?) Chet was known for what he called PHD (Pig-Headed Discipline), though, and he refused to give up.

Then, in his fourth month, something changed. He landed his first big account: Xerox. It was the biggest advertising buy ever for the company. By the sixth month, he had landed 28 of the 167 advertisers. And with those 28 advertisers, Chet doubled the sales over the previous year and went from number 15 in the industry to number 1. He kept doubling sales for the next three years in a row. By the end of year three, he had successfully brought in *all* 167 of his Dream 100 as advertisers in their magazine.

Chet said, "The goal of the Dream 100 is to take your ideal buyers from 'I've never heard of this company' to 'What is this company I keep hearing about?' to 'I think I've heard of that company' to 'Yes, I've heard of that company' to 'Yes, I do business with that company.'" Chet grew that company by using the Dream 100 to create one-to-one sales opportunities.

Chet also used this same strategy to penetrate Hollywood. He had written a screenplay called *Emily's Song*, and he had decided he wanted to try to sell the screenplay to Hollywood. The only problem was he didn't know anyone in the entertainment field. So he bought an issue of *Premiere* magazine that listed "The 100 Most Powerful People in Hollywood," which became his Dream 100 list. He used the same Dream 100 process to contact these people, and within months, he was able to get LeAnn Rimes to read the script. Together, they went to Warner Bros., where the screenplay was purchased!

THE DREAM 100 (ONE TO MANY)

Chet Holmes's Dream 100 for "One to One" selling strategy is powerful when your business model needs a small number of big customers. But for most of us, we're looking for *lots* of customers, not just 100. When I was starting out, many of the things I sold weren't very expensive, so it didn't make financial sense to send packages and make phone calls to try to sell a $20 product. That's why Chet's Dream 100 concept didn't make sense when I first heard it; I couldn't see how it applied to my online business. In fact, initially, I completely dismissed the concept and figured it didn't apply to companies like mine.

One day, though, as I was writing *DotCom Secrets* and thinking about how I was going to sell the book when I was finished writing it, I identified *who* my dream customers were that would want to read my book and *where* they were congregating. I made a list and wrote out *everywhere* that I could think my dream customers might be gathering. On that list I identified:

- 10+ top websites and forums they spent time on
- 15+ active Facebook groups they participated in
- 50+ influencers they followed on Facebook and Instagram
- 30+ podcasts they listened to
- 40+ email newsletters they subscribed to

- 20+ blogs that they actively read
- 20+ YouTube channels they subscribed to

After making the list, I added up how many subscribers, readers, and followers each of those channels had. I was so excited to find out that there were over 30 *million* of my dream customers on that little list alone, all congregated inside of those 185-plus communities!

Next, I tried to figure out how to get my message in front of those 30 million-plus people. I brainstormed ideas, and that's when the bolt of lightning hit! *The Dream 100!*

No, I couldn't do a Dream 100 campaign to all 30 million-plus people because it would cost too much. After all, I was trying to sell my book for $7.95, so if I did get a yes from a customer, it was only worth $7.95 to me. But what if, instead, I did a Dream 100 campaign to the owners of those 185-plus communities asking them to promote my book to their audience? If I could build a relationship with one of them and get just *one* yes, that could turn into hundreds or thousands of new customers!

So that's exactly what I did! I found the contact information for those 185 people, and I sent them each a copy of my book in the mail with a letter asking if they'd be interested in helping to promote my book on launch day. Within a week of sending out the packages, I started to get messages back. One message was from a podcaster on my Dream 100 list whom I'd been listening to for years but had never actually met: John Lee Dumas from EOFire.com. He told me he loved my book, and he asked me to be on his podcast to talk about it. I quickly agreed, and, within a few days, I was being interviewed by John Lee Dumas. He asked about my book, told people why he loved it, and then he told them to go buy a copy. Within a week of that episode airing, we had sold over 500 books from that one interview alone!

I didn't stop there, though. I kept following up with my Dream 100, and not only did I get on other blogs and podcasts, but people also promoted me in their email newsletters and more! I ended up landing over 30 of the 185 people as promotional partners.

The second part of the Dream 100 strategy (covered in more detail in Secret #4) works even for those who didn't respond or weren't willing to promote my book. Advertising platforms like Facebook allow you to target your ads to people with certain interests. For example, Tony Robbins was in my Dream 100, and while he didn't directly promote my first book, he did directly promote *Expert Secrets* after over 10 years of being on my Dream 100 list! However, even though he didn't directly promote *DotCom Secrets*, I still wanted to market to his (at the time) 3.2 *million*-person audience, as they were my dream customers too. On Facebook, I was able to buy ads that were only shown to his audience, and we were able to sell thousands of copies of my book to his people!

Our launch campaign for my book may have seemed massive from the outside as we sold over 100,000 copies in a very short period of time, but in reality, we just put a concentrated effort to market to the dream customers of 185 people.

Recently, I was at a mastermind event in Puerto Rico, and I had a chance to spend time with Rachel Hollis, the author of the #1 *New York Times* best-seller *Girl, Wash Your Face*. At the time, she was in the middle of launching her new book, *Girl, Stop Apologizing*. As I was in the middle of writing this book, I was curious about how she had sold over a million copies of her books. I asked her for the secret to selling that many copies, and she told me:

> We asked ourselves this question: "What are the tribes that my women are already in? What network marketing companies are they in? What Facebook groups . . . what Instagram channels . . . what hashtags are they following?" After we identified these things, we tried to figure out who are the tribe owners of these women. Who do we need to become friends with? Anyone who had over 200,000 followers, we would direct message (DM) them, tell them who we were, and ask them if we could talk. We started messaging everyone. Our focus was to find the tribes, and then figure out the best ways to infiltrate them.

The Dream 100! She didn't call it that, but that's *exactly* what she had done to quickly become one of the best-selling authors of all time! Now, I know what some of you are thinking, *Russell, this may work for you and Rachel when you're selling books, but I sell something different, so the Dream 100 can't work for me.* It always makes me laugh when people think these concepts will work for every business except their own, when the reality is that this concept works for every business. Period. Let me share some more examples.

Recently, I was listening to the *Foundr* podcast. They were interviewing Tom Bilyeu, the founder of Quest Nutrition, who had started his business with a few friends and quickly grew it into a billion-dollar company. During that interview, he was asked how he grew Quest Nutrition, and Tom replied:

> We had a very different approach that got a lot of people excited. Not just about the product, but they felt good about the way we treated them. We went old school, researching several hundred health and fitness influencers, then sending them handwritten letters and free samples. This was all about showing an understanding of what others were trying to achieve, and that Quest was interested in helping them connect with their audience.
>
> When people are building a community, they have a real sense of service to that community. We would send them free product and just say, "If you like it, tell people, and if you hate it, tell people that too." Not trying to steer people's comments gave us a pretty great recommendation. Some didn't like it and said so, but the vast majority loved it and were grateful we had showed an understanding of who they were and what they were trying to do, so they spread the word.[6]

Tom didn't realize it, but the Dream 100 struck again! It's the strategy that almost all successful companies (oftentimes without realizing it) are using as the backbone of their traffic strategies. When most people hear the title of *Traffic Secrets*, they assume I'm just going to show how to run Facebook or YouTube ads. While those tools are great, they're just small external tactics of a much larger strategy.

The core strategy to understand is that your dream customers have *already* been congregated by your Dream 100. If you focus on identifying them and marketing to them, your dream customers will start flowing into your funnels faster than by anything else you could do.

A DIFFERENT DREAM 100 ON EACH PLATFORM

A few years ago, I decided to rebrand my podcast from the *Marketing in Your Car* show to the *Marketing Secrets* show. When we did this, I set it up as a new podcast and invited all my old listeners to resubscribe and join me on the new show. I had a lot of my faithful listeners move over to my new podcast, and then I brainstormed other ways to grow my show. I first started by leveraging the traffic that I own. I sent emails to my lists asking them to subscribe, sent out messages to my Messenger lists, and posted on Facebook, Instagram, and about everywhere else that I had a voice. This did get a big influx of listeners as all my true fans came over and plugged in.

I was so excited about the immediate growth that I figured this initial surge would be all we needed as the catalyst that would grow the show. Unfortunately, it wasn't. In fact, the show quickly flatlined, and then it started to shrink. I was completely freaking out, wondering if I made a mistake starting a new show.

After I sat in my office with a few of the people on my team brainstorming for hours about how to get our podcast to grow and what things I could do to get people to share my message, it hit me, the big *"aha"*! It was so simple in my head, but as I blurted it to my team, it sounded stupid.

"People who listen to podcasts . . . Well, they listen to podcasts!" I said.

"Yeah . . . um . . . I'm not sure where you're going with this, Russell," my team responded.

I half laughed. "Think about it. We're trying to get people who love Instagram to move to Apple to listen to us. While our best fans did come, the majority didn't. Why? Because people who are on Instagram love to consume content on Instagram. The same is true for our blog: our superfans will move from Facebook and other places to read our blog, but our best blog readers are people who read other blogs. People who love to watch YouTube videos love to watch videos on YouTube, and people who listen to podcasts listen to podcasts.

"We can spend a ton of time and money convincing people on these other platforms to move to podcasts, or we can spend that same time and money focusing on the people who are already listening to podcasts. If they find a new show they love, they'll listen every day!"

That was the big "aha" that set into motion our strategy for building a special Dream 100 list just for our podcast through the other podcasts that our dream listeners were listening to. It also caused us to build out Dream 100 lists for every platform we've talked about already.

You see, prior to this big "aha," we only had one big collective Dream 100 list with people from all the platforms. We hadn't respected the fact that people like to consume media in their own favorite ways, and while it's possible to move people from one platform to another, there is much less resistance when you just migrate people to you who are already on the platform that they love.

WHAT ABOUT "BRICK-AND-MORTAR"- TYPE BUSINESSES?

At this point, some of you may be thinking, *But Russell, I'm not selling a book or a product online. I'm a local brick-and-mortar business trying to generate local leads online, so this won't work for me.* For all my brick-and-mortar business owners, don't worry, this strategy still works, even though you will need to look at it a little differently. When building your Dream 100 list, instead of identifying the national influencers or leaders in your niche, you need to identify your local influencers.

For example, if I owned a local juice bar, I would ask myself: Who is my dream customer and where are they already congregating? My dream customer would be someone who is trying to get healthier. To find these dream customers, I would create a list of the local gyms, health food stores, chiropractors, personal trainers, nutritionists, etc., and then start building my Dream 100 from that list.

We'll show more examples of how these concepts work for brick-and-mortar businesses throughout this book, but I wanted to address it quickly here before some of you thought that this concept wouldn't work for you.

CREATING YOUR DREAM 100 LIST

THE DREAM 100

Figure 2.2

If you would like to print the Dream 100 Worksheet for your own use, go to TrafficSecrets.com/resources to download your copy.

The next step is for you to build out your Dream 100 list. Everything we do from this point forward from paid ads to free traffic to joint ventures will all build from this core foundation of the Dream 100. But for some reason, even though I've been talking about this concept for years and it seems easy enough for people to understand, very few people ever sit down to do the work and actually build it out.

If you were to hire me today for a $100,000 consulting day, the first thing I would do with you is spend the first three to four hours building out this list. That is how important it is, so don't skip it! Yes, it's simple, but it's the foundation to everything!

In my friend Dana Derricks's book *The Dream 100*, I wrote the foreword, which includes:

> As the CEO and cofounder of the fastest growing, non-VC-backed software company in history, hitting nine figures in under three years, it would seem difficult to narrow down the ONE thing that really propelled us to where we are more than anything else . . . But, it's not. It's the Dream 100. The Dream 100 is the foundation for our entire company.
>
> At ClickFunnels, we don't just leverage the Dream 100 approach for traffic . . . we use it for EVERYTHING. How do we pick the market we want to enter? We use the Dream 100 to research different markets and niches, then we narrow in on the ones that suit us best. How do we decide on our blue-ocean strategy? We use the Dream 100 to find the red oceans and carve out our place in the market. How do we create our offers and figure out what's going to sell? We use the Dream 100 to model offers that are working in our marketplace, which takes out the headache and hassle of "blind guessing."
>
> Everything we've done has come off of mastering the Dream 100 and, specifically, knowing how to complement as opposed to compete. That's how you build your foundation. From there, you just get traffic (again, tapping into the Dream 100) . . . and the rest is history . . . The Dream 100 is where ALL traffic leads (whether it's Facebook Ads, integration marketing, you name it) to and from. It all circles back to the Dream 100. If there's one area to invest as much time and money into your business as you possibly can, from the beginning, it's the Dream 100.[7]

You see, the Dream 100 is the key foundation for traffic *and* the key foundation for your entire business because it helps you to figure out how to position your offers and tell your stories. I cover this extensively in *DotCom Secrets* and *Expert Secrets*, but I want to impress upon you here how important this key step is.

THE TWO CORE TYPES OF CONGREGATIONS

As you're building out your Dream 100 list, there are a few important notes I want you to remember. In Secret #1, we talked about how there are two ways that your dream customers will find you: either they're going to search for you or they're going to interact with things that interest them where *you* will interrupt them. I make these same two distinctions when I'm trying to identify where my dream customers are congregating.

Interest-Based Congregations: The first type of congregation is based on interests. In most social networks, after someone joins, the first thing the network tries to do is figure out what things you're interested in. Facebook is believed to automatically track over 52,000 data points on each user as they are using their platform, which is super annoying as a user but super awesome for us as advertisers.[8] On top of that, advertisers have the chance to select the interests that people follow, such as:

- Who are the people (influencers, celebrities, thought leaders, authors, etc.) you are following?
- What companies are you following?
- What movies, books, and brands are you following?

On the Dream 100 worksheet, I put a column for each of the main social networks. Depending on when you are reading this book, there may be new networks that have become super popular and/or some of these networks may be dead, so you should adjust the columns as needed. What matters most is that you are making a list of all the people, companies, movements, and interests that your Dream 100 are already following.

Start with your favorite social network and try to write down between 20 to 100 Dream 100 names for that network. Then do the same thing for podcasts, blogs, email newsletters, and any other important types of congregation. Although we call this the Dream 100, I like to try to make my list as big as possible, and I re-create my list two to three times per year as I pull off names that aren't bringing us the right customers and add new names as we find them.

After you've filled in as many names in the Dream 100 interest-based columns as you can find, then move on to the search-based congregations.

Search-Based Congregations: When someone goes to Google or any other search platform, they type in a keyword phrase looking for something like:

how to lose weight

emergency plumber Boise Idaho

best water filters

As soon as they type a phrase, they enter an existing congregation of people searching for the same thing. Before I created my first product (How to Make a Potato Gun), one of the first things I searched for was how many people were currently searching for phrases around that topic.

potato gun

spud guns

potato launchers

potato gun plans

At that time, there were over 18,000 people per month searching for all these phrases. Of course, that was a while ago, so the number has probably increased dramatically. In my case, this congregation of people were looking for something that I had the solution for.

This type of congregation is called a search-based congregation, and searches can occur on Google, Yahoo, or any other search platform. Some popular search platforms at the time of this writing are Quora.com, where people can ask questions on any topic; Pinterest.com, where people search for images; and YouTube.com, where people search for almost everything! (Later on, I'll show you how YouTube and a few other search platforms serve as both search *and* interest-based congregations.)

EXERCISE

To create your Dream 100 list, write out the phrases that you believe people are actively searching. There will be many ways that we will refine and use these congregations, from buying ads to doing SEO to getting those people's pages that are listed to push people into your funnels for you, but, for now, just build a list from your best guesses. We'll discuss some amazing software tools later to help you identify phrases you might never have thought of on your own, and we'll also explore how to find out how many people are searching for each phrase. For this exercise, though, I want you to write out the phrases offhand that you think either you or your dream customers would search for each day.

WHERE DO I START?

I've found that most people can grasp the concept of the Dream 100 pretty quickly, but when they try to actually find 100 people, they get stuck. Oftentimes they are able to build a dream dozen, but they struggle to get more than that.

At the end of the day, traffic is a numbers game. I want to find 100 (or more) people because even with 100 people, we may only get 5 to 10 of them who are willing to let us get in front of their audience for free. After that, we may only get 10 or so others for whom we're able to successfully target their audiences on the ad networks, so it's essential that you cast a wide net.

The easiest way to build a larger list is to go back to Secret #3 in *Expert Secrets*, where we explore the 3 Core Markets or Desires.

I'll quickly re-explain it here so you can see how it ties into the Dream 100.

It starts with the 3 Core Markets or Desires: health, wealth, and relationships.

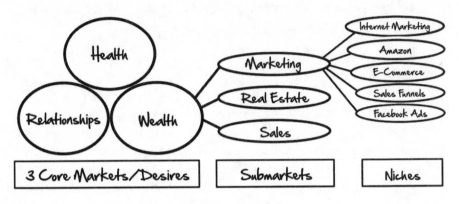

Figure 2.3:

Inside of the 3 Core Markets/Desires are submarkets and niches.

Each of the three markets have an unlimited number of submarkets. For example:

- Wealth → finance, investing, real estate, sales, marketing
- Health → nutrition, strength training, weight loss
- Relationships → marriage advice, dating advice, love

Inside each of the submarkets are the niches. So, for example, if my market is wealth, my submarket would be marketing, and the niche that I would create is "sales funnels."

- Wealth → marketing → sales funnels

Other niches inside of the marketing submarket could be marketing through e-commerce, Amazon, dropshipping, SEO, PPC (pay per click), Facebook Ads, or online courses. Honestly, other niches in my submarket would include any way that someone would use the internet to market or create a new business.

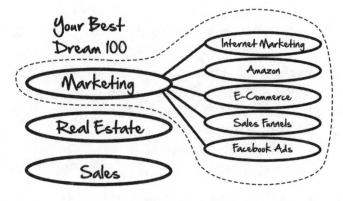

Figure 2.4:

To find your best Dream 100, look outside of your niche
and into your submarket for the warmest traffic.

With that in mind, when I build my Dream 100, I'm not just looking for other people who are selling "sales funnels" stuff. I do add those people, companies, and keywords to my list, but what I'm really looking for is all the other people, companies, and keywords that are within my submarket. They are my warmest traffic and where I focus first.

My goal is to provide my Dream 100's followers with my new opportunity. I can usually build my Dream 100 from this list pretty easily. But if you're struggling to identify all the niches within your submarket, just ask yourself this question: **What other vehicles are people trying to use to (insert result they desire) with (insert your submarket here)?** To illustrate this even further, let me give you some real-world examples.

- **In the WEALTH core market** with a real estate submarket, I'd ask: "What other vehicles are people trying to use to make money inside the real estate submarket?" The answers to these questions would include: house flipping, short sales, and wholesaling.

- **In the HEALTH core market** with a weight-loss submarket, I'd ask: "What other vehicles are people trying to use to get six-pack abs inside the weight loss submarket?" The answers to these questions would include: Keto diet, vegan diet, meatatarian diet, and bodybuilding.

- **In the RELATIONSHIPS core market** with a parenting submarket, I'd ask: "What other vehicles are people trying to use to have a better relationship with their kids inside the parenting submarket?" The answers to these questions would include: homeschooling, baby sign language, after-school sporting programs, and drama.

Each of these answers is a niche within a submarket with dozens of influencers, companies, and keywords that you can target! Your submarket is where you should focus all of your Dream 100 efforts initially because this is your *warmest* traffic.

After you've finished filling in your Dream 100 worksheet, then you'll be ready to discover the Hook, Story, Offer framework that you'll be using over and over again to pull people from your Dream 100 into your funnels.

HOOK, STORY, OFFER, AND THE ATTRACTIVE CHARACTER

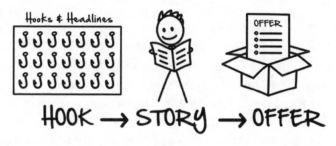

Figure 3.1:

Every piece of good marketing has a hook, a story, and an offer.

It was 9:27 P.M., and the last of Jessica's kids had just fallen asleep. It had been a long day that started way before the sun came up, and it was finally ending. While Jessica was exhausted, it was *her* time now, as she had a few precious moments to herself without kids pulling her in a million directions. Soon she would have to start her nighttime routine of cleaning up the house, getting herself ready for bed, taking off her makeup, and finally falling asleep for a few hours, before she had to wake up and start it all over again.

As she fell onto the couch, she reached into her pocket and slowly pulled out her phone. *What's been happening in everyone else's life today?* she wondered. She opened Facebook and swiped through the lives of her friends and family, hoping to find some comfort knowing she wasn't the only one who had a busy day.

Soon she started to get bored. But when she was about to close the app, she saw an image fly past her screen. She almost missed it, but she slowly moved her finger back up her phone, bringing the picture into the middle of the screen.

Yep, she thought she saw that right. It was a picture of a woman about her age in workout clothes, with gray shorts on. The thing that caught her eye wasn't the shorts, though—it was the dark gray spot in the middle of the shorts. A little confused, she looked above the image and read the words:

> Let me tell you about that time I peed my pants during a workout . . . I was filming for Dollar Workout Club and I have never been so embarrassed before.

Jessica was right! It was a picture of a grown woman who had peed her pants! She laughed for a second, but then that laughter turned into uneasiness as she realized that she knew exactly how this woman had felt. She had experienced the same thing earlier that year when her kids had wanted her to jump on the trampoline with them. She wanted to be a good mom, but after a few jumps she had to get off because she had peed her pants. She had quickly come up with a reason why she couldn't jump anymore, and after apologizing to her kids, she had run into the house to get changed. She knew the story she had told her kids wasn't true, which added to her mom guilt even more. This also made her think about other activities that she knew she would love to do but were off limits for the same reasons.

After a few seconds of looking at the image, Jessica decided that she wanted to see why in the world this woman would post a picture of herself on Facebook telling others that she had peed her pants. She clicked on the image and was immediately taken to a page that had a video from the same woman in the picture.

Jessica clicked on the video and started listening to the story. The woman's name was Natalie Hodson, and she was a fitness blogger and mom of two amazing kids who were both 10-pound babies. Natalie told her embarrassing story of when she accidentally peed her pants during a workout she was filming for her blog! She then talked about a doctor that she had met who specialized in helping women with this problem. She shared how this doctor was able to help her, and after she had success, she wanted to share it with other women.

Natalie mentioned she had worked with the doctor to create an online program that anyone could do from home with simple exercises to strengthen their abs, core, and pelvic floor. Together, Natalie and the doctor made an e-book that also came with bonuses like diet and nutrition tips, exercises and movements, and specific training programs. They wanted to make this offer for all the moms who had struggled with accidental leaks after having babies, but didn't have the ability to meet with the doctor in person. Instead, you could get the same advice without ever leaving the comfort of your home. And you could get the e-book and all of the bonuses mentioned for just $47.

Excited, Jessica jumped off the couch and ran across the room to find her credit card. After typing in her credit card numbers, within minutes, she had access to the e-book that would solve her problem forever.

Even though Jessica's story is fictional, this type of experience does happen each and every day to women who are embarrassed when they accidentally pee their pants a little bit when they cough, sneeze, or even jump on a trampoline. Over the past three years, over 120,000 women have purchased Natalie's e-book. This has made Natalie Hodson a household name, given her the ability to change the lives of countless women around the world, and made her very wealthy in the process.

The framework that Natalie used to get over 120,000 people to buy her book *Abs, Core, and Pelvic Floor* is called Hook, Story, Offer.

The hook is the image and the headline that Jessica saw as she was scrolling through her feed. It hooked her and stopped her just long enough to get her attention. It then asked Jessica to click on a link, which gave Natalie a moment to tell her story, build a relationship with Jessica, and explain the perceived value of the offer she would be making. Finally, Natalie made her an irresistible offer that would help Jessica to get out of pain and move toward pleasure. This Hook, Story, Offer framework is the pattern that you'll see over and over again in most ads and funnels online.

HOOK, STORY, OFFER

This framework of Hook, Story, Offer is something I talk about often. It's the core foundation for how we sell anything online. It's how we diagnose what's not working in every funnel that we set up. If an ad isn't working, it's always because of the hook, the story, or the offer. If a funnel isn't converting, it's always because of the hook, the story, or the offer. It really is that simple and probably the most important framework that I am teaching you to master.

In *DotCom Secrets* and *Expert Secrets*, I spend multiple chapters talking about Hook, Story, and Offer, where I fully explain how to make irresistible offers and the frameworks we use for story selling. I will be talking about Story and Offer in this chapter in relation to traffic and ads, but *Expert Secrets* is the definitive guide for mastering these concepts. With that said, let's jump into the Hook, Story, Offer framework.

Hook: Now that we know exactly where our dream customers are congregating, our job is to throw hooks to them to see if we can grab their attention. In the next secret we'll be talking more about *how* to do that, but for right now, I want you to understand *what* a hook is.

The hook is the thing that grabs someone's attention so you can tell them a story. You see thousands of hooks every day. Every email subject line is a hook, trying to grab your attention for just a moment so you'll read that email. Every post, picture, and video you see in your feed on Facebook is a hook that is trying to get you to engage so they can tell you a story and then make you an offer. Every picture on Instagram, thumbnail on YouTube, and headline on a blog is a hook designed to grab your attention. We see hooks all the time, yet it's hard to define exactly what they are. Are they words? Yes, they can be. Are they images? Yes, they can be. Are they the backgrounds of your videos? Or the goofy things you do in the first three seconds to get someone to stop scrolling? The answer is yes. Anything that grabs someone's attention is a hook, and the better you get at creating it and throwing it into your Dream 100's congregations, the more attention you will get.

I always picture my end customer sitting on the toilet or lying in bed, or sitting on the couch in the moments of their day that they are alone, holding their phone, scrolling through their feed on Facebook or Instagram. What hooks can I throw out that will cause them to stop scrolling and listen long enough to hear my story? Pay attention the next time you're scrolling to what hooks grab your attention. Why did you stop? Why did you click play? What did the hook say, and how did it make you feel? Answering these questions will help you to become amazing at developing hooks.

Story: After the hook grabs their attention, you now have a small window to connect with them through story. There are two core goals from that story that you are about to tell them.

- The story will increase the value of the offer that you are about to make. By telling the right story (or "epiphany bridge" stories, mentioned in *Expert Secrets*), you can show the perceived value of what you're selling and the story will create a desire for them to buy now.

- The story will build a connection with you as the Attractive Character and your brand. Even if someone doesn't buy something today, if they connect with you, they will become your follower, and then your customer, and eventually your raving fan. Your stories will help them to build a relationship with your brand.

Your personality (or "your Attractive Character," mentioned in *DotCom Secrets*) is becoming more and more vital to the success of your traffic campaigns. Anyone can throw up an ad and get someone to buy once, but if you are willing to share your stories, build a connection with your audience, and actually serve them instead of only selling them something, they will continue to buy from you over and over again. They will become your advocates and share your message and your ads with their friends.

Offer: The hook gets your customers' attention, the story creates desire, and the last step of every message, post, email, and video is the offer. The offer doesn't always mean asking people to buy something amazing, although this is my favorite type of offer. The offer could be as small as telling them if they "like this post" or "comment on my video" or "subscribe to my podcast" or "join my list," you'll give them a special thing in exchange. The better the offer is, the more likely someone is to do the thing that you actually want them to do.

If people aren't doing what you want them to do (joining your list, clicking your ads, or buying your stuff), the simplest way to fix it is often to increase the offer. For example, if I tell you that I'll give you $1.00 if you take out the trash, you may say no, because that effort isn't worth $1.00 to you. But if I increase the offer and tell you $10, you may say yes. If I increase the offer to $1,000, that offer would be too good for almost anyone to say no.

The same thing is true with your ads. If you hook someone, tell them a story, and make them an offer and they still don't buy, it's likely that the offer isn't good enough for them. You may need to tell a better story to increase the perceived value of the offer, or maybe you may need to make a better offer. Add more bonuses, increase how much they get, make it sexier—whatever they need for the offer to be irresistible.

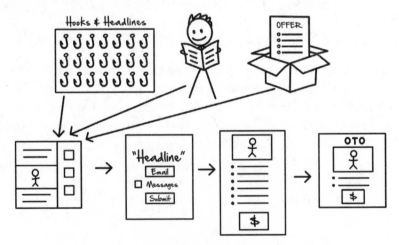

Figure 3.2:

Every page of your funnel needs a hook, a story, and an offer.

Yes, each ad has a *hook* (the image or video or headline that gets people to stop scrolling), a *story* (the thing that you show after you have people's attention) and an *offer* (typically, what they are going to get if they click the ad). If you can show customers what's in it for them, you will have success utilizing the strategies taught inside of *Traffic Secrets*.

If any of your traffic campaigns aren't working, it's *always* the hook, the story, or the offer. If the conversion on your landing page isn't working, it's *always* the hook, the story, or the offer. If the attendance to your webinar, the close rate on your pitch, your upsell take rate, or your email open rate is not working, it's *always* the hook, the story, or the offer. And if you want to solve all these problems, create better hooks, tell better stories, and make better offers.

WORK YOUR WAY IN, BUY YOUR WAY IN

It was just weeks before we were going to "officially" launch ClickFunnels.com to the world. For the past 12 months, my cofounder Todd Dickerson had spent almost every waking moment painstakingly writing tens of thousands of lines of code. I had spent every last penny I had earned trying to keep the doors of my little company open so we could feed our families, all the while waiting for the launch of our new company that we believed would change the world. It was almost go time.

With one month left, Todd and our other cofounder, Dylan Jones, flew to Boise to grind out the last 10 percent of the code before we went live. Fueled by Red Bulls and a fire to see their baby come to life, they would code each night until 3:00 or 4:00 A.M., go back to their hotels for a short nap, then be back to the office by 9:00 A.M. These were the days that I would never forget.

As the "nontechnical" cofounder who had no skills in code, I wasn't able to help during these hack-a-thons, but I knew my role. When the cart opened on launch day, I needed to have a pipeline of people waiting and begging to sign up for their free trials. So while Todd and Dylan were coding, I was working on the Dream 100. For every platform, I would research and find the people who already had my dream customers, add them to my list, and send them messages to introduce myself. My Dream 100 list grew into my Dream 200, then my Dream 500. By the time ClickFunnels was ready to go live, it had become my Dream 736. I remember looking at that list the day before the launch, thinking that these people had already congregated my dream customers and already had relationships with them. I just had to figure out ways to get my message in front of these audiences.

Looking back, just five years since that moment, it's amazing to see how far we've come in such a short period of time. This morning, as I'm writing this chapter, we just passed 100,648 active, monthly paying customers using ClickFunnels. The majority of those members, my dream customers, came from the followings of the 736 people that I identified as my Dream 100.

Now, if you skipped the exercise in Secret #2, please stop here to go back and do it. It's the key to filling your funnels with traffic. Remember, if you hired me for a $100,000 consulting day, this is the very first thing I would have you do. If you need help doing it, pretend you just wired me $100,000 and then go and do it. The reason I emphasize this so much is because I've seen the companies that make eight and nine figures a year complete this vital step.

STEP #1—DIG YOUR WELL BEFORE YOU'RE THIRSTY

Now you have your Dream 100, and they have your dream customers. The next question you should be asking yourself is the same question I asked myself: "How do I get my message in front of their audiences?"

The first key to the Dream 100 is that you need to dig your well *before* you're thirsty. In his networking book, *Dig Your Well Before You're Thirsty*, Harvey Mackay explains that if you want to build a business relationship with someone that's worthwhile, you have to start it before you're ready to make the deal.[9]

The most common mistake that entrepreneurs make when they start their Dream 100 is to wait to start building relationships with those people until their product is ready. As soon as I identify someone as being part of my Dream 100, I immediately start digging my well. I personally do this in a few ways.

First, I subscribe to everything that my Dream 100 are publishing. If they're on your Dream 100, they probably publish on at least one, if not many, different platforms. I'll listen to their podcast, read their blog, watch their stories on Instagram, and join their email newsletter because there will likely be a time in the near future that I'll have the chance to actually speak to them. I've met people in the past who have somehow made it through all of my gatekeepers and got a precious few minutes of my time, and I've figured out within seconds that they didn't know who I was and only cared about what they thought I could do for them. These conversations never turned into anything fruitful for either of us. To avoid that situation, do your homework so that when your moment comes with your Dream 100 person, you're prepared to talk about *them*. Ask them questions about their life, things they post, and topics they care about.

I also watch what my Dream 100 are publishing because, in the future, I might be creating ads for these same people. If I know the things that an individual member of my Dream 100 are saying to their followers, I can model the same language patterns in my messages.

Usually, when I tell people to subscribe to everything, they kind of freak out because they don't want to join over 100 people's email lists, subscribe to over 100 podcasts, or follow over 100 influencers on Instagram. After all, it would take several hours a day to manage that, right? But the truth is it actually won't.

For the email newsletters, I create a new email address that is set up specifically for my Dream 100 campaign, and I use that new email address to join everyone's list. I make a filter that pushes each person's emails instantly into a folder so my inbox stays clean. That way, when I'm about to call or message a certain person, I can log into that email account, click on their folder, and quickly look at the last dozen or so emails and catch up on what they are publishing.

I also only use my social apps (YouTube, Instagram, Facebook, etc.) for two purposes: to produce and publish content, and to spy on my Dream 100. I don't use them to be "social," because this is the fastest way to ruin your life. Okay, not really, but seriously . . . from this point forward, you should never look at yourself as a "consumer" of social media but as a "producer" of it. You produce content and you pay close attention to what your Dream 100 is doing on each of those platforms. That's it. Personally, I spend about 15 minutes twice a day quickly swiping through each app to keep my finger on the pulse of my market, and then I close my phone down and get back to producing.

After subscribing to my Dream 100's content, I try to buy some of their products. This allows me to see their funnels and what they're selling on their backend and get a good idea of what they are doing. We call this process "funnel hacking," where you go through their sales process to get ideas of what is working in this market as well as being able to get on their customer lists to see what types of things they send to their customers. When you're a customer, you can tell them why you love their products. Few things build rapport better and faster than being able to tell someone that you're a happy customer.

The third and last thing I do is look for ways that I can serve my Dream 100. Remember, right now I'm not asking them to do anything for me. I'm digging my well before I'm thirsty to see what I can offer them. One of the best things I can do to help someone after buying their product or listening to their podcast or reading their blog is to talk about it socially. I may make a post on my Facebook wall or on my Instagram stories talking about an awesome podcast I heard or product I bought, telling other people that they should go buy it while tagging my Dream 100 person in the post. I've found that this is one of the easiest things I do to get someone's attention and provide value to them, but it could be anything from sending them a gift to creating videos or images that they could use for their own marketing.

This process may seem like a lot of work—and it is—but it's the foundation for your entire company. Not only is it the foundation for getting traffic, it's also the best way to figure out your place in the market's ecosystem. What value do you have that you can provide to this market that is different? What problems are being unsolved by the others in your Dream 100 that you are uniquely qualified to do? Seeing what your Dream 100 is promising and trying to sell to your dream customers, what hooks they are putting out, what offers they are making, and what beliefs your market has, will become the best market research you could ever do to figure out what the gaps are in the market and what offers you need to create.

As discussed, when we launched ClickFunnels, I had built a very large Dream 100 list. My first goal was to dig my well before I was thirsty, which is a key step to do before you "work your way in." I started doing this through four very strategic phases:

Phase #1 (Day 1–14): I started the process of following my Dream 100 by subscribing and listening to the content they were pushing out. During my twice-a-day, 15-minute social media binges, I would watch what each of my Dream 100 were doing, and then I would look for things that resonated with me. I would quickly comment on what they were publishing, sharing what I thought was special, and looking for ways I could serve them.

Phase #2 (Day 15–30): I would then contact my Dream 100 (via email, direct message, etc.) and open up a dialogue. My goal was *never* to pitch them anything during this time.

Currently, I conservatively get over 1,000 messages a day among all my social platforms, and there are some huge red flags that keep me from responding to people, as well as a few green lights that give me an open door where I'll actually respond.

- **Red Flag #1: Don't send a templated message.** So many times I see the copy/paste emails that have been sent to 500 other "influencers" that day, and these messages don't get a response. Write each person a personal message or don't send anything at all.

- **Red Flag #2: Don't tell me your story yet.** There will be a day and time that your Dream 100 will care about your story, but it's not with the first message. You telling them your story is them serving you, and you have not built up the reciprocity yet. Serve first, or they will never have a chance to serve you later.

Pretend like you are trying to date your Dream 100, because you kind of are. Treat them right, and one good relationship can be worth millions of dollars to you. But now that you've seen the red flags, let's talk about some of the green lights that make me want to respond.

- **Green Light #1: This isn't the first time I've ever seen your face.** Most of your Dream 100 spend time publishing things they believe in, and if you don't think they read the comments on the things they publish, you're wrong. Make sure that they've seen your face actively participating in meaningful ways in the discussions they create, so when they see you pop in their inbox or as a direct message, they recognize you. During this phase you are selling you to the Dream 100, not your product. If they don't like you, they'll never want to know more about your product.

- **Green Light #2: They tell me how great I am.** I know that sounds shallow, but come on, there's a reason we're doing this. I personally feel very uncomfortable when people give me direct praise, especially in front of people, but I *love* reading it in comments or messages, and I remember the people who tell me how what I'm doing has impacted them.

- **Green Light #3: They've done their homework.** They know who I am and what I care about, so when we do talk, they ask me about stuff that's important to me. When people ask me about my wife or kids or wrestling or things that I'm really passionate about, I relate to them differently and I remember who they are.

- **Green Light #4: They don't ask for anything now.** Just don't do it. Trust me. If you ask too early, the answer will always be no. There will be a time, but that time is not now.

Phase #3 (Day 31–60): Make your Dream 100 your fan. I never ask someone to promote something for me if they haven't experienced it. When we were launching ClickFunnels, I gave my Dream 100 free accounts, no strings attached, so they could use the product. When I was launching my books, I sent free copies. With my courses, I provided free access. Your best promoters will always be your biggest fans.

After I have plugged into each person in my Dream 100 and started the process of digging my well before I'm thirsty, there are now two ways that I can get my message in front of my Dream 100's audiences. First, I can "work my way in" by getting traffic that I earn. Second, I can "buy my way in" by getting traffic that I control. Let me show you how each of these work.

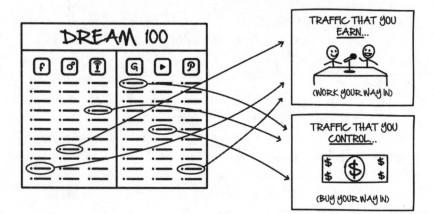

Figure 4.1:

You can get traffic from your Dream 100 by working your way in and/or buying your way in.

STEP #2—WORK YOUR WAY IN (TRAFFIC THAT YOU EARN)

I want you to think about the last big blockbuster movie that you were excited to see. Usually, it starts with a movie trailer getting leaked online. From there, they start showing that trailer before all the other movies leading up to the premiere. With all that marketing, I think that most of us consumers are aware it's happening. But then, usually about a week out from the big day, the covert marketing strategy that pushes everyone to watch the new movie on opening night begins. Hollywood knows that if they don't fill the theaters on launch day, then the sales for the life of the movie will suffer, so they pull out the big guns.

What is Hollywood's covert strategy? Well, it's simply working their way into the Dream 100 just like you do. Their strategy looks a little like this:

Figure 4.2:

To launch a movie in Hollywood, the actors and actresses show up on various TV shows to promote their movie.

Do you notice, what usually happens one week before a new movie or TV series premiere, music album, or book launch? Where do the lead actors, singers, or authors show up? They show up on TV! They put out a hook to grab curiosity, tell a story to create desire, and make an offer to get people out on opening night! That's it! They have their Dream 100, and they're working their way in.

I was talking to Tony Robbins after his last book launch, and he said that between TV, radio, and the internet, he did over 260 interviews during the week he launched his book. While I'm sure that week was intense for him, it helped him sell millions of copies of his books for free by allowing him to work his way into the shows that had already congregated his dream customers!

Now, while it's easy for Hollywood to get booked on the daily talk shows, oftentimes it's harder for smaller entrepreneurs like us. The good news is that you can utilize your Dream 100 in a way that is as powerful as (and sometimes even more powerful than) being on the big, nationally syndicated shows. These shows have a ton of people, but there is no targeting at all. By using your Dream 100, you're able to have your interviews shown to the exact target market who is likely to buy your product or service.

Figure 4.3:

You can work your way in to your Dream 100 by appearing on their own shows.

When I launched *DotCom Secrets*, I knew that I was going to spend a lot of money on paid ads (i.e., buy my way into the Dream 100), but I also wanted to get as much free initial traffic as possible. I started by sending a pre-release copy of my book to everyone on my Dream 100, including dozens of podcasters, bloggers, email list owners, and influencers. I wanted them to read the book, and if they liked it, I hoped they would promote it to their followings. A few days later, I sent them a certified letter in the mail (I could have sent an email, but I wanted to make sure I got their attention) telling them that if they liked the book, I would love to have them help promote the book on the launch date. I'd even be willing to pay them $20 for every book they sold!

Almost instantly, I started getting responses from people on my Dream 100 list who had now read my book and wanted to help me promote it on launch day! As I mentioned previously, one of the first to respond was John Lee Dumas from the *Entrepreneur on Fire* podcast! He said he loved the book and would love to do an interview with me about the book and have it go live on my launch day. We recorded an interview in the weeks leading up to our launch, and on our book launch date, his podcast also went live. From that one interview alone, we sold more than 500 copies of my new book! And that result was from just one of my Dream 100! We ended up getting dozens more people to help promote the book on their various platforms. On opening week, we sold tens of thousands of copies, and that book continues to be a bestseller to this day.

When we launched *Expert Secrets*, I wanted to take that same strategy to the next level. We took our Dream 100, and as soon as I had a cover designed for the book, I sent them a copy of the book with 300 blank pages inside. I hadn't started writing it yet, but I wanted them to be aware that I was writing another book. As I got closer to my launch date, I sent them a copy of the book with the first four chapters in it (to help get them excited), and as soon as I had the first, unedited draft, I sent them another copy. They had a chance to see me create this book with them, and because of that, many of them had a vested interest in its success.

We decided about a month before launch to coordinate a "virtual book tour" just like the bigwigs in Hollywood would do if they were about to launch a new movie. I asked each of the Dream 100 if they would interview me on their platform, but we added a twist. I asked if they would add the person who runs my Facebook Ads as a temporary user to their account so that I could put in my credit card and spend my money to buy ads through their ads account that pointed to the interview on their platform. Here is an example of how this worked:

About a decade ago, one of the first people on my Dream 100 list was Tony Robbins. To make a really long story short, I had the chance to meet him in person during one of his Unleash the Power Within events. I then went on to speak at his Business Mastery event in Fiji and was interviewed for his *New Money Mastery* DVD program. Yes, I had been digging my well for over a decade. I had tried to serve however and whenever he asked. And when *Expert Secrets* was done, I decided that I was finally going to ask Tony for something. I asked if he'd be willing to interview me about my new book on his Facebook page.

Now this step is very important. I didn't want to interview him on *my* page, because then only my people would see it. If he interviewed me on *his* page, all of his (then) 3.2 million followers would see it! He agreed, and the second that we started the interview, over 1,500 people watched *live*. When the interview was over, I asked Tony if I could spend my money to buy ads to that video through his profile and that I'd still pay him a $20 commission on every book he sold in addition to me covering the costs of the ads. I tried to make this a huge *win* for him, and he said, *"Yes!"* During our launch week, that interview was seen by Tony's fans over *2.8 million* times! Since then, it's had a total of 3.1 million views. And that result was from just one of my Dream 100.

Figure 4.4:

By getting interviewed on Tony's Facebook page, I was able to get in front of his huge audience. This one video alone has been viewed over 3.1 million times!

I ended up doing a countless number of interviews on every platform possible, and during launch week, we sold over 71,248 copies of *Expert Secrets*! (The average *New York Times* bestseller only sells about 10,000 copies during opening week.) This is how we "worked our way in" to the audiences of our Dream 100.

Not all promotions are an interview, although I think that is the easiest way to illustrate this concept. Many of my Dream 100 had an email list, and they promoted my books to those lists by sending out an email recommending purchase of the book. Some wrote reviews and posted it on their blogs, while others talked about it inside their Instagram stories. Everyone published to their own platforms in different ways, so I let them do what was most comfortable to them. I will always be grateful to them for putting me in front of their audiences: my dream customers!

Now, this concept isn't just a launch strategy. It can and should be a consistent part of your business. To this day, I still do multiple interviews each month for people who have a platform that want to have me on as a guest. I would recommend trying to do at least two per week as a starting goal. This may seem like a lot, but it's how you fill your funnels with consistent leads. Usually at the end of the interview, the host will ask me what I'm working on or where I would like people to go for more information, and I direct them toward whatever funnel we are focusing on at the time. Sometimes I will tell them to get a free copy of one of my books, while other times it's to get a free trial of ClickFunnels, download a free report, or subscribe to my podcast.

This can and should be a consistent part of your traffic strategy. This organic, earned traffic oftentimes converts at a much higher rate than almost any form of paid traffic. It's harder to scale, but your hottest, best buyers will typically come from an endorsement from your Dream 100.

We call this "earned" traffic because you typically aren't paying for it with money, but you are paying for it with your time. When people are getting started and don't have an advertising budget, I always recommend starting with earned traffic. The first eight years of my business were entirely fueled by earned traffic. I worked my way into my Dream 100, got in front of their audiences, and, with their endorsements, drove traffic into my funnels.

For those of you who are starting with a big budget who think that you can skip this part, I would be careful. I've found that paid traffic will get you started more quickly, but the second you turn off the ads, the traffic stops. On the other hand, when you have been constantly and consistently working on earning traffic, your traffic will hit a point of critical mass where you can't turn it off even if you wanted to.

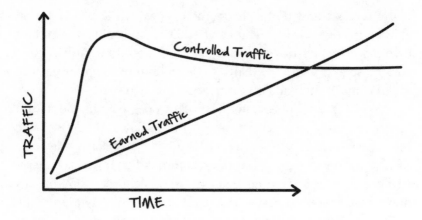

Figure 4.5:

While controlled (paid) traffic usually produces a quick spike, the traffic typically fizzles out. Earned traffic often produces a slower amount of traffic than paid traffic at first, but usually grows over time.

In Section Two, I will be going deeper into each of the platforms that we leverage, and I'll show you more specifics on how to get this earned traffic. For now, though, I just want you to understand the foundational concepts behind earned traffic and how it works.

Now, let me transition into the next type of traffic: traffic you control.

STEP #3: BUY YOUR WAY IN
(TRAFFIC THAT YOU CONTROL)

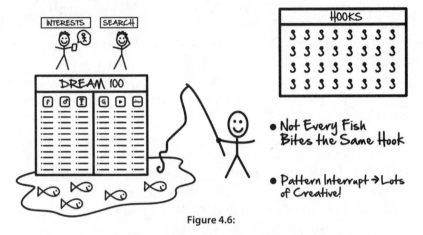

Figure 4.6:

While you're building relationships with your Dream 100,
you can still get traffic by buying it.

In a perfect world, every one of your Dream 100 would say *"Yes!"* and promote you to their audiences on all their platforms daily. You'd get unlimited free traffic, you'd never have to risk any money on ads, and business would be really easy. Unfortunately, it doesn't work that way. Typically, if I contact all of the 100 people on my list, I'll usually get about 30 that will say yes, they will help, and then usually only about 10 people will actually do any real promotion. Sometimes they're too busy or get caught at a bad time, while other times they might have a competing product. Honestly, sometimes they may just look at you as their competitor or maybe they just flat-out hate you, and that's okay too. Just because you can't get them to promote you for free doesn't mean you can't still get in front of their audience by running paid traffic. Yes, you can even get in front of the audiences of the people who hate you.

However, when I got started over 15 years ago and I was trying to sell my potato gun DVDs and other products I had created, this wasn't an option. You had to work your way in, and if the person who controlled the traffic said no, you had no other options. But now thanks to Facebook and now pretty much all social platforms, you can usually target the followings of your Dream 100 and show ads directly to them. Yes, that means that before Tony ever did the live interview and promoted *Expert Secrets* on his page, I had spent a decade buying ads on Facebook that only showed up to his followers.

Now while I'm digging my well and building relationships with people, at the same time I'm buying my way in to their audiences. I do this for a few reasons.

First: It's faster. Paid ads can give you immediate feedback. I can turn an ad on and within minutes have people flooding into my funnels.

Second: It gives me the ability to test out different hooks and see what things people in each of my Dream 100's audience are clicking on. Before I did the interview with Tony, we tested dozens of headlines and images and ideas with his audience as ads and saw what things got the most clicks and engagements. Then, when I had the opportunity to be interviewed by Tony, I knew what his people actually wanted to hear and I could craft my message around that.

Third: 90 percent of my Dream 100 will likely never actively promote me on their own, but I still want to get in front of their audiences, and this is the only way. It's not as powerful as an endorsed promotion, but it's the second-best thing.

Fourth: Paid ads are how you scale a company fast. My number-one goal with every funnel I create is to have a "break-even" funnel, where for each $1 we put into paid ads, we get at least $1 back. You see, this is the *big* secret that I shared in *DotCom Secrets*, which was proven with the launch of ClickFunnels.

About a year after we launched ClickFunnels, we were approached by the first big venture capitalist company who wanted to give us funding. They had funded another Boise software startup and wanted to add another hypergrowth company to their portfolio. I went to lunch with one of the partners of the company to find out what they had in mind. As we started eating, he started to ask me the questions that I had seen so many times while watching *Shark Tank*.

"How much money does it cost you to acquire a customer?"

I smiled, knowing he wouldn't understand my answer, and then said, "Well, we were paying about $250 to get a free ClickFunnels trial, but we turned those ads off."

"Wait . . . what? That is a great CPA (cost per acquisition)! With those numbers, if we were to give you $10 million, we could help add another 40K members. Not only would that make you worth a lot more, but we could also take on another round of funding afterward!"

I stuttered a little, then explained, "We actually turned them off because I'm paying for the ads out of my own pocket. I don't have the luxury to go $10 million in debt to get 40K members. Every customer I bring in needs to be profitable from day one."

Then I showed him the *DotCom Secrets* book funnel and explained that while it cost me about $23 on average in ads to sell a book, we actually made over $37 on average from every person who bought the book.

"Wait . . . that makes no sense. How do you make $37 selling a free book? You only charge $7.95 shipping and handling."

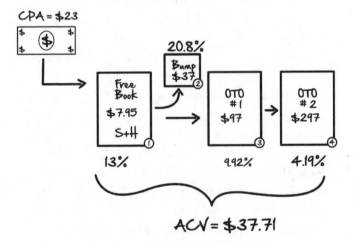

Figure 4.7:

When we create multiple buying opportunities for our customers
in our funnel, we usually break even or make a small profit on
the front end. It allows us to scale without limits.

I laughed and said, "That's the big secret of a funnel. People paid me $7.95 for each book, but then we upsell our courses after they buy the book." I went on to explain the concepts further, as I'm about to do for you right now. Because we can get lost in the weeds with numbers, I've broken it down as simply as possible into the four steps a customer goes through. Be sure to reference Figure 4.7 and read through this a few times until you grasp how "average cart value" works.

- **The Product:** We made $7.95 immediately from each person who bought the book.

  - Total cart value: $7.95

  - I spent $23 in ads to acquire a customer, which made for a negative: -$15.05

- **Order Form Bump:** On the order form, we had our first upsell for the audio book and 20.8% of our buyers added the $37 product to their order (otherwise known as a bump).

  - New money collected for each buyer: $37 x 20.8% = $7.70

  - Total average cart value: $7.95 + $7.70 = $15.65

  - I spent $23 in ads, which made for a negative: -$7.35

- **OTO #1:** After the buyer's order, they immediately see the first of our two special upsells, which are also called one-time offers (OTOs). Our first OTO was $97 for one of our online digital courses that helped implement what they would learn in the book. This first OTO had 9.92% order conversion in a one-click upsell that allowed them to add it to their order without having to re-enter their credit card information.

  - New money collected for each buyer: $97 x 9.92% = $9.62

  - Total average cart value: $15.65 + $9.62 = $25.27

  - I spent $23 in ads, and we finally made a profit: $2.27

- **OTO #2:** Then we offered a second OTO selling a course on how to get traffic into funnels for $297. This second OTO had 4.19% order conversion using a one-click upsell.

  - New money collected for each buyer: $297 x 4.19% = $12.44

  - Total average cart value: $25.27 + $12.44 = $37.71

  - I spent $23 to get each customer, but with an average cart value of $37.71 in sales, we made a net profit for each new buyer who came into our funnel: $14.71

I continued, "So when you do the math and add up all the orders, we averaged $37.71 in total sales for each book that was sold! We call that number the average cart value, or ACV. After the customer bought the book, we used a follow-up funnel via emails, retargeting, Messenger, and other follow-up tools to introduce them to ClickFunnels over the next 90 days. Because we acquired the customer profitably with our funnel before they were shown our software, we got a customer *first* and made a profit before we ever introduced them to our core product. That's how we've been growing so fast without any outside funding."

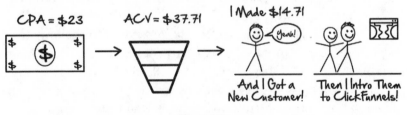

Figure 4.8:

By creating front-end offers, we're able to acquire customers for free (and sometimes for a profit), and then we introduce them to ClickFunnels.

He sat there for a minute and then stated, "If what you're saying is true, this will change business as we know it forever."

I smiled and told him, "Yes, that is the message that I've been called to bring to this world."

You see, there are really only two ways to scale a company fast. The first is to take on outside funding and then to use that money to either acquire other companies or pay to acquire customers. However, this way is lazy and inefficient, and I don't recommend it. I liken this strategy to taking steroids to win a bodybuilding contest. Yes, you won, but you cheated.

The better, smarter, and more efficient way to scale a business is to create a funnel that is profitable and then to put as much money into paid ads as possible. When you have a funnel that at least breaks even, then you don't have an advertising budget and you can spend as much money as you want without it ever costing you anything to acquire customers.

I remember when we had this realization with ClickFunnels. We had been buying ads into our funnels and slowly growing them. We went from spending $100 per day to spending thousands per day, and our front-end, break-even funnel that we were driving traffic to was making us money for each new customer that came in our doors. Even better, a huge percentage of those customers then joined ClickFunnels at $97 per month, meaning we no longer had an advertising budget. As long as we watched the ads closely and made sure that we didn't buy ads in places that weren't going to at least break even, we could grow fast. Soon we were spending over $25,000 per day and growing at a pace that no one had ever seen before.

You might still be asking yourself, "Which is better: controlled traffic or earned traffic? Is it better to work your way in or buy your way in?" The answer is, "*Both* are essential to the long-term success of your company." If you only focus on paid ads, you are left at the mercy of the networks that allowed you to buy the ads. If and/or when Google or Facebook slaps or snaps, you can lose the lifeblood of your company overnight. If you only rely on earned traffic, you are completely relying on other people to get your message out to the market.

While the blend of these two types of traffic is the key to building a solid foundation for your company, there is still one other type of traffic that trumps both earned and controlled traffic. Given the chance to have only one, I'd always choose this third and last type of traffic: traffic that you own.

TRAFFIC THAT YOU OWN

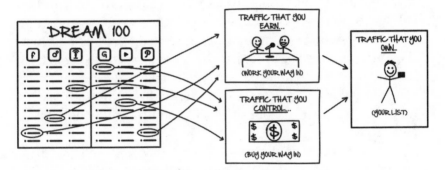

Figure 5.1:

While traffic that you earn and traffic that you control is good,
traffic that you own is the best type of traffic to have.

Those numbers couldn't be right . . . could they? I thought. I did the math again.

"If I had 10,000 people on my list, and I was selling a $50 product . . . if just one percent of them bought a product from me . . ." I mumbled under my breath. "One percent of 10,000 people was 100 people times $50." Then it hit me. *I'd make $5,000, right?*

No, that can't be right. Can it? I hadn't made that much money so far this year, let alone from sending one email. *But wait, what if I had 100,000 people and sold the same product? That would be $50K! And that was if just one percent of the people I sent an email to actually bought a product from me!*

But what do the numbers look like if two percent buy? $100,000? Whoa! That's more money than most people make in a year. I must be doing these numbers wrong. But even after running the numbers a second time, I came up with the same result.

Then a new idea flew into my head and I was so excited that my hands were literally shaking. The words that were in my head wouldn't stay there any longer and I actually started to say out loud, "Wait. This is from just one campaign. What if I did that once per month . . . or once per week . . . or even once per day? Is that even possible?"

Suddenly I realized that I was still in class, even though the bell had rung 15 minutes earlier. The teacher was gone, and most of the kids, outside of a few people lingering, were talking about their plans for the weekend. Luckily no one was close enough to hear what I was actually saying to myself. I felt like I was just given something illegal, some type of insider trading, where no matter how I did the math, as long as I focused on this one thing, I was going to win.

I looked around at those few people still in the room just long enough to see that no one was even aware that I was there, and I half smiled and started writing again. As I was scratching numbers on the back of a pad of paper, I had one of those experiences. You know what I'm talking about? That feeling when you found something that was too good to be true, but no matter how many ways you looked at it, you couldn't disprove it?

I had stumbled upon the key that could change everything for me. I was just trying to figure out how to play the game of online marketing when I came across a short reply to a forum post online regarding if people were really making money online or if it was all just a big scam.

I wish I knew who this author was so I could thank him for this insight. While I can no longer find the original post, it went a little something like this:

> Every so often I hear the skeptics ask this question, and I always smile because I know that they don't understand how leverage works. They're used to working eight hours a day and getting paid for those hours. If they want to

make $100K per year, they have to make at least $50 per hour, work 40 hours per week for at least 50 weeks per year. When they hear about the "gurus" online making $100K in a weekend, it doesn't make any sense to them and they think it's a scam, but it's actually quite simple.

When someone has spent the time to build a list of followers of 10,000, 100,000, or 1,000,000-plus people, they can send out an email to that list selling a product. To make $100K, they only need a small percentage of those people to buy the product, yet to someone working for the hourly wage it would take them all year to earn that amount.

Recently I sent an email to my list of 32,000 subscribers and offered them a chance to buy one of my $37 e-books. Of those 32,000 people, only 232 of them decided to purchase (just 0.7%), but that put a quick $8,584 into my pocket. That would have taken the skeptics more than 171 hours (at $50 per hour) to earn the same as I did from less than 15 minutes writing the email and sending it out to my list.

My heart was beating out of my chest. I needed a list, and I wanted it now. I turned to Google and started searching for the how. The next few days I learned all the secrets about how to send mass emails. I purchased the software, got the computers set up (mass emails used to be sent directly from a computer), and all that was left that I needed was a list of email addresses to plug into the software and I'd be rich.

But where did people get these lists? I couldn't understand that part of the puzzle, so I went back to good ol' Google for the answer. Within a few searches, I found the honey pot: a website that would sell me a CD with over 1 *million* "spam-free email addresses." I didn't know how they got them, but they guaranteed that they would be spam-free, so I was in. I sent them the money and patiently waited for my CD to arrive.

Everything seemed so easy. Each step was falling into place! Why wasn't everyone doing this? Was I missing something?

I waited and waited for the means to test my theories, but the days turned into weeks with nothing showing up. I emailed the company, asking them when I'd get the CD, but I didn't get a response back. Had I just fallen for a scam? *Where was my list?*

And then it happened! After a long day at school, and an even longer day at wrestling practice, I got home late, beat up and tired. My wife, Collette, was working two jobs to support her jobless student athlete at the time, and she was worn out too. I walked through the door and gave her a kiss. But right before I sat on the couch for a few much-needed minutes of rest before starting on my homework, I saw it! On the kitchen countertop was a cardboard envelope, just big enough to hold a CD!

All of my tiredness disappeared, and excitement flooded into my body as I ran over, ripped it open, and held in my hands the CD that would guarantee my freedom! *One million* names and email addresses of people who wanted to send me money for cool stuff I was going to sell them! I quickly started spewing out what I had written down a few weeks earlier to try to explain to Collette what this thin disc meant to us.

"This has a *million* people's email addresses on it! If we send out an email selling a $50 product and just one percent buys . . ." I grabbed a pad of paper and calculated the math again. "One percent of 1 million people is 10,000 people! Ten thousand people times $50 is $500,000—a *half million dollars!*"

"What?" Collette asked.

"I know, half a million seems like a lot, so let's say it's just 10 percent of that. That's still $50K! That's almost *double* what we made last year from *just one email*! We could literally send out emails every week!"

And then I dropped the bomb. "Collette, you should go and quit your job tomorrow! There is no way this could fail. Even if just a fraction of that one percent buy, we're gonna be rich!"

My wife probably tried to talk sense into this husband of hers, but I don't remember much of what she said because I was too busy running to the computer. I unplugged our phone line, plugged it into my modem in the wall, and started writing the email. I wrote about an amazing product that I had yet to create and ended the email with a "Buy Now" link to my personal PayPal account. I loaded the email addresses in, where all I had to do was click send.

I sat there for a few minutes, visualizing what was about to happen. I did the math one last time in my head, and then I took a deep breath, smiled, and clicked send.

0 of 1,000,000 emails sent . . .

1 of 1,000,000 emails sent . . .

5, 9, 21 of 1,000,000 emails sent!

It was going a lot slower than I expected, but knowing that $500K would be in my PayPal account soon, I was okay waiting a little longer for it. With that, we went to bed, and like a kid on Christmas Eve, I lay in bed dreaming about how much money would be in my account by morning.

The next morning, I was woken up by my wife. At first, I was a little groggy, but her getting ready for work reminded me that she was supposed to quit today. That is, as long as we woke up rich! I needed to check our sales! I ran to the computer and woke up the monitor.

6,423 of 1,000,000 emails sent.

WHAT?! Only six thousand emails had been sent so far. This was completely throwing off my calculations. Instead of sending a million emails a day, it was going to take weeks to send a full million. As I was rewriting my business plan in my head, Collette told me that she needed to use the phone, and, for those of you who don't remember dial-up modems, that meant I had to pause the email, crawl under the desk, unplug the modem, and re-plug in the phone.

Within seconds, the phone rang. I crawled out from under my desk, almost hitting my head as I answered it.

"Hello," I muttered.

"What the #@%#^$@ are you doing?" exclaimed the stranger on the other line. "In the past six hours, we've received over thirty spam complaints from *your* IP address, and we're going to shut you down."

Wait . . . what? "Sir, you don't understand. The people I'm emailing have spam-free email addresses. They want me to send them emails. I purchased the list of emails from—"

"Son, that's the definition of spam!" he yelled.

My heart sank. I vaguely remember him talking about lawyers and fines, but honestly I just wanted to get off the phone and hide.

After what seemed like forever, I hung up with a huge lump in my throat.

"Who was that?" Collette asked.

"Um, no one." But then I blurted out, "Just promise me that you won't quit your job today, at least not yet." Collette smiled, took the phone, and turned to make her call.

I was so frustrated. I thought I had cracked the code. Other people were emailing their lists, so why did I get in trouble when I sent emails to mine? I grabbed my backpack and started the trek back to the college campus, but I felt numb as I walked out the front door. Instead of going to class, I slipped into the computer lab, just to see if anything had happened during the night. I logged into my PayPal account with this question spinning through my mind: *Of the 6,423 people who did get my email, had anyone bought?*

I waited for the loading screen . . . loading . . . loading . . . and then I saw the dashboard. Every time I had logged into PayPal before, the balance always had a big fat $0.00 next to it, but not this time! This time the number was different! Seven sales made the most beautiful $70 I had ever seen!

It had worked! I was still a little confused, though. I knew that the way I did it was *completely* wrong and potentially illegal. But I *knew* that there had to be a right way to build a list that wouldn't get me labeled as a spammer.

And so the next step in my journey began. With the newfound hope that I now had, I searched for legitimate list owners so I could see what they were doing. I joined tons of lists and watched the process. What did they do to get me to sign up? What emails did they send? Why did some emails make me want to buy something, while others didn't?

And then, something happened that I had never experienced before. All on the same day, I got emails from dozens of these list owners about a guy whom they called "the godfather of internet marketing" and how he was retiring. I clicked on the emails and was taken to a long page telling the story of Mark Joyner, who was one of the early pioneers of online marketing who had made millions of dollars. He was selling off all his intellectual property, along with a course of him teaching how he had built his company so large so fast. In the course, he would reveal how he had built email lists with millions of people and how he had some of the most visited websites in the world.

I knew I had to buy this product no matter what it took. I had never felt this way before. Something about the way he told his story and made his offer was *so* irresistible. For just $1,000, I would get access to everything this man had ever created. I looked at that page for weeks until his campaign was almost over and he was about to pull this offer offline forever. The night before he was going to close it down, I lied in bed knowing that on the other side of that $1,000 investment was the key to helping me build a list. I didn't sleep that night, not for one minute.

As the sun started to rise and I heard my wife waking up next to me, I knew I had to ask her something, but I was scared. Every online venture over the past 18 months that I had tried had failed. Just a few months earlier, I had gotten our internet access shut off within hours of me telling her she could quit her job. Yes, 23 "tests" in 18 months, all in an attempt to make money online, had failed. We had no money to our name, I didn't have a job, and Collette was making a whopping $9.50 per hour at hers. I was about to ask her to let me spend $1,000 we didn't have on a hope and a dream.

I did that math. It would take her 105 hours of working to earn that money, and that was before taxes. We needed that money for food and rent and everything else, but as she opened her eyes and I asked her to make a sacrifice that I couldn't, she smiled and asked, "Do you think this will be the one that works?"

As I'm writing this now, I'm tearing up. I always say that you can only be as successful as your spouse or significant other will allow you to be. When Collette looked at me in that moment, I knew she believed in me, even though I had no track record of success, and I'm so grateful that she did. I told her that I felt that it was the key, and if I could figure out how to build a list, then we would be free, and Mark Joyner was the man who was going to teach us how.

She gave me a kiss, told me she believed in me, and, with that, I jumped out of bed, ran to the computer, and pulled out our only credit card and typed in the digits. Within seconds, it was done. A week later, I had the course. What I had assumed at this point and what Mark Joyner taught me were the same: the list is the key. That's the big secret. It is the only real asset in any company.

THE ONLY REAL SECRET TO BUSINESS: LIST BUILDING

When you look at the big online acquisitions, it's interesting to see what the companies are actually buying. In September 2005, eBay purchased Skype for $2.6 billion.[10] At the time, eBay was one of the largest online sites and their development team was arguably the best in the world. It would not have been difficult for eBay to clone Skype and make a better product. What Skype had that eBay wanted, though, was 54 million members in 225 countries and territories, increasing at a rate of 150,000 new users daily. eBay was purchasing the list.

In more recent times, Facebook purchased Instagram (and its 30 million users) for $1 billion.[11] Obviously, there are many reasons why Facebook made the acquisition, including acquiring their development team and gaining speed to market, but one of the main reasons was to obtain Instagram's member list.

We also see it in smaller, entrepreneurial-type companies. Your list is your key to your current and future success online. This is the *best* type of traffic: traffic that you own. As of the time I'm writing this, I have 1.6 million entrepreneurs who are on my email lists, hundreds of thousands on my Messenger lists, over a million following me on my social lists, and tens of millions of people on my pixeled lists.

In fact, my *only* goal with traffic that I control and traffic that I earn is to convert it into traffic that I own. That's what I learned from Mark Joyner. When I'm buying ads, sure, I want to sell a product, but, more importantly, I want to get those people on a list first. Because when I buy an ad, I'm getting them to click once. When they join my lists, I can email them as often as I like for free, instead of just getting them to click once. It's the same with traffic that I earn. I want to direct these people into funnels where I get their information and get them on to my lists. That way I can follow up with them over and over again.

Figure 5.2:

With traffic I own, I can follow up with my leads and customers anytime I like.

That's why the concept of the break-even funnel in Secret #4 is so vitally important. All of the traffic I control and earn is always pushed into a front-end funnel that will ask for the visitor to give me their email address, subscribe to a Messenger list, or both. That way, I can convert them from traffic that I control or earn into traffic that I own, where I can market to them for free, over and over again.

The different funnel types here are covered in great detail in *DotCom Secrets*, but for now, I want to show you how we use these front-end funnels to convert clicks into traffic that you own. In both traffic that I control and traffic that I earn, I have some type of call to action, or CTA, pushing customers into a front-end, break-even funnel. For example, at the end of a podcast interview, I might use three different CTAs to get people into my funnels:

If I'm using a lead funnel: "I'd love to give all of your listeners a free copy of my new e-book, *Marketing Secrets Blackbook*, where you can learn 99 marketing secrets that will change your business . . . And change your life. You can download your free copy at MarketingSecrets.com/blackbook."

With a lead funnel, you're giving customers something for free in exchange for their email address. We call the thing you are giving away for free a "lead magnet," because if you create something that is exciting for your dream customers, it will attract those leads just like a magnet. You don't sell anything in this type of funnel, but once they're on your list, the follow-up funnels are where you'll make your profit.

The Marketing Secrets Blackbook
"99 Marketing Secrets That Will Change Your Business... And Change Your Life!"

Free Instant Access!

Enter your best email below and I'll send you a FREE copy of my new book, the "Marketing Secrets Blackbook!"

Enter Your Email...

Send to Messenger
Kelsey Kodanko Not you?

Get Access Now!

🔒 Your information is safe with us and will not be shared with any third party.

Want To Know How We Took ClickFunnels From ZERO To Over $100,000,000 In Sales In Just 3 Short Years...? Then Get Your **FREE Digital Copy** Of The 'Marketing Secrets Blackbook' Now!

Figure 5.3:

My lead funnel gives away 99 marketing secrets in a free e-book.

If I'm using a free book funnel: "I just finished my new book *Expert Secrets*, and I'd love to send everyone a free copy if you'll just cover my hard costs of shipping. Just go to ExpertSecrets.com and let me know where to ship your copy today!"

With the book funnel, we give them an amazing deal to get a copy of my book when they cover the shipping. I send them the book, and then the upsells will cover my ad costs and hopefully make me a small profit. More importantly, though, I create a customer to add to my lists.

Figure 5.4:

My book funnel gives away a free book (with $7.95 shipping) called *Expert Secrets*.

If I'm using a webinar funnel: "I have a new web class coming up where I'm showing a new secret funnel strategy that almost nobody knows about, that once you understand, can take your business from 'startup' to 'Two Comma Club' winner practically overnight. You can register for this free web class at SecretFunnelStrategy. com."

With the webinar funnel, I invite them to the web class. When they register, they join my list. Then at the end of the web class, I make a special offer which covers my ad spend and ideally makes me a profit. (Note: this funnel and how to give the presentation is taught in great detail in *Expert Secrets*.)

Figure 5.5:

My webinar funnel gives away a "secret funnel strategy" in a one-hour presentation.

Do you see how this works? I earn my way onto a platform, and then my offer at the end pushes customers into one of my front-end, break-even funnels. Each of the funnels is created in such a way that there is value at every step of it.

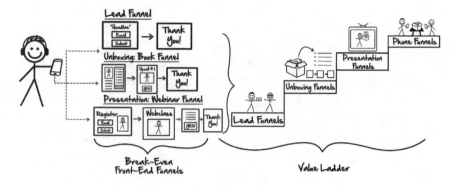

Figure 5.6:

With all of my front-end end funnels, the goal is to break even so I can
ascend my customers up my value ladder, thereby making a profit.

With the traffic I control, the process I take leads through is
similar. However, unlike earned traffic where I would be getting
in front of audiences by getting on to someone else's show, having
someone send an email to their list for me, or letting me guest
post on their blog, with paid traffic, I create and buy ads.

UNDERSTANDING THE VALUE OF YOUR LIST

It's been said that on the low end, you should average about $1
per month for each name on your list, and when I got started, that
was true. When I had 500 people on my list, I was making about
$500 per month. As I grew, these numbers held true for a while:

- 1,000 people on my list: $1,000 per month
- 10,000 people on my list: $10,000 per month
- 100,000 people on my list: $100,000 per month

But as I've gotten better at building a relationship with my
lists, these numbers have gone up dramatically. As a worst-case
scenario, though, they should follow these metrics. For example,
if you know you want to make $100,000 per year, make sure you
are focused on getting at least 10,000 people on your list (10,000

people x \$1 per month x 12 months = \$120,000). If you want to make \$1 million per year, focus on getting 100,000 people on your list (100,000 people x \$1 per month x 12 months = \$1,200,000).

Again, I want to note that these numbers change in every market. Most local businesses may only have 500–1,000 people on their lists, but because of their ability to build a better relationship with that list, they could be making \$50–\$100 per name per month, whereas with some types of lists (such as retargeting or social lists), you might only make \$0.50 per name. I suggest setting a benchmark of \$1 per name per month and then trying to beat it.

As a side note, if you think about traditional investments like real estate, I see people all the time spend \$250,000 on a rental house and hope that it brings in a positive cash flow of \$500 per month. Then they'll take up to 30 years to pay off the mortgage (i.e., "break even") while still having to deal with broken toilets, tenants, and more.

List building is a completely different investment model. I might have to pay anywhere from \$1 to \$5 per lead in Facebook. For this example, let's use the top number. If I paid \$5 per lead and only spent \$5,000, I would generate 1,000 leads. If I averaged \$1 per month per name, after five months I would break even, and after that I would have a positive cash flow of \$1,000 per month.

Having a list has also saved me multiple times in my company. Unfortunately, sometimes things happened that required me to get an influx of money quickly or I would lose everything. Traditionally, if I wanted to raise a quarter or half a million dollars in a weekend, it would be impossible. Because I had a list, however, I could write a few emails, send them to the list, and generate the needed revenue in days. Twice, my list has kept me from inevitable bankruptcy when the market changed and my business was failing. I created a new offer, sent it to the lists, and was able to quickly pivot and recover.

You might be wondering, "Now that I've added someone to my list, how does that grow my company?" Well, the answer is simple. Now that you have created the *most valuable* thing inside your company, you can then direct your subscribers into "follow-up funnels."

FOLLOW-UP FUNNELS

My mentor and friend David Frey wrote: "A study done by the Association of Sales Executives revealed that 81 percent of all sales happens on or after the fifth contact. If you're a small business owner and you're only doing one or two follow-ups, imagine all the business you're losing. Not following up with your prospects and customers is the same as filling up your bathtub without first putting the stopper in the drain!"[12]

Some say that the "fortune is in the follow-up," and I believe it's true. The way we follow up is to take the traffic that we now own and push them through follow-up funnels.

Last year, I pulled the stats from four of our most successful front-end funnels to demonstrate the power of driving people toward a break-even funnel and then using follow-up funnels. Let me give you a breakdown of what happened over a 30-day window. (Note: ACV stands for average cart value, i.e., how much we made on average from each person after they bought the front-end offer plus any upsells.)

- **Funnel #1: *DotCom Secrets* free + shipping book funnel**

    - Leads generated: **5,410**
    - Books sold: **2,395**
    - Average cart value: **$30.81**
    - Total gross sales: **$73,789.95**
    - Ad spend: **$69,026.31**
    - Profit: **$4,763.64**

- **Funnel #2:** *108 Split Tests* **book funnel**

  - Leads generated: **2,013**
  - Books sold: **1,357**
  - Average cart value: **$12.38**
  - Total gross sales: **$16,799.66**
  - Ad spend: **$13,813.57**
  - Profit: **$2,986.09**

- **Funnel #3: "Perfect Webinar Secrets" free + shipping funnel**

  - Leads generated: **1,605**
  - Product sold: **760**
  - Average cart value: **$34.38**
  - Total gross sales: **$26,128.80**
  - Ad spend: **$22,359.94**
  - Profit: **$3,768.86**

- **Funnel #4:** *Marketing in Your Car* **free + shipping MP3 player funnel**

  - Leads generated: **5,177**
  - MP3 players sold: **1,765**
  - Average cart value: **$14.79**
  - Total gross sales: **$26,104.35**
  - Ad spend: **$23,205.25**
  - Profit: **$2,899.10**

When you look at just these four "break-even" funnels during a 30-day window, the total stats look like this:

- Front-end revenue: **$142,822.76**
- Front-end ad costs: **$128,405.07**
- Total profit: **$14,417.69**

So while it looked like our company was doing about a million and a half dollars a year in top-line revenue, it was only actually making a little over $10,000 per month. From the outside, this looked like a failing business, and it would have been if we didn't understand the strategy behind traffic, funnels, and the value ladder. But when you do understand those core principles, then the stats look a little differently. This is how we looked at those stats:

- New leads added to my list (traffic that I *own*): 14,205 people

- How much I got *paid* to acquire those 14,205 people: $14,417.69

That's right. I didn't just get free leads, I actually got *paid* over $1.00 for each person who joined my list that month. After we plugged these leads into my follow-up funnels, we ended up making a total of $16.49 in sales from every $1 we made inside of our funnel within 30 days of each lead joining.

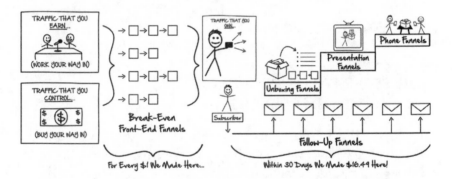

Figure 6.1:

With follow-up funnels, we were able to grow our profit from just $1 per customer to $16.49 per customer in a 30-day period.

Yes, those 14,205 people ended up collectively spending $234,240.45 within 30 days inside our follow-up funnels, and all of that money was pure profit because I didn't have to pay Mark Zuckerberg over at Facebook or Larry and Sergey at Google any of it. I wasn't trying to control the traffic or earn it; it was mine. Once someone is on my list, I can then send out follow-up messages to them anytime I want for free because I now *own* that traffic!

In my follow-up funnels, I sent those 14,205 people emails with free videos to build a relationship with them. A few days later, I invited them to come watch my webinar where I taught them how ClickFunnels worked to grow as a company. Not all wanted to watch the web class, but 1,129 did and registered for it. At the end of the web class, we sold a product for $2,997, and 57 people bought it (grossing us $170,829). Over the rest of the month, some signed up for the ClickFunnels trial, some bought other books, and some bought courses and coaching. In the first 30 days, we multiplied our profits by more than 16 times. When you look over the next 60, 90, 360 days and beyond, you'll see that each lead can and should be worth thousands of dollars to you, and if you can break even (or even make a little profit) to generate that lead, you should do it all day every day.

VC-backed companies will go in the hole for 6–12 months or more to generate a customer. That's right, they sometimes don't break even for over a year, but they can do that because they're burning someone else's money.

THE SECRET TO QUICKLY GROW YOUR LIST WITH PAID ADS

Ideally, we break even in our initial funnel, but sometimes it might take us a few days or weeks to break even using our follow-up funnels. Many times, people will lose some money inside of their front-end funnels and not break even immediately, and because of that they get scared and walk away from it. If they looked closer at their numbers, though, they'd see that they might have been just a few days away from breaking even and that they could still have kept running ads to those funnels profitably, even at a loss. Let me show you how this works.

Let's say that you decide to buy Facebook Ads to a lead funnel that doesn't actually sell anything immediately. You're just giving away a free report of some type of lead magnet with a goal to generate a lead that you can plug into your follow-up funnels. In this example, let's say that you're spending $3.00 to generate each lead.

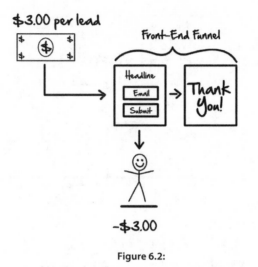

Figure 6.2:

If all we had was a front-end funnel, we would lose money on every lead we acquired.

As of right now, this funnel seems like it's a dud, right? Well, without the follow-up funnel, it would be. When someone joins my list, I'll build a relationship with them. I might send them a few emails making sure they're able to download the lead magnet I gave them for free, and I might even send a video or an article helping them to get more value from the thing I just offered them. At that point, I would still be $3.00 in the hole for each lead, but I would be building a relationship with them, which means they would be more likely to open my emails and buy things from me in the future.

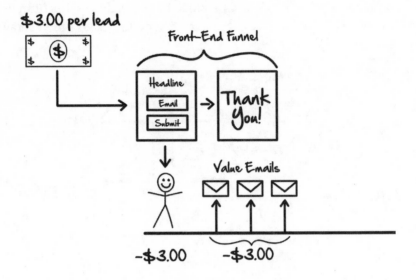

Figure 6.3:

With a follow-up funnel in place, we're able to
continue the conversation with our leads.

Here's where the fun begins. The next set of emails in my follow-up funnel would be focused on introducing them to the next funnel in my value ladder. For this example, let's say it was one of my free book funnels. I would send them three emails inviting them to get a free copy of my book when they cover shipping. Those who get a free copy will be taken through that sales funnel, and I should make some profit from each book buyer. In this example, on average, I would make $1.00 from each lead who went through this second step. As of day six in this follow-up funnel, I would still be -$1.50 in the hole.

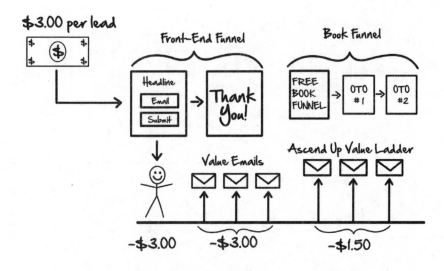

Figure 6.4:

When we offer our leads the opportunity to ascend our value ladder
and buy our book, we start recouping some of our ad spend.

The next step in the follow-up funnel would be to move
them into one of my higher ticket funnels. We call this "funnel
stacking." In this example, the next thing I would invite them to
is one of my web classes. I might send a few more emails inviting
them to register for the webinar. After they went through that
webinar sequence and I made an offer for one of my higher ticket
products, the average dollar per lead would increase past the $3.00
I spent for the lead. At that point, I would break even and start
making a profit. That means within about a week of paying for
that lead, I would be in the black! Anything that those customers
bought from me in the future would be *pure profit*.

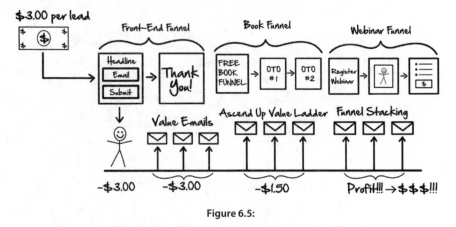

Figure 6.5:

After we stack multiple funnels back-to-back in our
follow-up funnels, we make a profit.

Are you seeing how this works? Sometimes the break-even happens inside of the initial front-end funnel, but other times it happens within the follow-up funnel. As soon as I know that I break even on day X of my follow-up funnel, then I go back and spend money to acquire customers, knowing that I'll have a return on that investment at an already established point.

When I first started on my online journey, I heard Mike Litman say, "Amateurs focus on the first sale."[13] I didn't really understand what that meant until I started using follow-up funnels and realized that I could spend way more money to acquire a customer than I initially believed. Dan Kennedy once said, "Ultimately, the business that can spend the most to acquire a customer wins."[14] With good funnels and a strong follow-up funnel, you can increase how much money you can spend to acquire a customer.

MULTIDIMENSIONAL FOLLOW-UP FUNNELS

So far I have only talked about emails inside your follow-up funnels. In a perfect world, everyone who got an email would read it and click on the links inside. Unfortunately, with people's attention spans today (down from 20 minutes in the '90s to just seven seconds today!), a lot of the people you send emails to will never actually open them. Some stats show that as much as 87 percent of emails go unopened! You're battling for attention every time you send anything.

As the war for attention has grown, a lot of amazing tools have been created that we can plug into our follow-up funnels to make sure people actually see our message. My hope is that this list of tools will continue to increase, but I'll share with you the ones that I see as the most powerful today.

Retargeting: The first, and one of my favorite tools to plug into my follow-up funnels, is retargeting ads. We'll go deep into our retargeting strategy in Secret #9, but for now, I want you to be aware of what they are and how they work. Have you ever been to a website, and then over the next few weeks, it seems like they're stalking you online? Everywhere you go, you see their banner ads following you around? That is retargeting, and it's one of the most powerful ways to push someone through your follow-up funnels and ascend them up your value ladder.

Messenger: In 2011, Facebook created their Messenger program which, for many people, has replaced email as their favorite communication tool. You can add Messenger subscriber boxes into your funnels and get people joining your email list to also join your Messenger lists. This gives you the ability to follow up with people through a different channel than email. It's a very powerful tool that has a much higher open rate than email. However, because of the intimacy of people's Messenger inboxes, I've found that unlike email, where I can send email daily and not have many people upset, with Messenger, I can only send one or two messages a week without losing many subscribers. We strategically place Messenger messages within our follow-up funnels to create a conversation about once or twice per week with a goal to direct people back into a funnel or ascend them into the next one.

Text Messages: We don't normally try to get someone's phone number on a traditional landing page, because each new field traditionally lowers conversions, but I do try to grab a phone number when people buy something from us or when they register for a webinar. We can use text broadcasts to make sure people don't miss the webinar they've signed up for, let them know the statuses of their orders, and help move them into the next step in our value ladder.

There are always new communication tools being developed, but their goal is the same: build a relationship with your subscriber and ascend them through your value ladder.

Now that you see how follow-up funnels work, I want to spend a minute on the psychology and sequencing of follow-up funnels.

THE 3 CLOSES: EMOTION, LOGIC, FEAR

As you have seen, we have a lot of tools that we can use to try to get someone to buy from us. But what should go inside of each message? We've found that the ones that give you the most leverage include messages based on:

- Emotion
- Logic
- Fear (urgency and scarcity)

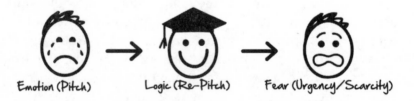

Emotion (Pitch)   Logic (Re-Pitch)   Fear (Urgency/Scarcity)

Figure 6.6:

Whenever you close someone, make sure to include
in your message emotion, logic, and fear.

The most powerful way to get someone to take action is by using emotion. It's often been said that people buy things emotionally and then try to justify their purchase logically. If you've read *Expert Secrets*, the entire book is focused on story selling, which shows you how to tell stories to break false beliefs and put people into an emotional state where they are ready to change and ready to buy. This is the most powerful way to create emotion in the minds of your visitors and get them to take action. That's why most of our ads lead with emotional stories. The lead of any sales letter, the stories in my webinars, the first emails in our follow-up funnels, and the first ads in my retargeting sequences always speak to people's emotions. This is where the majority of your sales will happen too.

For example, take this sketch of a very basic "free book"–style sales page, like the one you may have seen before you purchased this book. The top of the page has a headline that appeals to one's emotions, a video telling stories to get one emotionally interested in the product, and then an order form for one to take action. Fifty percent of my sales will come immediately from people who only see this top block and never scroll. They're my emotional buyers.

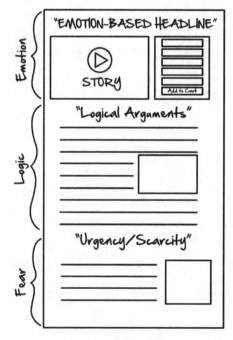

Figure 6.7:

Every sales page we create has this same style because it addresses the
emotion, logic, and fear messages in the order required to create the sale.

The next 30 percent of buyers are a little bit harder to convince. They're the analytical buyers. They may have felt something emotionally, but they need to be able to logically convince themselves that the purchase is right for them. Often they're afraid of what others will think if they buy it, because they have a fear that their status will decrease if the product doesn't work for them. So under this top section of the page, I transition my message to speak toward their logic. I explain why this is a good deal and compare it to other investments they could make. I also let them know about the money-back guarantee if it doesn't work so they won't risk a decrease in status. Lastly, I try to use as much risk reversal as possible.

The last 20 percent of buyers aren't as motivated by emotion or logic, but they are motivated by a fear of missing out (FOMO). The only thing that will get them to take the leap is for them to be afraid that you're going to take it away. Urgency comes from you giving them all the reasons why they need to buy it now, and scarcity comes from all the reasons why this will be gone soon. For this last group, I close almost every sales presentation, letter, and sequence focusing on urgency and scarcity.

I just showed you how the process of Emotion → Logic → Fear works on a landing page, but it also works inside of every follow-up funnel and retargeting sequence.

Figure 6.8:

We build emotion, logic, and fear messaging into our follow-up
funnels to help our audience purchase our products.

When someone joins a follow-up funnel, my first set of messages focuses on the emotion as I tell stories of other people who have used the product and share the hidden benefits. After a few days, I switch all my messaging to logic, and then the last set of messages will switch to fear.

If I'm only sending out three emails in that step of the follow-up funnel, then I have one for each of the three closes. If I have five emails, I might spend the first three days on emotion, one day on logic, and one day on urgency and scarcity. The number of messages matters less than making sure you hit each of the closes, because each one will bring in a different group of buyers.

As I make my transition to the next funnel in my follow-up funnel, I start over with emotional story selling again and get people engaged about the next funnel in the value ladder. This process is true in *every* type of messaging you put out. When your goal is to move people through a process or funnel, every type of communication you send should start with emotion, move to logic, and end with fear (urgency and scarcity).

FOLLOW-UP FUNNELS (SOAP OPERA SEQUENCES) VS. BROADCASTS (DAILY SEINFELD EMAILS)

In *DotCom Secrets*, I talk about the two types of communications I have with people after they join my list: Soap Opera Sequences and Daily Seinfeld Emails. I've found that a lot of people get confused on how those types of communications work and how they tie into follow-up funnels, so I wanted to spend a minute showing how these concepts fit together.

When someone first joins my list, I take them through a process called the Soap Opera Sequence. We call it that because the emails aren't stand-alone messages, but instead we will use multiple emails to tell a story, where each email hooks you to read the next email in a way that is similar to how a good soap opera will use their storyline to pull you from episode to episode. In these emails, we tell our readers a story that will build a relationship and rapport. That way, they'll be more likely to keep reading our emails, clicking on our links, and buying our products.

The second type of communication is the Daily Seinfeld Emails that are more similar to episodes of the Seinfeld show. Each email is a stand-alone message that has a hook, tells a story, and then pushes back to your core offer. We use these each day as we send a broadcast to our list with a goal of getting them back into our funnels. Some people have thought that these two ideas were opposing, and others have asked how they fit into the follow-up funnel framework. The truth is they both work together inside of your value ladder.

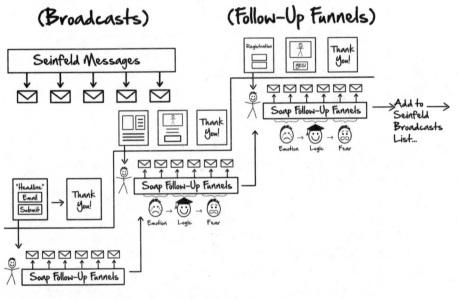

Figure 6.9:

After a lead has gone through your entire Soap Opera Sequences for all your funnels, then you can send them your Daily Seinfeld Emails.

When someone first joins your list, we plug them into a follow-up funnel. Immediately, they're put on a Soap Opera Sequence where we tell them stories (providing an emotional close) and lead them through our follow-up funnel. The first set of emails are all about building rapport. Readers usually connect with your story (as you're the Attractive Character in your business) because you're the one who will likely be communicating with them.

Then we transition to the first funnel we're going to promote in our sequence. We start "Season Two" of our Soap Opera Sequence (SOS) with the stories behind the new product/funnel that we're introducing them to. We transition the SOS from us (the Attractive Character) to the first product we want to introduce. The SOS moves through emotion, logic, and fear, and it guides people into and through that first funnel. When it's over, we move to "season three" of our SOS and start our new story about the new product/ funnel that we're introducing them to.

The Daily Seinfeld Emails come *after* someone has moved through all the Soap Opera Sequences inside of the value ladder and they are done with our follow-up funnels. In a perfect world, we'd have follow-up funnels that lasted 40 years, but the reality is that most good follow-up funnels are effective for 30–60 days. After that, people drop off the core list that has ascended your people through your value ladder, and then they're moved to our daily broadcast list. This is the list that we use to send our daily story-based (Seinfeld) emails to lead people to our new front-end offers and get them to re-register for our webinars and promote our blog posts, podcast episodes, and affiliate offers. This is the bucket we put people into after they have dropped out of the back end of our follow-up funnel.

The next secret will show you how to infiltrate your Dream 100, build your own distribution network (your own show), and find your voice.

INFILTRATING THE DREAM 100

From 1989 to 1994, there was a late-night talk show called *The Arsenio Hall Show*. My parents didn't watch it, so I never had a chance to watch it at home. I do remember, though, that my friend's parents watched it every night, and often my best friend would tell me about it. One summer night during a sleepover at their house, we stayed up late and I had my first chance to see the famous Arsenio Hall in action, running around doing his "Woof! Woof! Woof!" chant as he pumped his fist in circles. We used to mimic this on the playground for years afterward every time we would score a touchdown or a home run. His shtick became ours, and we thought we were so cool every time we did it.

Over the years, I had a chance to see his show a few other times. I remember being amazed at the energy of his show and the amazing guests he'd bring on. In June 1992, he had Bill Clinton on while Clinton was running for president. Clinton played "Heartbreak Hotel" on the saxophone, an act considered by many to be the most important moment in his political career for helping to build his popularity among minority and younger voters.[15]

Just two short years later, the show went off the air, and, for most of us, we never heard Arsenio's name again. That is, until 2012 when he showed up as a contestant on *Celebrity Apprentice*. I watched that season, trying to learn business lessons for growing my company from Donald Trump and the contestants. Each of the episodes gave me a few ideas, but the biggest gold nugget was dropped in episode seven.[16]

It was so simple that I think almost everyone missed it. For some reason, though, it caught my ears, and it's been running through my mind now for almost a decade. Let me set the scene for you. The two competing teams were tasked with raising money for charity, and all the contestants were making phone calls to their rich friends and asking for donations. Penn Jillette was able to get the Blue Man Group to perform on the streets of New York City and to donate money. Every celebrity was able to raise some money, except for one: Arsenio Hall.

I watched as Arsenio opened his Rolodex of celebrities and made calls for hours. Each call went to voicemail. He got one commitment from Jay Leno, but the check showed up past the deadline and didn't count toward the competition. In the final scene before the boardroom, Arsenio's frustrated teammates tried to figure out why he didn't raise any money.

Defeated, Arsenio explained that everyone used to answer his calls when he had his own show. But when he didn't have his own talk show, his so-called friends avoided him.

And *that* was the big takeaway! When you have your own show, everyone answers your calls. Earlier we talked a lot about the Dream 100, and how you can work your way in or buy your way in. In either of those situations, you have more leverage when you have your own show, or your own platform. When Arsenio had a talk show, if he called anyone (even the future president of the United States), they would take the call because they knew that he could provide a platform for them that they couldn't get otherwise.

Your platform is the true value that you have to provide your Dream 100. It's more valuable than money, gifts, or anything. The Dream 100 want exposure, and your platform can provide that for them.

As cool of a person as I think I am, I'm sure that if I didn't have my platform of over 2 million entrepreneurs among my email lists, social lists, and podcast listeners, it would have been very difficult to get Tony Robbins, or any of my Dream 100, to return my calls, respond to my emails, or be interested in working with me. None of these people needed another friend. They did need, however, access to my platform, and so that gave me the ability to get my foot in the door, build friendships, and start partnerships. This is the key to working your way in.

Recently, I heard Gary Vaynerchuk speaking at an event for digital marketers where someone asked him where the future of marketing and attention is going. His response was very profound:

> I think this [holding up his cell phone] is the television in 1965 . . . And the TVs, they're the radio, right? . . . The one thing I do study is history, because history loves to repeat itself. So, if you go look at the brands (the beer brands) that were romantic about staying on the radio, because that's how they did it and didn't shift to television, while things like Miller Lite (that nobody had ever heard of) went TV only and became the brand.
>
> If you look at TV in 1965, that's what I think this [the cell phone] is, and I think that YouTube, Instagram, Facebook, and Snapchat are ABC, NBC, and CBS . . . And then I think I, within it, [am] *M*A*S*H** and *Happy Days*. So that's the system . . . And so what you need to do for your business is figure out the channels where you could be the star of that network.[17]

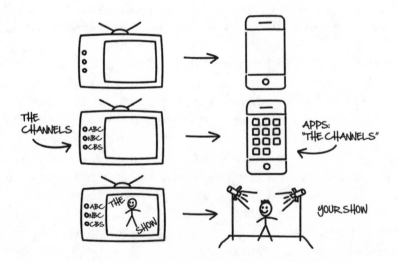

Figure 7.1:

Find the "channel" where you can be the star, then build your show there.

As powerful as that statement is, the more powerful thing to understand is that today you don't have to convince a network that you should have your own show. Instead, you can click a few buttons and *that fast* you can have a show on all the major apps.

Right now, the ABC, NBC, and CBS's on people's phones are:

- Facebook (talk show)
- Podcasts (radio)
- YouTube (sitcom)
- Instagram (reality TV)
- Blogs (newspaper)

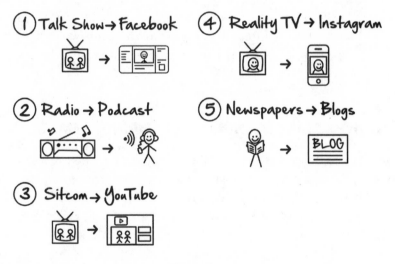

Figure 7.2:

All the previous forms of communication have modern-day applications.

More apps/channels will pop up, but as of right now, the majority of eyeballs are focused on these apps, which each gives you the ability to create your own show for free.

But is having your own show the same as having your own list? I would say that the answer is, "Kind of." With your own list, you own the traffic, but with your own show, you're renting space and trying to earn eyeballs on someone else's network. That was the problem for Arsenio. When Fox dropped his show, it was over. If Facebook decides they don't like your show for some reason (and they've been known to do it), they can cancel your show or your account without a warning. The same is true with podcasts, Instagram, and YouTube.

Now, imagine if Arsenio Hall understood the principles you learned in Secret #4, and if, during each episode of his show, he had told his viewers to go to his funnel and opt in to get his top 100 favorite jokes for free. In that case, he could have built a list of millions of subscribers on the network's dime, and when the show got canceled, he still would have had a platform because he still would have had his list. He could have moved to a new channel, launched a podcast or a blog, emailed his followers, and guided his followers to his new show. Until you own the traffic, you're always left to the whims of the network. So even when starting your own show, remember that the goal is still to turn that traffic that you're earning into traffic that you own.

YOUR PRIMARY DISTRIBUTION CHANNEL: EMAIL

The key to success with your show is how many people you can get to actually consume what you're creating. You might be able to rely on each platform promoting you for free, but I never like to include that as part of my marketing plans. Sometimes we'll create an episode that goes viral and we'll get millions of views for free, but that's not something we bank on. Instead, we need to ask ourselves, "After my new episode is live, how can I get people to go and consume it ASAP?" The best way to do that is to leverage the list that you've already been building.

Figure 7.3:

The modern-day application of direct mail is email.

We spend all our efforts to convert all traffic we control and traffic that we earn into traffic that we own (our own list) because when we have our own list, we control our own destiny. I've had friends who relied 100 percent on Facebook or YouTube's algorithms to promote their videos. A lot were blessed with amazing reach, many of them getting tens of millions of views for each video they would publish. Unfortunately, each platform's algorithms changed (as they always do), and many of these same people now struggle to get a few hundred views. For that reason, I always look at free, viral traffic as the gravy on top of what might come if I promote the video to the best of my abilities, and I make my number-one goal first and foremost to promote each episode I publish.

In addition to email, you'll want to continue to build up other lists and distribution channels, such as direct messenger lists on Facebook and followers on Instagram, so you can do "swipe-ups." Each platform has its own version of a list, but email is the only one you own; you're renting all the rest and you could lose them at any time.

YOUR PRIMARY SHOW CHANNEL: TEXT, VIDEO, OR AUDIO

The next logical question you might be asking yourself is, "Which channel do I create my show on?" My response would be, "It depends on you." To begin with, you shouldn't try to create a show on every channel. Doing that will hurt your ability to grow at all. For now, the key is to focus on one channel. In Secret #15, Conversation Domination, I'll show you how to leverage your primary show to get distribution across all channels, but, for now, you need to focus on just two channels: your primary distribution channel (email) and your primary show channel.

The channel you should be growing your primary show on depends on you, your personality, and your talents. For those of you who love writing, I'd focus on creating a blog.

Newspapers → Blogs

Figure 7.4:

The modern-day application of newspapers is a blog.

If you hate writing, but you *love* the idea of being on video, then I'd recommend you build your show on one of the video channels (each one has a different strategy that we'll go deeper into in the next section).

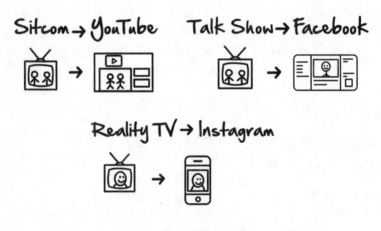

Figure 7.5

The modern-day applications of sitcoms, talk shows, and reality TV are respectively YouTube, Facebook, and Instagram.

For those who have a voice for radio or who may be a little nervous about being on camera, then I'd recommend starting your own podcast.

Figure 7.6:

The modern-day application of radio is a podcast.

If you're still not sure which platform you'd like to create your show on, I'd recommend looking at which platform you consume the most content on. Typically, if you love YouTube and spend a lot of time watching videos, you're going to have the best success creating videos for that platform, because you understand it. If you listen to podcasts a lot, that's probably the best place to start. Similarly, if you read a lot of blogs, that's probably the best place to start.

Because we spent so much time talking about your "Primary Distribution" channel (email) in Secret #7, I will spend the rest of this chapter talking about your "Master Show." Remember that for now, you should *only* be building one show on one channel. Do not try to build more than one at this point. In Secret #15, I will show you how to leverage this one primary channel into all the secondary channels, but that does not come now. Focus all your efforts on making your first show successful.

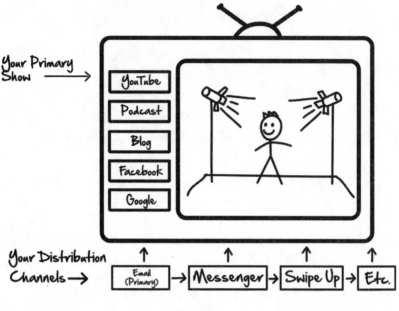

Figure 7.7:

Once you have your primary show, you'll use your distribution channels like email, Messenger, and "swipe-ups" to notify your audience there are new episodes.

STARTING YOUR SHOW (FINDING YOUR VOICE)

On March 26, 2013, I launched my first episode of my *Marketing in Your Car* podcast, which later became the *Marketing Secrets* show. It seemed as good a day as any to launch it, outside of the fact that in the prior few months I had almost bankrupted my company, fired about 100 employees, found out that I owed over $250,000 to the IRS (which if I didn't pay soon would mean even more fines and possible jail time), and had almost no money left in the bank account with tons of credit card debt piling up. Looking back now, it seems like the worst possible time to have launched a podcast teaching people my "secrets of marketing," yet that's exactly what I did.

I knew that if I was going to do my own show, I had to be consistent or it wouldn't work. Out of all the types of shows that I could publish (audio, video, or text), I knew that it had to be simple or I'd never stick to it. When I considered how to work it into my everyday routine, I realized that every day I had a 10-minute commute to my office. I figured that I could record each episode on my phone as I drove to work. In the episodes, I would share my thoughts about what I was doing to market my business and the lessons I was learning each day. That's how it got its original name: *Marketing in Your Car.*

The first episodes were not good. In fact, years later, my friend Steve J Larsen told me, "The first 45 or 46 episodes weren't very good, but then around that time is where it seemed like you found your voice, and they started getting better and better after that." The good news for me (and also for you) is during your first episodes, the ones where you are the worst, no one is listening to you yet! If I hadn't done the first 45 episodes, I never would have gotten to episode 46 where I started to hit my stride. That's why it's so essential to start publishing your show now, even when you're not good at it. In the process of doing your show, you will find your voice. I am so grateful that I actually had no idea how to check the download stats to see if anyone was listening to me when I first got started, because I'm sure that I would have been discouraged and stopped. Don't look at your stats, downloads, or numbers at first, because you're just trying to build the foundation for something great, and it will take time.

About three years into my podcast, I learned how to check the download stats and discovered that I had tens of thousands of people listening to every episode. I also found out that the majority of the people who had joined my highest-level mastermind groups and coaching programs had all been podcast listeners first. When I asked our coaching members about it, the pattern of how most of them came into our higher-end programs was shockingly similar. So many told me that they would listen to a few episodes, and then for some reason, an episode would connect with them. It made them want more, so they would go back to episode one and binge listen to every episode over a week or two period of time. During the episodes, I documented my journey as I was building back up my company. I'd share stories of the people that I had a chance to work with; usually before these listeners had finished binging, they had applied to work with me.

Without selling ads in my podcast, promoting my own or other people's products (both things that you can and probably should do to make money from your show), I was just telling stories of my own and from my clients. Yet that podcast has converted more casual followers into raving fans than anything else I've ever done. But it didn't start that way; it took over three years of consistent publishing.

Let me walk you through the steps that will make your own show a success.

Step #1) Publish daily for at least a year: The first commitment that you have to make is that you will be consistent. I knew when I started that if I didn't find a platform that was easy for me and easy to create the content, I wouldn't be consistent. What platform makes the most sense for you? How and when are you going to publish? Do you wake up each morning and write a 1,000-word blog post before lunch? Do you do a Facebook Live before you go to bed each night sharing the day's lessons? What works for you that will help you to be consistent? If you can publish every day for a year, you'll never have to worry about money problems again. During the process, you will find your voice, and your audience will have time to find you.

One of my friends, Nathan Barry, wrote this post recently, "Endure Long Enough to Get Noticed":

> How many great TV shows have you discovered in season three or later? I started watching *Game of Thrones* after they had released five seasons. Pat Flynn had released at least 100 episodes of his podcast before I even knew he existed. I discovered *Hardcore History* years after Dan Carlin started producing it.
>
> This is such a common experience. There is so much content being produced that we can't possibly discover it all. So instead, we wait for the best content to float to the surface after time. If step one in building an audience is to create great content, step two is to endure long enough to get noticed.
>
> Seth Godin is very generous with his time and will appear on almost any relevant podcast—but you have to

have recorded at least 100 episodes first. His filter is creators who have shown they are willing to show up consistently for a long time.[18]

For those of you who have been around me for any amount of time, you know that this is a soapbox that I'm very firm on. You must be publishing or you will never become relevant, and you must continue publishing if you want to remain relevant. This part of the traffic flywheel does not go away.

Steve J Larsen knew when he bought his first tickets to Funnel Hacking Live that I was probably going to tell everyone this eternal truth, but as he packed his bags, he told his wife, "I will do everything that Russell says at this event . . . except publishing my own show. I won't do that."

Before lunch on day one, I told everyone that the number-one thing they could do from now until next year's event would be to pick a channel and publish daily on it. I told them that if they did that every day for a year, they would never need to worry about money again. And then I did something I hadn't before; I made everyone in the audience commit to me that they would start publishing that day.

Most of the people in the room raised their hands and were excited to take the challenge, but very few took what I said at face value. But when one person, Steve J Larsen, made the commitment, the one that he went in knowing he wasn't willing to make, he decided to go all in. He decided to start a podcast, and at that event, he started creating his first episodes.

About a week later, he applied for a job at ClickFunnels and became my new head funnel builder. He sat next to me every day for the next two years. As I was working on my projects, he watched me share (publish) all the lessons I was learning along the way. I was podcasting, posting on Facebook, doing Periscope shows, and more. He told me that he was shocked at how much I published, and so he modeled what I was doing.

For the next two years that he worked at ClickFunnels, he kept publishing his show; after a few months it started getting some traction. It kept growing over the years, and when he decided to make the jump from being an employee to becoming his own entrepreneur, he had a large following of people who were consuming everything he was publishing. That show and his following became the launch pad he needed to launch his career. He had the fans and a following, so he simply introduced them to the new offers he had created, and he became an "overnight success."

Step #2) Document the journey: The biggest question and the largest fear that most people have when I tell them to start their own show is they have no idea what they will talk about. One of the most powerful things I learned from Gary Vaynerchuk is a concept he calls "Document, Don't Create." I'm sharing an article from his blog going deeper into this concept:

> If you want people to start listening to you, you have to show up. What I mean by this is there are a lot of you out there who aren't producing enough articles or videos or pieces of content that should be produced to build your influence. Too many "content creators" think that they only have one at bat—they have to make the one, most beautifully created video or image or rant on Facebook.
>
> But what they don't realize is that their hunger to make the perfect piece of content is what's actually crippling them.
>
> It's true that if you want to be seen or heard on social media, you have to put out valuable content on a regular basis. You should be doing a YouTube vlog or podcast or some sort of long-form audio/video series at least once a week. You should be posting on Instagram and/or Snapchat stories at least six to seven times a day.
>
> Now you're probably thinking, *Whoa, that's a lot. How do I create six to seven meaningful things a day?*
>
> I'll give you the biggest tip when it comes to content creation: Document. Don't create.
>
> In very simple terms, "documenting" versus "creating" is what *The Real World* and *The Kardashians* is to *Star Wars* and *Friends*. And don't get confused—just because you're "documenting" doesn't mean you're not creating

content. It's just a version of creating that is predicated more on practicality instead of having to think of stories or fantasy—something that's very hard for most people (including myself).

Think about it: you can ponder about the strategy behind every post and fabricate yourself into this "influential person" . . . or you can just be yourself.

Creating this influential persona might seem especially hard if you're just someone starting to climb the ladder. And I get it—for some of you there's a lot of pressure in that. You think that some 30- or 40- or 50-year-old is going to listen to your rant video with cynicism and think, *What does this kid know?*

But, one of the biggest mistakes people make when creating content for their personal brand is trying to oversell themselves because they think that's what's going to get people's attention. Whether you're a business coach or motivational speaker or artist, I think it's much more fruitful to talk about your process than about the actual advice you "think" you should be giving them.

Documenting your journey versus creating an image of yourself is the difference between saying "You should . . ." versus "My intuition says . . ." Get it? It changes everything. I believe that the people who are willing to discuss their journeys instead of trying to front themselves as the "next big thing" are going to win.

So, when I say to put out those six to seven meaningful pieces of content a day, pick up your smartphone, open Facebook Live, and just start talking about the things most important to you. Because in the end, the creative (or how "beautiful" someone thinks your content is) is going to be subjective. What's not subjective is the fact that you need to start putting yourself out there and keep swinging.

Starting is the most important part and the biggest hurdle that most people are facing. They're pondering and strategizing instead of making. They're debating what's going to happen when they haven't even looked at what's in front of them.

So do me a favor and start documenting.

"Okay, I started, Gary. Now what?" you ask. Keep doing it for another five years and then come back to me before you ask again.[19]

People who are tuning into your show are typically doing it because they're looking for some type of result. It's the same reason why they buy your products, open your emails, and engage with your content. People listen to my podcasts, read my books, and watch my videos because they're trying to figure out more ways to market their business. I'm not publishing because I know everything about this topic, I'm publishing because I'm obsessed with this topic. I'm in a constant search for new and better ways to market my own company, and as I run across them, have ideas, and read cool things, I'm sharing them with my people. As my friend Rich Schefren once told me, "We get paid a lot to think for other people."

So my first question for you as you start your show is this: "What is the big result that you're obsessed with? What are you trying to learn for yourself anyway that you can document as you're discovering it in real time?"

Figure 7.8:

On your show, you can document your journey, test your material, and find hooks.

When you listen to the introduction to my podcast, I call out the big question that I'm answering on my show:

> So, the big question is this: "How are entrepreneurs like us, who didn't cheat and take on Venture Capital, who are spending money from our own pockets, how do we market in a way that lets us get our products and services and the things that we believe in, out to the world, yet still remain profitable?" That is the question, and this podcast will give you the answers. My name is Russell Brunson, and welcome to the *Marketing Secrets* podcast.

Figure 7.9:

In my podcast, I document my journey in real time.

Inside of this frame, I can talk about, share, and interview people on anything related to helping people sell more of the things that they believe in. Since I started this podcast on the back of a huge business failure, most people would have thought it was the worst time ever to start a podcast, let alone one about marketing a business, but looking at it through the "Document, Don't Create" lens reveals that it was the perfect time to start the podcast. In fact, I wish I would have started it 10 years earlier when I had first gotten online, because I would have had so many more interesting things to share as I was learning them all the first time. In any case, how cool is it now, six years later, that I have documented the entire journey from business failure to growing ClickFunnels to being an over $100-million-per-year company? Even more importantly, tens of thousands of people have been able to follow us on that journey and learn the lessons as I was learning them!

Step #3) Testing your material: Recently, I was at a private mastermind retreat in Wyoming with a handful of influencers who had collectively made billions of dollars online and influenced hundreds of millions of people. One night as we were sitting around a campfire, Dean Graziosi shared an insight that has changed how I look at the material that I'm publishing. His story, from the best of my memory, went something like this:

> You know how when you watch an amazing comedian perform onstage on a late-night talk show, every joke he tells lands perfectly? You find yourself wondering, "How is this guy so funny?" But what you don't realize is that over the last 10 years, as he started his journey to become a comedian, he would write out 10 jokes, go to the closest dive bar, stand up on stage, and deliver his jokes. He probably watched as one or two of the 10 jokes landed, and the rest bombed. He would then go back home, take the two jokes that landed, and then write eight new ones. The next week he would find a new place to perform, deliver his 10 jokes, and maybe find that one of his new jokes actually landed. Now he has three jokes in total that

he can use. He goes back to his apartment and starts the process over again, doing this week after week, year after year, until he's found his 10 jokes. Now he's ready. That's when we get to see him, after he's perfected the material, when he stands up on stage, and lands every joke on the biggest stage in the world.

I look back at my journey and think about my first book, *DotCom Secrets*. I was so scared when I finished writing that book that I didn't want to give it to people to read. But what most people didn't realize was that a full decade before I wrote that book, I earned that book. I was obsessed with marketing, and I read, watched, and listened to everything I could get my hands on. After that, I would test the concepts and ideas on the little businesses I was creating. I also tested the concepts on other people's businesses as a consultant. Some ideas worked, while others failed.

I started teaching at small seminars and workshops. I would explain concepts and watch to see which ideas made sense to people and which ideas were confusing. At each event, I would teach the concepts again, over and over, tweaking and refining the ideas and stories every time. I did interviews, podcasts, videos, and articles testing my materials over and over again. From this work came the frameworks like the value ladder, the secret formula, the three types of traffic, funnel hacking, and the Attractive Character. I was testing my material for over a decade, and so while I was nervous for others to read the book, I was also confident knowing that it was ready.

The same thing happened with *Expert Secrets*. I spent two years talking about the concepts on my own podcast and on other people's podcasts. I developed ideas on Periscope and then Facebook Live. I ran events, workshops, and coaching programs testing the ideas on others' businesses as well as mine, and the end product was the book.

Today, as I'm typing this current book in the passenger seat of an RV while my wife is driving and the kids are playing in the back, I'm just as nervous about putting it out into the world as I was with my very first book. Yet I know that I've been testing this material for the past two years on every platform that I have had access to, and it's ready.

Publishing your show daily, as you're documenting your journey, will give you a chance to start testing your material. You'll discover what messages connect with people, which episodes get shared, and which ones don't. You'll see which messages get people to show up and comment and which messages don't connect. It's this very process of you showing up consistently and publishing that will help you to refine your message, find your voice, and attract your dream customers to you. It doesn't matter if your end goal is a book, a webinar, a keynote presentation, a viral video, or something else, the more you publish and test your material, the clearer your message will become and the more people you will attract.

Step #4) Introduction to Your Dream 100: When you start your show, typically you'll use the first few episodes to tell your origin story, why you created the show, and what people should expect. These initial episodes are important because there will be people who find your show a week from now, some a year from now, and others won't find it for years, but when they do, and when they get hooked, most people will go back to episode one and binge-listen (or read or watch) to catch up on what they missed. Even though these early episodes are old, they'll still likely be a starting point for many people that fall in love with your content.

After the initial episodes, it's time to start using your show to infiltrate your Dream 100. This is the secret to getting amazing new content for your show, and it also gives you the ability to leverage your Dream 100 as guests to grow your show.

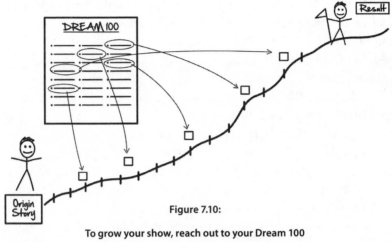

Figure 7.10:
To grow your show, reach out to your Dream 100
to see if you can be a guest on their show.

Think about how this works on TV. Let's say that *The Tonight Show* wants to get a lot of people to watch their show. What do they do? They try to find the most relevant, interesting guests possible to be on the show, right? But they don't stop at that. All week leading up to that interview, they're promoting their guest on every distribution channel they have access to. You'll see commercials all week leading to the interview talking about who's going to be on the show, and you'll see clips during the commercial breaks leading up to the show, showing the funniest or most intense parts of the interview. The host is leveraging the guest to attract more viewers. The same will be true for your show.

Who are the people on your Dream 100 that have an interesting story they could tell that will relate to your show *and* have a following of people that you can promote their episode to? You have a platform that you can now leverage to get people on your show, and they have a network that you can advertise their episode to. It's a huge win-win. In a perfect world, they would promote their episode to their entire following when it goes live (and that does happen at times), but even if they don't promote, you can still buy ads targeting their audiences on Facebook, Instagram, YouTube, or wherever their following is.

Now, I know what you're probably thinking, *That's great, Russell, for people who already have relationships with their Dream 100, but what about me? I'm brand new. My show has almost no followers, so why would any of them want to let me interview them?* The reality is that many people you ask will say no, and that's okay, because you don't need everyone. You just need one: one guest that you can then leverage to get the others.

Typically, most markets have a "good ol' boys" club atmosphere, and usually a lot of your Dream 100 will be in one or more clubs. To infiltrate and get access to that club, you don't need to get access to all of them; you just need to have one of the cool kids think you're cool, and then you're in.

One of my favorite illustrations of this point was in the movie *Never Been Kissed*, starring Drew Barrymore (Josie) and David Arquette (Rob).[20] In this movie, Josie is a writer for the *Chicago Sun-Times* and gets a job to go undercover back to high school to get a story on teenage culture. She struggles to get in with the cool kids, and her brother Rob tells her the secret: If she can get one person to think she's cool, then she'll be in, because everyone else at school will be too scared to challenge it. Rob then demonstrates this principle as he registers for school, becomes popular within a day, and uses his popularity to get Josie into the cool kids' club.

A few years ago, I got a phone call from a guy named Tellman Knudson who was just starting his own company. He knew I had a list of subscribers (apparently I was on his Dream 100 list) and he wanted to ask if I would promote a summit he was creating to my list. I decided the idea he was pitching me on wasn't a good fit, and I told him no.

I assumed this was going to be the last that I heard from him, thinking that most of the people on his Dream 100 probably would have told him no as well. He didn't have a list or a platform; he just had an idea and some hustle. About six months later, out of the blue, I started getting dozens of emails from some of the most respected list owners in our industry, all promoting Tellman's new summit.

Interested in what happened, I gave Tellman a call and asked him how in the world he was able to get all of these huge list owners to promote for him.

He responded, "I made a list of the people I wanted to be part of this promotion, and then I started calling them. The first person told me no, and the second person said the same thing. I kept calling and kept getting noes. Somewhere in that list I called you, and your answer was the same, but I was determined to make this work no matter the cost, so I kept calling."

"How many people did you end up calling?" I asked.

"Forty-nine."

"You called forty-nine people?"

"No, I got forty-eight noes, but the forty-ninth person said yes! I knew that after I had one yes, I was in. I asked him if he knew anyone else that might be interested, and he gave me three names. I called each of them, and they all said yes. I asked them for referrals, and they all said yes as well! As my list of yeses grew, I started calling people who told me no and showed them the people who were now involved and had said yes, and many of the noes I had received earlier turned into yeses. I received forty-eight noes in a row, and then the next thirty people all said yes."

That promotion ended up building Tellman a list of over 100,000 people in just a few short months, and that list generated him over $800,000 in sales during his first year online. This is the power of infiltrating your Dream 100.

So your job now is to look at your Dream 100 and start asking them to be on your show. Many will say no, but don't let that stop you. You only need one yes.

As you have a chance to interview your Dream 100 on your podcast, you'll be giving them a platform for which they'll be grateful. You'll be able to spend time building a relationship as you interview them on your show (digging your well before you're thirsty), and you can tap into their audience to promote their episode, build your show, and get access to their followers.

PUTTING IT ALL TOGETHER

I've explained a lot of concepts in this chapter, so I want to recap it all into something a little more tangible.

Step #1: The first step is to figure out what type of show you want to have. If you're a writer, then you should start a blog. If you like video, then you should start a vlog on one of the video platforms. Lastly, if you like audio, then you should start a podcast.

Step #2: Your show will be you documenting the process of achieving the same goal that your audience will be striving for. As you're documenting your process, you'll be testing your material and paying attention to the things that people respond to. If you commit to publishing your show every day for a year, you'll have the ability to test your material and find your voice, and your dream customers will be able to find you.

Step #3: You'll leverage your Dream 100 by interviewing them on your show. This will give you the ability to build relationships with them, give them a platform, give you the ability to promote their episode on your show to their audience, and get access to their friends and followers.

Step #4: Even though this is your own show, you're renting time on someone else's network. It's important that you don't forget it and that you focus on converting it into traffic that you own.

Figure 7.11:

As you create your own show, focus on converting traffic that you earn and control into traffic that you own.

And with that, I will close out Section One of this book. So far, we've covered a lot of core principles to traffic. We:

- Identified exactly *who* your dream client is.
- Discovered exactly *where* they are congregating.
- Talked about how to work your way into those audiences (traffic that you earn) and how you buy your way into those audiences (traffic that you control).
- Learned how to take all the traffic that you earn and all the traffic that you buy and turn it all into traffic that you *own* (building your list).
- Discussed how to plug that list into a follow-up funnel so you can move them through your value ladder.
- Prepared to infiltrate your Dream 100, find your voice, and build your following by creating your own show.

In the next section, we'll shift our focus to mastering the pattern to get traffic from any advertising networks (like Instagram, Facebook, Google, and YouTube) and how to understand their algorithms so you can get unlimited traffic and leads pouring into your funnels.

FILL YOUR FUNNEL

In the first section of this book, we focused on truly understanding who your dream customers are, finding out who has already congregated them, and learning how to get access to those people and get them onto your lists. In this section, we'll be shifting more into the tactics of how to fill your funnels with your dream customers on the following four advertising platforms:

- Instagram
- Facebook
- Google
- YouTube

I could have gone deep into dozens of other platforms, including LinkedIn, Snapchat, Pinterest, TikTok, and Twitch, but I'm only exploring these four platforms in order to show you a framework and pattern that you can learn and use on any platform that you'd like to get traffic from in the future. Depending on when you're reading this book, admittedly, some of these platforms may no longer be relevant, and there will likely be many to come that no one has even heard of yet.

Showing you the strategy and tactics on one platform is the equivalent of "giving a man a fish," and teaching you the framework to get traffic from every platform is the equivalent of "teaching a man how to fish." As you read the following chapters, you'll learn the pattern and see its practical application throughout the four most important networks today, helping you to master the frameworks that will fill your funnels with your dream customers.

THE "FILL YOUR FUNNEL" FRAMEWORK

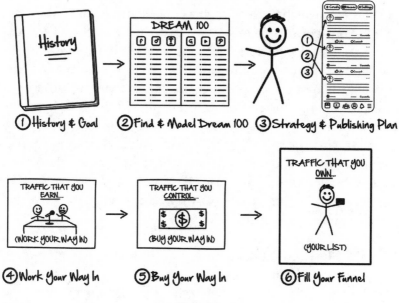

Figure 8.1:

This quick sketch will help you remember the six steps
inside the "Fill Your Funnel" framework.

Step #1—Understand the history and the goal of the new platform: If you want to know where the platform is going, you have to know where it came from. How did Google start? Where did Facebook come from? How did the algorithms change and, more importantly, why did they change? What was the purpose behind them? If you can understand why they made the changes, then you can start thinking like them. You can understand their goals and intentions.

This is so important because by the time you are reading some of these chapters, the algorithms may have already shifted, so it's essential that you understand the history so you can see where we are today.

As you start getting a layout of each platform's history, you'll quickly start to see what their end goals are. Each platform has a goal to make the best user experience for their end user as possible. That's what keeps their people coming back again and again. Google wants to make sure that they give their users the best search results possible. Facebook wants to make sure you love the things that show up in your feed. Once you understand that creating the best user experience possible is their goal, then you can start asking yourself how you can align with their goals. The goal of spammers is always to hack the algorithm to get what they want, which always provides short-term gains, because as soon as the spammers are identified, the loopholes that they have been exploiting are taken away. Instead, if you align with the wills of the network and give them what they want, then they'll give you what you want: tons of traffic.

Step #2—Find and model your Dream 100: The next question is, who on this platform has already figured this out? Who has already identified your dream customers, who is publishing to them, and who is getting rewarded by the platform by getting tons of views or likes (or whatever the reward system is for that network)?

As you start this part of the journey, I want to bring you back to the core questions we asked in Section One.

Question #1: Who is your dream customer?

Question #2: Where are they congregating?

Asking these two questions should then get you to ask the next question:

Question #3: Who are your Dream 100 on this platform who have already congregated your dream customers?

When I first went onto Facebook or Instagram (and I did the same things on other networks like Twitter and LinkedIn), I looked to see the Dream 100 who had already mastered that platform.

Who had the big followings and tons of engagement with my dream customers? Then I built out a new Dream 100 list specifically for each of those platforms, and I followed each of them. I needed to be able to see exactly what they were doing, because if they were having success, it meant that they were in the front of the algorithm. They're doing what the platform wants, so if you want to know what the platform wants today, in real time, then you have to be watching closely what they're doing in real time.

Here are the three things it will take to funnel hack social algorithms:

1) Follow each of your Dream 100 and spend 10 minutes each day watching what they are doing. Write down the answers to these questions:

   What are they posting?

   How are they getting people to engage with what they post?

   What paid ads are they running?

2) During these 10 minutes, try to comment, like, and engage with as many things they are doing each day as possible.

3) Notice the pattern of what is working right now and model it for your posts (funnel hacking). This will give you a pulse on what is working in the market on that platform right now. **It gives you the ability to see in real time what the algorithms are rewarding today.**

Before we go further, though, I want to talk about modeling and funnel hacking. Unfortunately, too many people will read what I wrote above, and, if I'm not careful, they'll start copying the inspirational quotes or videos they see other people posting. Then they'll come to me and say, "Russell, I copied it like you said, and it's not working."

Funnel hacking is not copying. Funnel hacking is modeling, and there is a big difference between copying and modeling. Every day, I look at over 100 people's posts, videos, ads, and quotes, and that helps me to gather inspiration for unique things that I can create. You're looking for the types of things the platforms' algorithms are currently rewarding that you can then model.

For example, a few years ago on Facebook, I noticed that some of the people I follow in the fitness market had created what are now called "memed videos," where they added a headline in the actual video, usually above and oftentimes below the video. They were new at the time, and not many people were doing them. For some reason, though, that style and layout got tons of views, comments, and shares—all of the things that we know Facebook loves.

Figure 8.2:

These memed videos got us a ton of comments, likes, and shares.

I saw this new pattern interrupt working, so we quickly modeled or "funnel hacked" this concept and started making our own memed videos. We were one of the first, if not the first, in the marketing world to use these. Because no one had seen them, every video we published in this format got more comments and engagement than anything I had ever seen before. Soon, though, others noticed how well this pattern interrupt worked, and they modeled it. Within a few months, hundreds of marketers were doing it, and most of my feed was filled with memed videos.

When the pattern interrupt becomes the pattern, it stops being as effective. Notice that I didn't say they stop working; they just become less effective. So if you are starting right now, and you see all of your Dream 100 doing something, you should still model what they're doing. It may not be as effective as a new pattern interrupt, but it is the current pattern that is working, so that's where you start.

After you model the pattern that's working, the next phase of funnel hacking the social algorithms is to look for and test ideas that will become the next pattern interrupt. For example, a few weeks ago I noticed that some of my Dream 100 started posting strange posts on Instagram that looked like this:

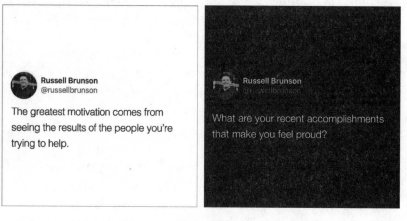

Figure 8.3:

We realized that quote cards like these created a pattern interrupt for our audience.

I had never seen anything like that before, and, honestly, I didn't really like it. It was different, though, so we decided to test the pattern interrupt and see if it would work for us. I made my first post modeling this style, and, sure enough, it was a winner. We now post images similar to this on Instagram a few times per week, and we'll continue to do that until we find a new pattern interrupt that works better. Following your Dream 100 lets you have your fingers on the pulse of what's working currently in each platform. You can model ideas that they're trying, come up with your own unique ideas, and test them both to see which ones stick.

Because the algorithms are always changing, it's essential that you network with and stay close to your Dream 100. They will be the ones who will also have a vested interest in staying in front of the algorithm changes, and it can be super useful to have a sounding board of people in your market during the inevitable changes that will come.

Step #3—Identify the publishing strategy and create your publishing plan: Each platform has multiple ways that you can publish your content, so it's essential to understand the strategy for each section and how you can weave it into your daily publishing schedule. For example, Instagram lets you do stories that are similar to a reality show, but also have your profile, which is more like a picture gallery. Questions I would start asking myself are: "How often should you be doing Stories and what do you post on your profile, and how often?" Instagram also lets you do "Lives" that are similar to a talk show to your following and they have IGTV for your "how to" content. There are a lot of possibilities, so you want to understand all the publishing opportunities on each platform, decide which you want to focus on, and figure out a plan to make it simple to consistently publish on your chosen platform.

Step #4—Work your way in: After I start publishing on each platform and I have content that my dream customers can see, I look for ways to work my way into the Dream 100. I start asking myself the question, how can I get organic, free exposure to the audiences of the people who have already congregated my dream customers, and then get these people to join my lists and become traffic that I own?

Step #5—Buy your way in: While I'm working my way in, I want to stimulate growth as fast as possible. The best way is to buy ads targeting the followers of my Dream 100 and then get these people to join my lists and become traffic that I own. I discuss buying your way in to audiences throughout this book, but Secret #9 goes a lot deeper to help you understand the paid advertising frameworks that you can use to master paid ads on each platform.

Step #6—Fill your funnel: As you're publishing, working your way in, and buying your way in, the goal is always to convert all the traffic and attention into traffic that you own. You do that by pushing people into your funnels where you can get their contact information, sell them your front-end products, and then push them through a follow-up funnel to ascend them up your value ladder.

These six steps make up the "Fill Your Funnel" framework and will help you to master every platform and stay on top of what's working in the moment. I've taken a snapshot in time of how each of the following platforms work and then applied this framework to them. That way, you can see how I think, and then you can understand what I'm looking for as I create my publishing plans and figure out how to work my way in and buy my way in to the following of my Dream 100. My goal is to help make this pattern so second nature to you that by the time you're done reading, you will know "how to fish."

FILL YOUR FUNNEL ORGANICALLY
(Working Your Way In)

It's hard for most of us to remember, but it wasn't too long ago that we used the internet differently than how we use it today, back when there was no social media. There were forums and message boards that allowed people to share their thoughts and ideas, but, for the most part, we went online to search for things we were looking for.

When the social movement started and sites like Friendster first popped up, followed shortly thereafter by Myspace, Facebook, and Twitter, we marketers all knew there was an opportunity to make money by leveraging these platforms, but we didn't know how. Most of our early attempts, if we are completely honest, were us just posting links to our funnels and other things that nowadays people would consider spam. We saw a huge congregation of people, and we tried everything in our power to get our messages in front of them. Most things we tried didn't work, at least not long-term.

I was frustrated with the new social platforms, thinking that they didn't work as a good vehicle to get traffic. Inevitably, I stopped trying to figure them out for a few years altogether. Instead, I focused my energy on free and paid search, banner ads, and email marketing, and I stayed away from social media like it was the plague.

Around this time, Twitter started to make its big run. It became the fastest growing new social network at the time, and everyone was jumping onto its bandwagon. In fear of missing out on the next big trend, I jumped on and started tweeting. At first, it made no sense to me, but all the cool kids were doing it, so I tried. I grew my following, and then I did the only thing I knew how to do as a marketer: I started to promote my products. To my annoyance, not only did I make very few sales, but my marketing also killed the engagement that I had built up with the few people who followed me.

Then I watched as Perry Belcher, one of the people on my Dream 100, joined Twitter. In a matter of months, he built a following of over 100,000 people, set up a webinar for those followers, registered over 20,000 people, and made over a million dollars in sales from that one webinar!

I watched in awe as he did it, and so I did what any good funnel hacker would do: I tried to reverse engineer his process. The more I dug into what he was doing, the more confused I became. He wasn't posting any ads. He wasn't talking about his products. Every post he made had thousands of people commenting, sharing, and growing his brand for him.

I finally reached out to him and asked if he'd be willing to explain his strategy to me. Luckily for me, he agreed. We quickly jumped on a phone call together, and it went a little something like this:

"Hey, Perry," I said. "I've been trying to figure out how to make money with all this social networking stuff, and it's not working. I see on the outside what you're doing, but it all seems backward. You're not promoting anything, you're not selling anything, yet you're making a ton of money. What are you doing?"

Perry kind of laughed and said, "That's your problem, Russell. Guess how much money I try to make with social networking."

"As much as possible?" I guessed.

I could hear him grin on the other end, and then he said, "Zero. None. That's how much I try to make with social networking. Social networking is not about making money; it's about making friends. It's just like how we do business in person. Let me show you how I view social media and how we use it to grow our companies. If you look at the social networks, we have Facebook, Twitter, YouTube, etc. . . . I view all of these networks like I'm going to a party. So, if I'm on Twitter posting messages and responding, it's like I'm at a party. Does that make sense?"

"Um . . . kinda," I replied. "But I'm still not sure how that makes us any money."

"Well, when you go to a party, do you just talk about what you do? 'Hey, I'm Perry, and I sell stuff. Would you like to buy some stuff from me?' No, of course not. If you did, you'd be the biggest jerk at the party. Everyone would avoid you. And that's what you've been doing on social media, Russell. I've been watching you, and that's why it's not working for you."

"Okay, then what do we talk about on the social networking sites? As an introvert, I've never really networked in real life, so I'm not sure how or what I should be saying."

"You talk about what's going on in your life," Perry responded. "You talk about your family, tell them stories, entertain them a little bit, ask them questions, and introduce them to other cool people who are at the party. Basically, you do everything you would do if you were hanging out with them in real life. Social networking is just a great big party. That's part number one."

I doodled an image to make sure it was clear in my mind. I also made a note to watch how Perry and everyone else in my Dream 100 was posting and making conversations on each social network so I could start modeling these "party" interactions.

Figure 8.4:

The goal of social networking is to invite people back to your home and, from there, to introduce them into your funnels.

"The second part of the process is how I use my personal profile on each social platform," Perry continued. "My personal profile is my house, it's my home, it's where I live. It has most of my thoughts, my information, and stuff that is interesting to me. I archive pictures, videos, fun stuff I've done with friends, and stuff like that. When people come into my house, they know what I'm about. They can see the things that I like to talk about."

"Now, this is how it works. When I go into groups and start networking, or I see someone else's posts in my feed, I go and participate in the conversations and make friends. As they see me consistently show up, they will want to drop by my house and see what I'm all about. Give them some free stuff like chips and dip (free content) to get them to come to your house. Then when they're at my house, that's where I invite them to take action with me: register for my webinar, attend my next event, read my new book, or join my newsletter list. That's how I invite people from my house into my funnels. Those selling conversations don't have a place on social media, but they do at your house. You can direct people into your funnels from the posts you make on your own personal profile. If you provide value on the social platforms, people will come running to your house because they want more of you, and from there, they will flow into your funnels."

This was the big "aha" that I needed! Social wasn't about selling. It was about making friends. I changed my tactics, deleted all my posts that were trying to sell my products, and started serving, interacting, being entertaining, and having fun with my followers. All the friends, fans, and followers that came afterward were a direct by-product of me being the life of the party.

I wanted to give you this context before we discussed any of the specific networks, because this is how we "work our way in." It's the core concept that you have to master if you want to have success with social media, no matter which platform you are focusing on. Those who just spam their message to their followers will always think that social media doesn't work. Even if they do get some short-term results, they won't last. On the other hand, those who play the longer game and plant seeds with their followers will end up with a constant stream of traffic flooding into their funnels.

PRODUCER, NOT CONSUMER

I want to give you one quick warning because I know that some reading this are probably already thinking, *Russell, I already spend way too much time on social media right now. If I'm going to become the life of the party, my whole life is going to be wasted on social media.*

I'll start by saying that yes, you are currently spending *way* too much time on social media. I don't care who you are; you are probably already spending way too much time consuming social media. If you're spending more than 10 minutes a day consuming social media, then you are wasting your time. The keyword here is "consuming."

As of today, you are no longer a consumer of social media. You are a producer of social media. There is a big difference. Consuming social media doesn't serve you or the audience you've been called to serve. Producing social media does serve them.

The first step in this process is to do a social media reset. That means unfriending and unfollowing almost everyone on every platform that you'll be using to generate traffic. That way, you won't be distracted by the nonsense that everyone around you is posting. From here on out, you'll use social media as a business tool, not a social tool. After you unfriend everyone, I suggest only following your Dream 100 on each platform. That way, when you log in to any of the platforms, you'll be able to quickly get a glimpse of what they're posting and get ideas for things that are working well that you can model. Also, you will be able to start digging your well with these people by commenting on their posts and messaging them through direct messages.

Now that your social feed has been cleaned up, go and look for the social parties that have the most people engaged in them. You wouldn't go to a party that only has a few dozen people; instead you would look for the largest parties in town where you can get the most exposure for your efforts. Depending on the platform, you'll be looking for the largest groups, podcasts, blogs, videos, and Fan Pages that you can go to and become the life of the party. As you participate in these groups and serve their audiences, the people will naturally start coming back to your home.

In the following secrets, I'll be giving you a specific publishing plan for each network that will show you how to effectively be a producer of social media in a way that won't consume your whole life. I want to bring up the concept of producer versus consumer now so you will be able to look at everything that happens in the next few chapters through this lens. This way, you can focus on serving your audience, not wasting your precious time.

Next we will cover how to fill your funnels with paid ads, and then we will move into the two largest social networks at the moment: Instagram and Facebook. I'll discuss how to find your Dream 100 on both platforms, understand the platforms' strategies, create your publishing plan, grow your followings and fill your funnels.

FILL YOUR FUNNEL WITH PAID ADS
(Buying Your Way In)

Now that you've seen the overarching strategy for "working your way in" and getting free organic traffic, I now want to lay out the strategy for how to fill your funnel with paid ads. After you have an understanding of these two core principles, then we'll dive into each traffic platform (Instagram, Facebook, Google, and YouTube) and show you how to use both of these strategies to find your dream customers and bring them into your funnels.

As you can probably tell, I spend the majority of my personal time working with my Dream 100, building and communicating with my lists, and publishing content to build fans and followers. In fact, during the first 10 years of my companies, we didn't run any paid ads. We paid affiliates to promote our products and used a lot of the growth hacks that you'll learn about in Section Three, but we never actually paid for an ad.

We were able to drive a lot of traffic with these methods, but there was never much consistency. We would set up a big promotion, drive a lot of traffic, and make a bunch of sales. But after the promotion was over, our traffic would slowly dry up, and we'd have to go back to the drawing board and create the next new offer to promote. It was a traffic roller coaster that lasted for years, until one day I decided I wanted off.

I came into the office and told our small team that we had to figure out paid advertising so we could get off the traffic roller coaster and get more consistency in our marketing. I asked if anyone was interested in diving in and mastering Facebook and Google, and one person raised his hand and said, *"Yes!"*

His name is John Parkes, and he started the first division of our company focusing on paid ads. Initially, it was just him for a few years, and after he figured out the model that worked for each network, he built a team that has been the backbone for the growth of ClickFunnels to where it is today.

Adding paid ads into the strategies you've been learning about is like adding lighter fluid to a pile of charcoal. You will get results faster on any funnel you want to promote and be able to more predictably control sales over the long-term.

Throughout this chapter, I'll be quoting John in a few sections, but it should be noted that everything I'm showing you here came from the methodologies he pioneered within our company. As always, we'll be staying away from the exact tactics that often change and focus instead on the overarching strategies that will help you to build out your paid traffic plan.

One thing John told me as we were mapping out this chapter was: "While it's true that each advertising network has little intricacies and nuances that can take a while to get used to, and there are definitely tips and tricks that can incrementally improve your performance, the good news is that the strategy of advertising on these networks is the same. The specifics of the platforms can be learned with online tutorials, or they can be hired out, but the strategy needs to be understood by you (the entrepreneur) in order to succeed."

WHAT IS MY ADVERTISING BUDGET?

The number-one question I get from people every time I start talking about paid ads is always related to how much money they'll need to budget to actually run ads. I always smile and tell them that if they have been following my advice so far and they've created a break-even funnel, then every dollar that they spend in ads comes back to them immediately. If they have a funnel that is break even or profitable, then they don't have an advertising budget. Their goal is to spend as much money profitably as possible because each dollar they spend turns into more dollars.

Let me tell you a quick story to illustrate how this works. Recently we launched a new front-end funnel at LeadFunnels.com. It was a $7 report that had a $37 order form bump and a $100 "one-time offer" or OTO. After the funnel was live, we wanted to test it to make sure it was working, that there were no technical issues, and that it actually was going to be profitable. So we created an initial "advertising budget" of $100. We started running Facebook Ads, and within about a day, the $100 was spent.

We then looked at the sales to see if we had made at least $100. From our first ad spend, we ended up getting about 100 clicks, selling 7 reports ($7 x 7 = $49), two people bought the order form bump ($37 x 2 = $74), and one person bought the $100 OTO. The total sales equaled $223. After we subtracted our $100 ad cost, we had made $123!

As you can see, this funnel no longer has an advertising budget. We'll keep running ads for as long as it stays profitable. If, for some reason, we lost money on this test, we would turn off the ads, rework the funnel, and then test again with another $100.

I never like putting very much of my money at risk at any given time, so with each new funnel, as soon as it's live, we set up a few ads, give it a small test budget, and see what happens. The funnels that flop are sent back to the drawing board to get reworked, and the funnels that work are scaled to see how much money we can profitably spend.

PROSPECTING ADS VS. RETARGETING ADS

Before we start talking about ads, I need to take a minute to explain the difference between "prospecting" ads vs. "retargeting" ads. Once you understand the difference between them and how they work together, we'll dive deep into how to use each of them together.

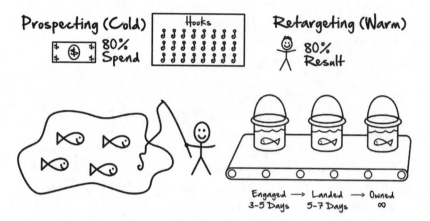

Figure 9.1:

To get your best results for paid ads, don't stop with prospecting ads. Continue with retargeting ads to give your warmer audience another opportunity to buy.

John explained, "Prospecting ads are the act of reaching out into the networks to find cold traffic or people who aren't familiar with you or your offers and hook them long enough to get their attention. After we've gotten their attention and gotten them to engage with us (engage could mean they watched, liked, or commented on an ad), then we move them from the 'prospecting' pool into the 'retargeting' buckets. We then advertise to these people differently and work to warm them up and then get them into our value ladder."

John continued, "Let me give you an example of how these work together. Let's say you have a book about effective parenting that you'd like to sell. A prospecting ad would be one that you run to a specific group of newlyweds who are likely new parents (or soon to be), introducing them to concepts from your book. As people engage with those ads, you'll be able to see which people are interested in what you have to say. A small percentage of those people may go and buy your book immediately, but the majority of them won't buy right then. It's those people who have engaged, but not purchased, who you would put into the retargeting buckets. Once they're in those buckets, we can warm them up, test other hooks, tell other stories, and remind them of the great offer we've made them in order to persuade them to click through and go into your funnel."

STEP #1: CREATE LOTS OF PROSPECTING ADS TO "HOOK" YOUR DREAM CUSTOMERS

When we first started using paid advertising, we made the mistake of thinking that we needed to create a great ad, and if we got the ad right, it would bring in thousands of our dream customers. I would spend a ton of time trying to create the perfect hook, and then once we threw it out into the ad networks, half the time it would fail. Other times it would work, but only for a little while. It was frustrating because I had set my expectations wrong. After a few months, we ended up with a few dozen ads that were working, and then I shifted my focus to other things.

John would get frustrated with me and ask me to take more pictures or make more videos that he could run as ads. I did a few every now and then, but for the most part I just assumed that paid ads didn't work as well as I had hoped.

A few months later, I called up my friend Dean Graziosi and we started sharing notes on what we were doing to sell our books and our coaching programs online. I had known who Dean was since I was a teenager; after all, I used to watch him on late night infomercials first selling his Motor Millions product and later selling tons of different books on real estate. I was probably the only kid my age who would sit up late at night and watch Dean while taking notes in my notebook about *how* he was pitching. I know, I know, I'm such a nerd, but it was amazing to see how good he was!

As I started to grow my first company, Dean was one of the first people on my Dream 100 list. I still remember that awkward moment when we first met; I explained to him that when I was a teenager, I used to watch his infomercials and study how he sold. He laughed, and we've grown a mutual admiration for each other as we've gotten to know each other better. I have become so grateful for times when we had a chance to just brainstorm on what was working at the moment.

Once when I was speaking to Dean on the phone, I started to brag, "We're selling about 1,200 copies of our book each week through paid ads right now . . ." But then I realized I didn't know how many books he himself was selling. "How about you guys?"

"We're at about 5,000 a week right now and have been holding steady at that number for the past few months," he replied.

Whoa, that's more than four times what we're selling, I thought.

Still talking to Dean on the phone, I shot a text to John to see what we were doing wrong, and if he could tell if Dean was really selling that many. A few minutes later I got a message back from John: "Five thousand?! I see his ads everywhere, but there's no way they're buying more ads than us. Ask him what he's doing to sell that many."

Dean and I talked for a while longer, but I still couldn't identify how he was getting four times the sales volume that we were. At the end of our call, we decided that it was best for me to fly out to spend a day with Dean and his team. That way, I could show them some of the cool funnel stuff we were doing, and they'd show us deep behind the scenes of what they were doing.

A few weeks later my team and I were in a plane, flying to Arizona, excited to see if we could figure out how to multiply our book sales four times over. Once both of our teams were gathered around a conference table, we showed them our best stuff, and then they opened up and let us look into their ad accounts.

At first, it was hard to find the needle in the haystack. Their ads looked similar to ours, and the targeting looked similar too. It seemed we had the same strategy . . . And then we saw it. Something we almost overlooked and couldn't have known at the time looking from the outside in. Dean and his team were running four times more creative (ads) than us.

"How many ads are you guys running?" I asked.

"Lots," Dean said. "They have me make a few new ads each day."

"Each day?"

"Yeah. Through my day, I carry my book with me, and every time I find a cool spot, I pull out my phone and make a new ad. Here is one at my daughter's softball game. Here is another at my house. This one is at the airport, and this one is when I went out to dinner."

I couldn't believe this was the big secret. More creative. More hooks. More ads. When you're thinking about prospecting ads, you're looking at a huge ocean of people—all who need your product or service but all who have a different reason why. If you try to create just one hook, it may last for a while and grab the people who are looking for that hook, but it will dry up very fast. You've got to become prolific at creating ads. The phone in your pocket will become your ad-making, creative-generating, hook-developing machine. Everywhere you go, you should be looking for opportunities to record a pitch for your offers that you can then turn into ads. After leaving Dean's office that day, we learned the gold nugget we needed to take our advertising and our company to the next level. My guess is that if you're reading this book, you probably saw one or more of the hundreds of creatives I made with my phone selling this book and the entire Secrets trilogy. You've probably seen the same thing with me selling ClickFunnels, our coaching, and just about everything else that I'm part of. The more creative you can put into the prospecting ocean, the more fish (dream customers) you're going to be able to pull out.

Targeting for Prospecting Ads

The next step after you have made your creative is to figure out who to show it to. John explains:

> **Dream 100:** The best place to start is your Dream 100 list for that platform. When you're running ads on Facebook and Instagram, you can target people who have an interest in a certain thought leader, brand, or celebrity. You'll find many (but probably not all) of your Dream 100's followers targetable this way in the Ads Manager. For YouTube, you can specify that you'd like your ads to show

in front of your Dream 100's videos both individually or their channel as a whole.

Ideal customer avatar: Second on your targeting list is your ideal customer avatar. Think about their interests, their age, their career, their home life, and anything else you can identify. Most of these ad platforms will allow you to get pretty specific on who you show your ads to.

Overlapping sections of multiple audiences: Some ad networks let you get more specific in targeting your audiences by layering on multiple criteria and then just targeting the overlapping sections. Think of three overlapping circles, each representing one of the audiences above and then imagine a center area where they all overlap. This center area represents the sweet spot where your dream customer is most likely to be. An example of this would be to not just target Tony Robbins's followers in one campaign, business owners in another, and women between the ages of 35–55 in a third campaign, but instead to have one campaign that requires the viewers be in all three of those categories in order to be shown your ad. Being smart with your audiences and layering them can really help bring your costs down and improve your results.

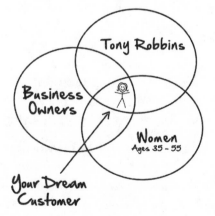

Figure 9.2:

When you target overlapping sections of people, meaning you layer your audiences and only target those who have multiple things in common, you can bring down your ad costs and get better results.

Algorithms: The last thing, and honestly where the networks are working toward, is for you to rely on the algorithms to do a lot of the legwork for you. You see, once you have a few hundred people engaging with your posts, clicking through to your funnels, and becoming leads and buyers, you've generated a pool of data. You've begun to prove exactly who it is that is responding to your advertising efforts.

The platform algorithms can work with that data and actually start lending a hand in your targeting efforts. In Google and YouTube, they're called Similar Audiences, and in Facebook and Instagram, they're called Lookalike Audiences. In both cases, you decide which bucket to use as the source, the algorithm then looks deep into who those people are, and then matches up others in your specified geographical range who are most similar to them (and thus more likely to care about what you have to offer).

80/20 Rule for Prospecting

One thing to note when running prospecting ads is that these types of ads are the most expensive, but they are vital for two reasons. First, it's through prospecting that you find out who is actually responding to your ads so your targeting becomes more on point (which brings your costs down). Second, it's prospecting that fills your retargeting buckets. If you stop prospecting, you'll soon find yourself with no one to retarget to. Here is a word of warning from John before you start running your first prospecting ads:

> I've been coaching small business owners and entrepreneurs for many years on their paid traffic. One thing I consistently come up against is a business owner who thinks it's too expensive to make sales using ads. If they're too hasty, they'll prematurely turn their advertising campaigns off. I've found, though, that if they understand how the 80/20 rule applies to ads, they'll better know what to expect.

When you put up your first ads, they're almost always going to a colder audience, a group of people who don't know you and don't know what you have to offer. It will always be more expensive and less efficient to advertise to this crowd, but when you're getting started, you have no other choice. Results will come slower with these prospecting efforts and costs to get a lead or a sale will be much higher (sometimes even so high that you're losing money to begin with). In fact, don't be surprised if you spend 80 percent of your advertising budget in this category and it only generates 20 percent of your results.

But if you hold strong, there is a light at the end of this tunnel. You see, while one purpose of the prospecting campaigns is to generate some leads and sales upfront, the bigger purpose is to fill all your retargeting audiences (which include your social followings and lists). As people begin to engage with your ads, they may subscribe and follow you (which you don't have control over) as well as be added to specific retargeting audiences (which you do have control over). It's from these new followers and retargeting audiences that you'll often see 80 percent of your results while only using 20 percent of your budget. As you use both of these strategies in tandem, you can make the sales you want at the cost you want and grow your business effectively.

STEP #2: USE A RETARGETING FUNNEL TO CREATE CUSTOMERS

As you've been spending money on prospecting ads to find your dream customers, the cream off the top has probably already come and purchased your products. However, there are so many people who would likely buy if they just had a little extra nudge. In Secret #6, we talked about the power of following up with your prospects through follow-up funnels using their email address. But what about all of the people who watch your videos or come to your funnel but don't give you their email addresses? How do you follow up with all of them? The answer is through retargeting ads.

Here's an example from John to show you how this works.

- Let's say you spend $2,000 on ads.

- From that, you get 100,000 people to actually see your ad.

- The ad performed well and 4% of these people engage with the ad (4,000 people).

- And 2% of the original 100,000 click the link in the ad and go to your funnel (2,000 clicks).

- Of these people, 30% of them give you their email address (600 leads).

- And 10% become buyers (60 buyers).

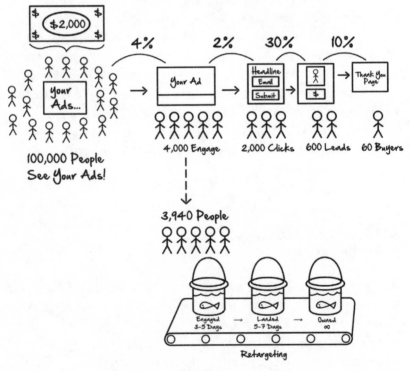

Figure 9.3:

Through retargeting, you can reach those who didn't buy when they first saw your ad.

That leaves 3,940 people who engaged with your ad but didn't become a lead or a buyer. While you'll never be able to capture everyone's attention, you can in fact reach a *lot* more. How? This is where retargeting comes in.

Since your efforts to reach people only resulted in a tiny fraction buying, you need specific campaigns in place to reach back out to those who were a good fit but just didn't take action (or enough action) for whatever reason. In order to do this properly, you need to build custom audiences. There are three specific audiences that are essential to a high-performance retargeting plan. Each is based on how far viewers got along the customer journey.

Audience #1—Engaged: The first audience you'll want to build is an audience based on viewers having engaged with you. Did they watch your YouTube videos this week? Did they watch one of your prospecting ads and make a comment recently? These people interacted with your post but never left the platform to pursue your offer. While they have made a minor commitment to you, it's nothing serious. These people are worth some continued ad dollars but not too much or for too long. I tend to run an ad to this audience for up to five days. If they haven't visited my landing page by that point, I let them fall out of the audience and return to the prospecting pools from whence they came. Maybe I'll hook them again in the future and they'll pop back into my retargeting bucket, or maybe I'll never see them again.

Audience #2—Landed: The second audience you'll want to build is made up of the people who clicked through and landed on your page. These people took a bigger commitment, left the platform, and visited your sales funnel. While they trusted you with their curiosity and visited your page, they didn't take any further action by opting in or purchasing. I tend to run an ad to this audience for up to seven days trying to get them to come back and take me up on my lead magnet. Again, if they don't opt in or buy within seven days, I just let them fall out of this audience.

Audience #3—Owned: The third type of audience you'll want to have is made up of those who did take your lead magnet and those who purchased. These people have made a large commitment and have entrusted you with email addresses and credit card numbers in exchange for your goods. This is the traffic that you now own, and it becomes very useful and lucrative in many different ways. Not only are they now on your follow-up funnel sequences, but they're also prime candidates for seeing ads for your next offer or an offer one step up the value ladder.

Figure 9.4:

The three types of audiences to include in your retargeting ad campaign include: engaged audience, landed audience, and owned audience.

Unlike prospecting ads where I'm making new creative as often as possible, with your retargeting campaigns, you're focusing on creating them once and you will never touch them again. It's similar to a Soap Opera Sequence inside of a follow-up funnel that you write once, and it lasts forever. As we move people through the retargeting buckets, we use the same three closes you learned about earlier: starting with emotion, then moving to logic, and ending with fear (urgency/scarcity). That is how we pull people into action throughout each retargeting campaign.

In order to implement retargeting, you have to place a pixel (a block of tracking code) on your sales funnel. This is a simple copy/paste procedure that allows the network to see how far along the customer journey your viewer got. This is important for two reasons. First, it provides feedback for you on what's working and what's not (what's converting these prospects into traffic that you own and what isn't) so you can pivot in either your targeting or your messaging. It also provides feedback for the algorithm to learn and optimize advertising efforts along with you. Second, the pixel is what allows us to put viewers into the different audience categories, so we'll know *when* to put specific ads in front of them.

To summarize, effective retargeting has at least three audiences (engaged, landed, and owned), and the end goals should be based on the type of audience the ad is targeted to.

- **Engaged → Sell the click:** Tell the network you want to collect a custom audience of everyone who has interacted with your posts in the past five days. To this audience, you want to show an ad with a hook and story that sells the click.

- **Landed → Sell the opt-in or purchase:** Tell the network you want to collect a custom audience of everyone who has clicked through to your landing page in the past seven days. To this audience, you want to show an ad with a hook and story that sells the opt-in or purchase.

- **Owned → Sell the next step:** Tell the network you want to collect a custom audience of everyone who has converted into a lead and/or sale. To this audience, you want to either offer another front-end product or walk them up the next step on your value ladder.

To understand this better, think of people as moving on certain conveyor belts. While they're on a specific conveyor belt, they're shown the ad appropriate to them; you're hoping they take the hook and find themselves in a new audience on the subsequent conveyor belt. If they don't take the hook, they move off that particular belt and find themselves back in your prospecting pool awaiting the next hook that intrigues them.

The lowest hanging fruit in the advertising world is running ads to your subscribers, followers, and ever-growing lists that you own. And while only a third of the emails you send may get opened, you can always run ads to your lists, often reaching those who didn't originally open the emails and greatly increasing your overall conversions from these lists.

What I've outlined here is a very effective strategy that will work on Google, YouTube, Instagram, and Facebook as well as other ad platforms. There are many different tactics and little things you can do to increase your ads' effectiveness, but by following the strategy outlined here, you can always be sure that you're hitting the right people at the right time with the right message.

INSTAGRAM TRAFFIC SECRETS

Over the past few years, one of my favorite social platforms to spend my personal time on has been Instagram. One of its core features, Instagram Stories, has become my favorite way to document my daily journey. Personally, I believe that it's the most powerful of all social tools to build a relationship between you (the Attractive Character) and your audience. A lot of the strategy I learned originally when I set up my account was from my friend and amazing entrepreneur Jenna Kutcher. In this chapter, with Jenna's permission, I'll share many of the concepts we learned from her. I'm so grateful to her for allowing me to share them with you.

STEP #1: UNDERSTAND THE HISTORY AND THE GOAL

Created by Kevin Systrom and Mike Krieger in San Francisco, Instagram launched on October 6, 2010.[21] Its fast-paced growth was unheard of: 100,000 members in the first week, 1 million members in the first two months, and 10 million members in the first year.[22] And in June 2019, it passed over a billion members![23]

In 2012, Facebook bought Instagram for $1 billion in cash and stocks.[24] While that story is fascinating, I think the more exciting story occurred in 2013, when Mark Zuckerberg offered to buy Snapchat for $3 billion.[25] After Snapchat's founder said no, Facebook decided that instead of buying them, they would just try to beat Snapchat at their own game. Over the next few years, they added all of Snapchat's core features into Instagram. Then in August 2016, they threw the death punch: they replaced

Snapchat's signature feature by launching Instagram Stories. Soon Snapchat's stocks plummeted, users migrated in droves from Snapchat to Instagram, and, almost overnight, Instagram became the second largest social networking site in the world.

Mark Zuckerberg's goal when acquiring Instagram and ripping off Snapchat's features was to find more places to leverage attention and place ads where you are spending your time: looking at your feed, exploring various things, and watching other people's stories.

If you are "working your way in," then you win this game by:

- Attracting followers
- Creating content that engages them and keeps them coming back to the platform for more

As you do that, you can use that attention to get free, organic traffic into your funnels.

If you are "buying your way in," you win by showing your ads to your Dream 100's followers and pushing them into your funnels. As with all platforms, I believe we should be playing both sides: working our way in and buying our way in.

STEP #2: FIND YOUR DREAM 100 ON THIS PLATFORM

The first step, as you'll soon see with every platform, is to identify the Dream 100 that have already congregated your dream customers on the platform you are starting on. Follow each of them and set up a plan to spend a few minutes each day viewing all their Stories, posts, and ads. This will help you to identify the patterns that are making these people successful.

Each day, I spend three to five minutes viewing my Dream 100's posts looking for:

- What pictures "hook" me and make me want to read the caption
- Which captions make me want to take an action

At the same time, I:

- Like the posts from my Dream 100
- Comment on at least 10 of my Dream 100's posts each day (digging my well)

I also spend five minutes watching Instagram Stories from my Dream 100:

- Looking for cool ideas on ways they're engaging people
- Checking out where their swipe-ups push me to
- Messaging (DM'ing) on at least 10 of their videos (digging my well)
- Looking for the swipe-up ads that are shown to me and funnel hacking them (swiping up on them)

Remember, you're now a producer of social media, not a consumer. Don't get caught in the trap of following tons of interesting people who will distract you and waste your time. Follow only those people who are already successfully serving the market that you want to serve, so you can understand what message they're sharing. Then you can figure out your unique angles inside of that ecosystem and unfriend or unfollow everyone else.

STEP #3: IDENTIFY THE PUBLISHING STRATEGY AND CREATE YOUR PUBLISHING PLAN

There are many ways to publish content on Instagram, and each section of the platform has a different strategy for how to publish and how to monetize. To make it simpler, I'll break down each of the core sections in Instagram and explain the strategy for how you can use each one. Here are the core areas of the platform we'll be focusing on.

The first I call "content hooks," where you are producing images and videos in a way to grab your dream customers and turn them into your followers. We rarely, if ever, actually sell anything in this content; we only focus on getting people to like, comment, and follow. We do this in two sections in the app:

- Instagram profile (your gallery)

- Instagram TV (your produced video content)

The second section of the app is your home. This is where you're able to direct people into your funnels and actually sell. I'll show you the strategies behind how we sell in this chapter, but for now understand that the areas that you'll be able to sell your products and services are:

- Instagram Stories (your reality show)
- Instagram Live (your live show)

Again, I want to mention that these platforms, their features, and the strategies for them are always evolving, so view this chapter as a baseline, and watch your Dream 100 closely so you can model and innovate on any and all algorithm changes as they come.

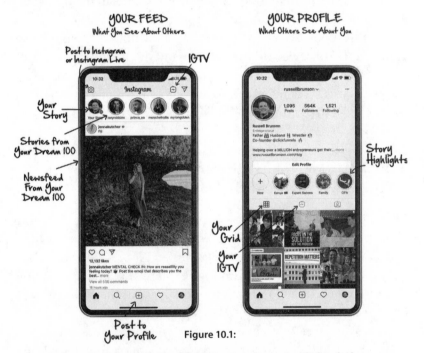

Figure 10.1:

On Instagram, you have two different ways to interact with the platform: by viewing other people's content or by posting your own content.

My biggest fear in telling people to model their Dream 100 is that they'll think it means they should "copy" their Dream 100.

Again, copying is not the goal; on the contrary, copying is illegal and unethical. Modeling is watching what others in your market are doing so you can get ideas on what *you* can create. To have success on Instagram or on any platform, you have to be you. Your brand and your personality are the keys to getting people to follow and engage with you. The differences you bring into the ecosystem that you serve is the secret that will create your true fans.

Jenna Kutcher said once, "A brand is the image and personality the business applies to its offers." The Attractive Character is the voice of your company, and what you're doing on social media is creating the image and personality that can connect with people and lead them into your funnels and to your offers.

The first step, then, when setting up Instagram is to quickly communicate in your bio who you are as the Attractive Character. When people find you on Instagram, the first thing they'll do is check out your bio. You only have 150 characters to make your first impression and get them to click on the "Follow" button. You also get one link that you can use to direct people back into one of your funnels (converting them from traffic that you've earned into traffic that you own). There are a lot of thoughts and beliefs on what you can or should write in your bio, but I suggest looking at your Dream 100's bios, seeing what's working, choosing what you like, and modeling them to create your own unique bio.

Instagram Profile Strategy (Your Gallery)

Your Instagram profile is the core foundation of your Instagram strategy. I'll focus on this first section of the platform because it is the key to increasing your followers and will fuel your Instagram Stories with their powerful swipe-ups, Instagram Lives, IGTV, and more.

The hook (your pictures): After someone looks at your bio, the next thing they'll see is a grid of all the pictures and videos that you've posted. Each picture is a hook that can potentially grab someone who is scrolling on Instagram and pull them into your funnels. People are automatically able to see all the pictures on your profile, and if you post them correctly, they'll also be able to see them inside of their own news feed.

When I started using Instagram, I had no clue what types of pictures I should post. If you scroll back on my profile to the very first pictures, you'll probably get a good laugh seeing all the random stuff I posted. As a result, I had low engagement because I had no idea what I was doing.

Shortly afterward, I heard Jenna Kutcher give a presentation on her "JK5 Method" framework. I started using it a few years ago, and I still use it to this day because it makes posting to my profile simple and fun. Using the JK5 Method will help you to create connection beyond just what you're selling, and to do that, you will need to post more than just your "work."

To implement the JK5 Method, you first need to create five main categories of things you're passionate about. This will help to give you a recognizable brand, and as you post images, you'll simply rotate through these categories so your followers get a good understanding of who you are beyond what you sell.

For Jenna, her five categories are marriage, body positivity, photography, fashion, and travel. If you scroll through her profile, you'll notice that she cycles through these categories. As I was creating my categories, I thought about the things most important to me that I wanted to share with the world. The categories I came up with for my brand were *family, funnels, faith, entrepreneurship,* and *personal development.*

Jenna explained why the JK5 Method helps to grow your brand and increase your audience:

> When you adopt this method, you'll not only create a versatile, well-rounded, and connected brand, but you'll also create an interesting feed that earns you the ability to sell. No two categories live next to each other in the grid, giving you extra visual element, but also giving people a way to find a way to connect with you, even if they currently aren't on the market for what you're selling. Oftentimes someone will follow you for just ONE of the categories while they get to know you, like you, and trust you, priming them to become a paying client in the future.

It's important we talk about the overall vibe of your "grid." Essentially, your grid is what users see when they scroll through to see multiple images all lined up in rows of three. It's easy to get obsessive about your overall grid aesthetic but what I love about the JK5 is that it gives people an overarching view of your brand when they click to see your full profile. If you truly follow the five-category rotation, viewers will see more than just what you sell but be able to also see if they can connect to your account enough to FOLLOW you. When someone lands on your page, they have about 10 seconds to make a decision on whether or not they want to follow you, and so we want this overall grid to create connection right off the bat!

Figure 10.2:

Because I simply rotate between my JK5 categories when I post, my followers can clearly see what I care about: family, funnels, faith, entrepreneurship, and personal development.

When you're posting on your profile, never post in real time; your posts should be thought out and strategic. (Real time posting is for Instagram Stories.) To curate photos for your profile, most phones will allow you to set up albums for your pictures. I suggest creating a new album for each of the five categories in your JK5. Then look back through your camera roll and move all the existing pictures you've taken in the past into these albums. Chances are this exercise alone will give you a few months' worth of the perfect images that you could start using today.

Moving forward, when you take new pictures with your phone, always add them into these albums. Each day, as you're looking for a new picture to post, go into that album on your phone and quickly grab the perfect picture. On top of pictures, Instagram also allows you to post videos on your profile that are under 60 seconds, so as you capture short videos that fit into your JK5, save them in your albums as well.

Before posting any picture or video, though, I highly recommend using Jenna's "ABCDQ Test" to see if it is "on brand" and therefore worthy for your profile. Here is the test:

- Aesthetic: Does it visually show something that fits the personality of my brand?
- Brand: Is it aligned with my dream client or something they will engage with?
- Consistent: Is it consistent in terms of color or quality to fit within my overall feed?
- Diversity: Is this something different than my last post? Does it create recognition beyond what I sell?
- Quality: Is this up to the quality I want my clients/ followers to expect? If this stood alone, would it fit my brand?

The story (captions): After you run it through the ABCDQ Test and you're ready to post the image, you need to think about arguably the most important question of all: "What am I going to say about this picture?" The picture is the hook that brings people in and grabs their attention, but the caption tells your story and tries to engage the reader before you make your offer or CTA.

Goal of Post. Each post you make should have one goal. As I post any picture and write its caption, the first thing I do is decide if the hook is meant to inspire, educate, or entertain:

- **Inspire:** It compels others to feel inspired and capable of big things.
- **Educate:** It teaches or educates your followers on a subject.
- **Entertain:** It provides entertainment for your followers.

Type of Caption. After I decide the goal of the post, I try to figure out the type of caption to post. According to Jenna, the three most common types of captions and how to use them in business are:

- **Tell a story:**

  The posts that do the best on Instagram have one thing in common: they invite you into the story and make you feel a part of the moment, as if you're experiencing it beyond the screen. I often pay attention to the little things or thoughts that happen in my days and turn those into short Stories I tell through captions. I'm not talking "once upon a time"–type stories but relatable life experiences that others can connect with.

- **Ask a question:**

  Having an audience (whether it's 10 people or 1,000 people) gives you access to people that can help you create the perfect offer! When you're not sure what to post, ask a question. People love to feel heard and be able to share their opinions. At least once a week I love to ask a question. Often, it's as simple as: "What is the best book you've read recently?" or as complex as: "Tell me what you're struggling with when it comes to Instagram so I can help you!" Questions can be directly related to your offer or just another way to connect with your audience. Plus, questions invite engagement onto your feed!

- **Make a list:**

    You can have a lot of fun with captions by sharing a short list! Some examples include: three things people might not know about you, five facts about your business, three ways to use your products, or the seven best books you've ever read. Lists are a fun way to deliver a caption that is easy to read or interesting; they can also further connect you to your followers in unexpected ways beyond the traditional brand stories you tell! We love sharing lists of our favorite things or writing an "introduction"-type post where we share more about us. After all, new people find and follow our account each week.

Hashtags. So what is a hashtag, and why do you need it? If you think of Instagram as a huge filing cabinet, then the hashtags are the filing folders. When someone searches a hashtag, Instagram finds all the images that use that same hashtag and gives you a gallery of only those images. For example, if I post a picture with the hashtag #potatoguns and someone searches for that hashtag, the picture I post will show up in the #potatoguns gallery. If they follow that hashtag (because they *love* potato guns), any new picture I post with that hashtag could show up in their news feed!

You can use up to 30 hashtags with each post to help your images, or hooks, show up in the searches and feeds of your dream customers. Hashtags are the equivalent of keywords in search engines. Sometimes, you can put your hashtags in your actual caption (we call these overt hashtags) where your audience will see them, but typically most of your hashtags will be posted in the first comment after you post your image (we call these covert keywords).

Figure 10.3:

To increase our reach, we place a few overt keywords in our post
and the majority of our covert keywords in the first comment.

There are many online research tools that can help you to figure out the best hashtags for your posts, and I do recommend using them, but the easiest way to research what hashtags you may want to use is to go back to your Dream 100. They're already serving your dream clients, so what hashtags are they using to get in front of them? Look at their hashtags each day as you're doing your research and keep a list of the ones that will work for you too.

The offer (your call to action): The last step in creating your post is your CTA. Every single post needs a CTA, and it can vary from being a very small ask to being a big CTA. Examples of small asks include: "Double tap," "Hit the 'like' button," "Post an emoji," or "Comment below." Examples of bigger calls to action include: "Share this post," "Tag 3 friends," "Click the link in my bio," or "Sign up for ____."

Calls to action are important for a lot of reasons. Ultimately, they help you get people off Instagram and onto your lists, but, maybe even more importantly, they help the algorithms know if people like what you're posting. If your audience comments, likes, and engages with what you post, the algorithms will assume you're creating content that people want and they'll reward you by giving you more exposure. When people comment, you should be responding to their comments. This will get them more likely to comment in the future, and it gives other people extra motivation to comment as well.

Now, let's quickly recap the basic process to follow when making posts on your Instagram profile:

- Follow the JK5 Method and create five main categories of things you're passionate about.

- Each day, post two pictures on your profile (rotate through your JK5 categories).

- Decide the goal of each post: Inspire, Educate, or Entertain.

- Decide the type of caption to use: Story, Ask a Question, or Make a List.

- Choose the hashtags that will make your post show up for your dream customer.

- Add a CTA to get your audience to engage with you.

If you need more examples on how to do this, then look no further than your Dream 100. If they're successful, you'll see this pattern within their posts, and you can model it for your own posts as well.

Instagram TV Strategy (Your Produced Video Content)

Instagram TV was originally created to be a competitor of YouTube. Most people used Instagram as an app that you scrolled through during your in-between moments, and they wanted to create something that would keep you in the app for longer stretches of time.

Figure 10.4:

IGTV episodes are longer videos that usually answer
a question or dive more deeply into a topic.

Part of our consistent publishing plan is to test out hooks and test our material. As I'm posting pictures and publishing Stories, I'm looking to see what people respond to. What questions do they keep asking me? What subjects and topics are interesting? When they see behind the scenes of my life, what parts do they want to understand more?

After identifying their interests, I'll create a more produced piece of content that answers these questions or expounds on certain subjects. These videos become episodes on Instagram TV. Typically, anything over 60 seconds is made into an IGTV post, and they can be up to 60 minutes long. In our market, we found that the sweet spot for video length is three to five minutes, so we'll spend that time answering a question or diving more deeply into a topic. These videos become our IGTV episodes.

The episode will show up to your fans and followers just like a normal picture or video that you post on your profile would. After people watch the first 60 seconds, Instagram will ask if they want to continue watching the rest of the video inside IGTV, making it vital that the first 60 seconds hook them into watching the full video or you'll lose people before they see your full message. Watch the IGTV's from your Dream 100 and see what types of videos they are creating and how they hook people and pull them into their content.

Instagram Stories Strategy (Your Reality Show)

When Snapchat first came out, they became famous for their core feature: letting you create short, 10-second videos that disappeared after 24 hours. I spent over a year growing my Snapchat following and had mild success with my Stories there. The platform was hard to use, it was almost impossible to grow an audience, and the stats they showed you were almost useless. However, early trends showed that it was going to be the next big social network, so we put in the time to try and make it work.

About a year into my Snapchat journey, I embarked on a charity trip to Kenya with a bunch of big influencers to help build schools. On the second day, after we had finished working and playing with the kids, we came back to our camps and checked our phones. That very day, Instagram launched their new Stories feature. At first, we were skeptical. Honestly, we didn't want to make a switch to this new platform after we had spent so much time building up Snapchat. Reluctantly, though, we decided to test the new platform. The next morning, we each made the same posts on Instagram and Snapchat. Then, we watched our stats closely to see which of the two platforms brought us the most eyeballs and engagement.

Knowing that this was a new feature to Instagram, I had a gut feeling that Zuckerberg was going to bribe us early adopters with tons of free engagement so that we'd switch platforms. And that's exactly what he did. Despite the fact that my Instagram audience was small (about 30 percent the size of my Snapchat audience), I got four times more views on each of my Instagram Stories than I did on Snapchat! As I shared my stats each night with the other influencers on the trip, we found that all our stats were about the same. Over the next few weeks, I started posting more and more on Instagram, and less and less on Snapchat, until, one day, I stopped logging into Snapchat and eventually deleted the app altogether.

So what exactly are Instagram Stories, and how do they fit into your Instagram strategy? At the top of the Instagram app, above your feed, you'll find a section showing the "Stories" for each of the people that you follow (your Dream 100).

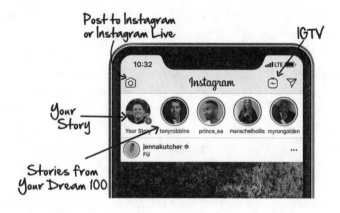

Figure 10.5:

Instagram Stories are short, 15-second-long videos that only stay on the platform for 24 hours and allow your fans and followers to see behind the scenes of your life.

If you click on one of their pictures, you'll see all the short micro videos that they've posted in the past 24 hours. Each video is just 15 seconds long, and you can post as many each day as you'd like. Because they disappear after 24 hours, you don't have to be as methodical about each post, caption, and CTA as you are with your profile posts. These Stories are more freestyle.

Personally, I look at my Instagram Stories as my personal reality show where my fans and followers can see behind the scenes of what I'm doing each day. I'm literally documenting my journey through the day in short, 15-second mini videos. When I wake up in the morning, I may make a quick post as I'm walking into the gym, quickly mentioning why I'm excited or what I'm dreading for the workout. I may make another post during my workout if I'm doing something new or funny that I think would be fun to share with my audience. After I leave the gym, I may post a quick video with one of my kids who just got out of bed and had funny bed head, or I may have them share their funny or scary dream. Then I get ready for my day, and I may make a post when I get in my car telling them quickly about what I'm excited about for that day or what I learned during my morning study.

Do you see how this works? I'm taking them on my journey during my day and sharing the highlights, giving them a glimpse of what I'm actually doing behind the scenes. As I get to the office, I may show them something I'm working on as I'm doing it. For example, I've posted Instagram Stories almost daily for the past few months showing my followers the process of me writing this book.

Each day, I know there are tens of thousands of people who watch these quick videos of me talking about this book and showing them new concepts or sketches I'm developing as I'm doing it in real time. Can you imagine how many of them are anxiously waiting for the second this book is done so they can buy their copy? By letting them participate in the process, they're more invested in what I've actually been doing. They're more likely to buy what I am creating when it's ready. Instagram Stories are the most powerful way I've ever seen to have your audience build a relationship with you as the Attractive Character.

Another great way to use Instagram Stories is to promote things you're working on in a cool way. I can show people my product or behind the scenes of how I fulfill my service, and then I can give people a CTA to go and buy one. Each day, I usually try to make at least one pitch for something I'm excited for. Instagram stories are my home where I'm able to push people into my funnels and actually sell to them.

When you first get your Instagram account, it isn't as easy to promote products; usually you have to tell your followers to click on the link in your bio to get taken to your funnel. After your account grows to 10,000 followers, though, you can unlock a really cool feature called "swipe up." If you've been following others on Instagram, you've undoubtedly seen people do this before. They'll make a pitch for something and tell you to swipe up to get access to it. When they swipe up on the screen, they will be redirected to any link you want.

Every day, I try to make 10–30 posts on Instagram Stories throughout the day documenting my journey. I'll typically make one that directs people to my profile to comment on whatever picture I posted that day. I'll also make one with a swipe-up CTA such as getting them to visit a funnel, listen to a new podcast episode, watch a video on YouTube, or engage with me in a way outside of the Instagram platform.

Story Highlights: These show up under your bio and above your grid. The way you use Highlights ties back to the JK5 Method, where you pick the five categories that your brand will be known for and create a "Highlight" for each one. As you make cool Stories that tie back to one of these five categories, you can save them as Highlights, and they will automatically save in that folder. This is a really cool way for people to see the Highlights over the past months or years tied to your core categories.

Figure 10.6:

Your Story Highlights allow you to keep your Stories "alive" longer than 24 hours and are usually organized into categories that are important to you.

"Highlights" mini webinar hack: We have a little trick that we use to leverage Highlights to sell a lot of products. About once per month, I pick one of my products that I want to promote. I block out a full day in my Stories devoted to promoting that product with a mini webinar. Basically, throughout the day, I'll post 15–50 Stories going through a scripted presentation to sell one of my products. Of course, I'll usually make a ton of sales on that day. But because I save it as a Highlight, it will continue to sell for me every day. Let me walk you through the script for this mini webinar.

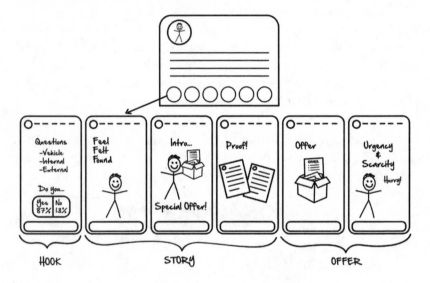

Figure 10.7:

My mini perfect webinar script still follows my Hook, Story, Offer framework.

In the first three Stories, I ask three yes or no questions that I know will hook my viewers. For those who have read *Expert Secrets*, these questions will seem familiar as they sync with the perfect webinar script. Question one is about the vehicle that I'm trying to put them into, question two relates to their internal struggle, and question three deals with their external fears. I ask each question, and then I let my followers answer yes or no.

My next few Stories will relate back to the questions I just asked. I like to use the framework: Feel, Felt, Found. I might say something like:

I understand how you *feel* . . .

I *felt* the same way . . .

This is what I *found* . . .

Then I make a few Stories introducing a special offer I created that will solve the problems people said yes to in the first three Stories.

Over the next 5–20 Stories, I'll show the proof. I'll say something like, "Don't take my word for it. Check out what others are saying." Then I'll post as many proof images, slides, and videos that I have related to the offer.

After all my proof, I'll make a few Stories recapping the offer they're getting that day.

Finally, I end with a few Stories talking about any urgency and scarcity that I have related to this offer.

This is one of my favorite ways to get consistent sales from Instagram. As people land on your profile and start following you, one of the first things they look at are your Highlights, so having a few in there that push your front-end funnels is a powerful way to make the conversion into traffic that you own.

Instagram Live Strategy

The last way to publish on Instagram is Instagram Live. Because Instagram Live and Facebook Live are so similar in their functionality and use, I won't be spending much time on Instagram Live. In fact, I purchased a second phone with the sole purpose of being able to go live on Instagram at the same time I went Live on Facebook. That way, I can stream the same message at the exact same time to both platforms.

One difference between Facebook Live and Instagram Live is that all Lives on Instagram are stored on the platform for only

24 hours, and then they're gone. On Facebook, however, your Lives are stored on the platform forever, so you can continue to boost and promote your Lives. I'm eagerly waiting for the day that Facebook and Instagram will just let you stream one message to both platforms at the same time. Until then, if you don't have a second phone, you may just have to borrow a friend's phone anytime you go live to get the extra eyeballs to your message on Instagram, or you can also do your Facebook live from a laptop, and then your Instagram Live from your phone. If you're not able to live stream on both platforms, I suggest you focus all your Live efforts on Facebook as your message can get more views over the long run. We'll talk more about the strategy of Lives in the next chapter with Facebook, but just know that this is the other area of the app that I treat like my home, i.e., I can use this feature to sell things to my existing followers.

Your Publishing Plan

Each section inside Instagram has different strategies on how you should be publishing. It's a lot, I know. I get it. When I first started looking at this platform, I thought that publishing on it would be another part-time job. So for me to get this to work, I had to build out a publishing plan that I could do in less than an hour each day and that was simple and effective enough for me to stick to it. Using this publishing plan will help to make sure that you're using every second on Instagram to its fullest. You can follow my publishing plan to a T, or you can tweak it to fit your own process.

INSTAGRAM PUBLISHING PLAN

DAILY: approx. 45 min.		
Research & Network: 10 posts & 10 messages/day	5 min./day	Scroll through your feed to look for your Dream 100's hooks, captions, and hashtags. Like and comment on at least 10 posts each day.
	5 min./day	Watch the Stories from your Dream 100 and look for how they're engaging people and what their swipe up CTAs are. Send a message to at least 10 of their videos. Swipe up on their offers and funnel hack them.
Instagram Profile: 2 posts/day	20 min./day	Pick two pictures from two of your JK5 categories, write captions, add hashtags, and schedule two posts per day.
	5 min./day	Throughout the day, reply to comments on your posts.
	5 min./day	Throughout the day, take pictures on your phone that relate back to your five categories and store them in your JK5 phone folders.
Instagram Stories: 10-30 stories/day	5 min./day	Post 10-30 15-sec. Stories throughout your day. On one Story, tell your audience to interact with a post on your profile (like, comment, etc.) On a different Story, give a swipe up CTA to promote one of your products or new published content (like a podcast episode, blog post, or YouTube video).
WEEKLY: approx. 40 min.		
Instagram TV: 2 videos/week	5 min./week	Pick the #1 most asked question and answer it in a 3- to 5-min. video. Reply to comments.
	5 min./week	Pick the post your audience was most interested in and teach the concept in a 3- to 5-min. video. Reply to comments.
Instagram Profile: 2 collabs/week	30 min./week	Collaborate with your Dream 100 by shouting each other out in your posts. Some collabs you could rotate through include answering each other's questions and sharing photos you've taken together.*
MONTHLY: approx. 25 min.		
Instagram Stories: 1 highlight/mo.	25 min./mo.	Create a product Story "Highlight" by scripting out a mini Perfect Webinar for one of your products and posting 15-50 Stories going through the presentation.
WHEN YOU GO LIVE ON FACEBOOK		
Instagram Live	n/a	Any time you do Facebook Live, go Live on Instagram as well. Reply to comments.

Please note: The time requirements shown are variable. It may take you less or more time.

* This strategy will be discussed in the upcoming section: "Step #4: Work Your Way In."

Figure 10.8:

Use this publishing plan to see at a glance where you should focus your efforts on Instagram.

STEP #4: WORK YOUR WAY IN

As you're following your publishing plan and posting your content hooks using the right hashtags, you will start showing up in the feeds of your dream customers. Having great content for a consistent period of time is the baseline strategy for growth.

The next level of growth starts when you tap into your Dream 100 and their followers using the power of Instagram TV. I told you earlier that we use IGTV to publish produced videos answering questions that our audience has been asking us. The only problem is that the only people who see these videos are the ones who follow us or those who happen to see our hooks in their feed. As we thought about this problem, we wanted a way to stimulate growth of our channel a lot faster, and that's when it hit us! We should do Question-and-Answer Collaborations (or collabs) with our Dream 100.

Let me explain how it works. A while ago, I got a question from one of my followers who was trying to figure out why they were struggling with growing their company. I could have easily made a video response and posted it, but then I had an idea. There were other people who were actually more qualified than me to respond to parts of this question. I messaged Steve J Larsen and told him that someone had asked me a really good question and that I was going to answer it on video, but I'd love if he'd also answer it too. He agreed, made the video response, and sent it to me. I also made a video response, and then I took our two responses and created an IGTV video, posted it on my profile, and tagged Steve in the video. A huge number of my followers watched the video, heard Steve's response, and went and followed him. I then gave him the same video and asked him to post it to his IGTV. He posted it, tagged me, and I got a huge stream of new followers from his account as well. This collab added over a thousand new followers to my account almost overnight.

We now try to do these collabs with my Dream 100 as often as possible. Often we'll do question swapping, where I'll ask them a question and then they'll ask me a question back. We post it on our feeds and both our channels grow.

You can do similar things when you meet your Dream 100 in real life, at conferences and events. Take a picture with them, post it to your profile tagging them, and have them post it to their profile and tag you. The possibilities are endless. Creative ideas like this are the key to working your way into the followers of your Dream 100.

STEP #5: BUY YOUR WAY IN

To quickly grow your Instagram following, you need to show up on your Dream 100's channel. Our favorite way to buy our way in is by getting a "shout-out." A shout-out is exactly what it sounds like it is. Basically, one of your Dream 100 posts on their profile or in their Stories about you. In their shout-out, they'll usually mention your name, tell people to follow you, and tag you. The tag makes a clickable link on Instagram where people can click on your tag and be taken immediately to your profile, which is why it's so important to optimize your profile page.

For example, we found someone on our Dream 100 list (@prbossbabe), sent her a copy of my *30 Days* book when it first came out, and paid her to do a shout-out. She posted a picture of herself with the book, told the story of the book, and then "shouted me out" by tagging me. This tag directed people back to my profile to find out more. She made this post on her profile, and she also published a few Stories with swipe-ups that took people directly to the book funnel. This post was shown to her 82.8K followers, received 4,978 likes, and drove hundreds of people to start following me.

Figure 10.9:

You can pay influencers to do a "shout-out" and mention you on their profile.

You can approach people in your Dream 100 to do paid shout-outs, but there are also a lot of agencies that specialize in getting shout outs for you. You can hire them, and they'll do all the work to find the people, get you the shout out, and get people to your profile page.

STEP #6: FILL YOUR FUNNEL

The last step in this framework is to then use all this exposure and engagement to convert all of this traffic into traffic that you own. The first phase is creating your publishing plan and putting out your content hooks to start to grow your following and build a relationship with them. We use your Instagram profile and TV to find people and turn them into subscribers. We can work our way in with collabs and buy shout-outs to speed up our growth.

As your following is growing, you can then start using your Instagram stories and get people to swipe up and push your followers into your funnels. You can also use our "Highlights mini webinar hack" to create mini webinars on your Highlights that will presell your people on the products or services you are selling in your funnels!

The last step is to start running prospecting ads (as shown in Secret #9) to find more of your dream customers and move them into your retargeting buckets so you can get them into your funnels. Everything you are doing now is all for the purpose of moving those people into your value ladder and ascending them up so you can serve them at a much higher level.

FACEBOOK TRAFFIC SECRETS

Around the same time that Google was trying to figure out how to create the best search engine ever, other entrepreneurs were trying to solve a potentially bigger opportunity. Everyone was starting to plug into this world wide web, so there had to be a way to socially connect all these people together in a user-friendly interface. There was a race to create the social network that would stick, and with hundreds of millions of dollars being thrown at the opportunity, the reward for the winner of this social arms race was huge.

STEP #1: UNDERSTAND THE HISTORY AND THE GOAL

The first attempt to create a website-based social network started back in 1997 with a startup called SixDegrees.com, which was based on the concept of six degrees of separation.[26] People were able to create an account, add their friends, and message people within their first three degrees of separation. They could also see how anyone on the platform connected back to them. It was one of the first attempts at social media that looked similar to what we now have today.

The next wave of tools that were created to connect us socially were online messengers. It started with ICQ in 1996, followed by AOL Messenger, Yahoo Messenger, MSN Messenger, and finally Skype in 2003.[27]

In 2002, we saw the launch of Friendster and the concept of "social circles," which mimicked how people were really connected in the real world. This algorithm eventually beat out

SixDegrees.com, which went out of business just four years after it started. One year later, other companies showed up based on this same "social circles" concept, such as LinkedIn, Hi5, and Myspace. Myspace quickly became the most popular social networking site around. For many people like me, who watched as Myspace crushed Friendster and the other fledgling social sites, I had assumed that they would be around forever.

Over the next few years, even more social sites emerged. Flickr became the first large photo sharing social site in the world, later dethroned by Pinterest. YouTube became a video sharing service that was later acquired by Google. Twitter launched with the ability to share micro content, while Tumblr became a micro blogging site.

In the midst of so many new social startups popping up every day, there was one that silently launched in 2004 that would soon grow to overshadow all others. Even with giants like Google trying to dethrone them with the short-lived launch of their social network, Google Plus, no one has been able to beat this social media king. Of course, the social network I'm talking about is Mark Zuckerberg's Facebook.

The story of Facebook's rise has been documented in movies and books and talked about so much in the media that I won't spend much more time here on its history. Mark's launch strategy started by allowing only people with a Harvard email address to get an account. Then he slowly extended access to other colleges, and eventually he extended access to everyone. At the time of this writing, Facebook has 2.7 billion users, and 2.1 billion people use one of Facebook's core services, including WhatsApp, Instagram, and Messenger, every day![28] Yes, over one-quarter of the world's population is plugging into the Facebook network daily. It's the biggest social party of all time, and unless some type of government regulation breaks up their monopoly, it will continue to grow.

Facebook has had a lot of scandals around how they handle their users' privacy and data, which can be super annoying as a user of Facebook, but it can be a huge blessing as an advertiser on their platform. Facebook tracks everything you do: What do you like? Which things do you comment on? Which types of posts do you engage with? All in all, they have up to 52,000 data points on every individual that they accumulated as you were scrolling, clicking, and commenting.[29] Their goal is to figure out what you like and show you more of that in your feed. The better your experience is on Facebook, the more likely you'll spend more time there; the more time you spend there, the more ads they can sell to marketers like us.

Because Facebook is tracking so many aspects of your behavior, it gives us as advertisers the ability to target people based on what they'll probably like (their interests). As mentioned in Secret #1, Facebook was the platform that originally gave us the ability to start using "interruption" marketing, where we could target those who were interested in what we were selling. We could interrupt them with a great hook, tell them a story, and then make them an irresistible offer.

Over time, the algorithm that judges which posts or videos get the most exposure on Facebook's platform continues to change. Five years ago, it was all about making a video that was sharable. If you knew how to get shares, your videos could get millions and millions of views overnight. As soon as everyone collectively learned the algorithm, then agencies started to pop up everywhere, guaranteeing to make you a video that would go viral, because they knew the algorithm and it worked.

Then Facebook went public, and they needed to raise more money, so Zuckerberg "snapped his fingers" and changed the algorithm. The new algorithm no longer rewarded people for having amazing, shareable content. That didn't make them money, which was necessary for stock prices to go up. He needed to change the algorithm so that Facebook could show higher returns for the investors. Overnight, the majority of "free viral videos" died, replaced with a new algorithm that required you to buy ads to boost and promote your videos. With these changes, it required you to buy views to your video. If those people who saw your paid video liked it, and a certain percentage of them shared it, then Facebook would reward you with free viewers. When this would happen, for every paid eyeball you got on your video, you would get two to three views for free. We used to call these videos "forced viral" videos, and they became the new standard for each video we created.

Around this time, there was a land grab for each platform to be number one with live video. Twitter bought Periscope, and it started to become the number-one place to stream live videos. I remember those days, because I was on Periscope streaming live almost daily, that is, until Facebook launched Facebook Live. To this day, I still like Periscope's app better; personally, I think that their streaming service, and pretty much everything else about it, is way better than Facebook Live, but Facebook wanted to become *the* platform for live video streaming, so they changed their algorithm. After the change, when you would go live on Facebook, you could get hundreds or thousands of people to show up for free in just seconds. They rewarded us for going live to force us all to switch to them; then after they won and beat out all the competitors, they took away much of the organic reach and made us pay to get more viewers to our videos.

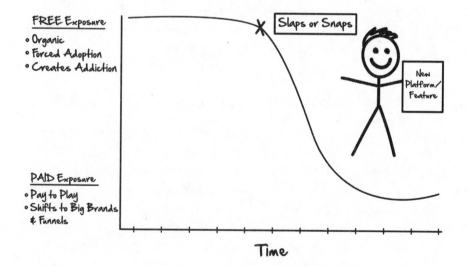

Figure 11.1:

When a new platform is released, they reward people for using it by giving everyone free exposure. Over time, your free exposure lessens and you have to buy ads in order to get as much exposure as you did for free before.

Facebook is a growing platform, and although I'm taking a snapshot of how it works today, it will continue to evolve. The good news is that even though Facebook's features, tactics, and user interface change often, your overarching strategy does not. Whenever I'm diving into a new platform, I always begin by asking myself these three questions:

- What is the goal of the platform?

- What is the strategy that I can use to help the platform with its goal?

- What are the tactics that the platform is rewarding people for right now?

For example, the *goal* of Facebook is to have its users create content that will keep people on their platform for as long as possible so they can show them ads. Our *strategy* is to figure out what content Facebook is rewarding people for right now and how Facebook wants that content to be promoted (both free and paid), and then for us to try to create the type of content they want. The *tactics* are what that content looks like. This changes daily, but we can get a glimpse of what is working right now by watching our Dream 100, seeing the things showing up consistently in our news feed that are getting the best engagement, and then modeling these things.

STEP #2: FIND YOUR DREAM 100 ON THIS PLATFORM

Surprise, surprise. The first step when you start using Facebook is to identify your Dream 100 that have already mastered this platform and congregated your dream customers. If you haven't yet, be sure to clean up your Facebook feed by unfollowing everything that isn't tied to your Dream 100 and your dream customers. This will keep the noise down as you step into this next phase.

Your Dream 100 are the people, experts, influencers, and brands in your market that have already congregated your dream customers. It is also the owners of the groups in your market. Each of these people and groups have their own social party happening, and your goal is to first identify the party's attendees (e.g., people, brands, interests, and groups) and then to leverage Facebook to get these people into your funnels.

There will likely be a few big names in your market that you're already familiar with, which is where I would start. Find their Fan Pages and "like" and "follow" those pages. Then find their personal pages and try to friend request them and follow their personal profiles too. Typically, after you do that, Facebook will find other people who have similar followings that you could follow. Go down that rabbit hole and start following every influencer you can find in your market that has a following. The same is true with groups. You can search for groups in your market and join them, and as you do, more groups will be "suggested" to you by Facebook. Join the ones that your dream customers are already congregating in.

Finding your Dream 100 is not a one-time activity but instead an "every time" activity where every time you're on Facebook, you should look for these new congregations or people and plug into them as they start showing up in your feed. As you do this, your Facebook feed will become the best market research tool in the world. You'll see every important conversation that your dream customers are engaging in. You'll see every ad being run to your customers. You'll see the messages they're exposed to, the people they connect with, the pains they have, the questions they want answers to, and the opportunities you can create to better serve them. This is what your Facebook feed is for: mastering your market.

My goal when following all influencers in my market is to plug into an ecosystem of at least 1 million people. For example, if I'm able to find 20 people to follow, and each of them has a following of 30,000 people, then I'm plugged into about 600,000 people. That means I need to keep finding influencers or brands or groups until that whole universe of people is at least 1 million people. For some of you, especially local-based companies, it may be hard to find 1 million people, so you can set a smaller goal; for others who have larger target markets, 1 million may seem too small. Set your goals to match your market size and then follow the influencers and brands you need to get to your magic number.

STEP #3: IDENTIFY THE PUBLISHING STRATEGY AND CREATE YOUR PUBLISHING PLAN

It's important to remember that Facebook is the biggest social party in the world. It's happening 24 hours a day, 7 days a week, and the majority of your dream customers are already there. You don't have to create traffic; you have to find the existing streams of traffic and figure out how to funnel those people into your world. While there are a lot of things that you can do inside of Facebook (and they'll continue to add more things), there are four areas of the platform that you must master.

- **Your personal profile (your home)**—As you are "working your way in" (e.g., going out and commenting on people's posts, joining groups and posting content and more), the friends, fans, and followers of your Dream 100—as well as the members of those groups—will see your profile picture, click on your face and be taken from the social party to your personal profile. This is your home, and this is where you'll be able to direct people into your funnels.

- **Your Fan Page (your show)**—I know, Facebook no longer calls this a "Fan Page," they call it a "Page," but I'm old school and still call it a Fan Page because it helps me to identify its goal in my marketing plan. This is where you are "buying your way in." After you post content on your Fan Page, you will be paying ("buying your way in") to boost it to the followers of your Dream 100.

- **Groups (your hangout)**—This is where you throw your own social networking party and build relationships with your tribe.

- **Messenger (your distribution channel)**—This is one of the most powerful distribution channels that you have to get your message quickly to your most hyperactive followers.

I will now dig deep into the publishing strategies of each of these four areas of the Facebook platform.

Your Personal Profile Strategy (Your Home)

Before we start our social networking, we need to make sure that our home, or personal profile, is ready when people start coming over. Most of your interaction online will be happening through your personal profile. As you comment, share, help, and engage with other people, they'll see how much value you're providing and click to see your profile page. If you structure your profile page correctly, it will grab your dream customers who are looking for more information about you and turn them into traffic that you own. Facebook allows people to "follow" your personal profile, but you have to turn it on in the settings. Make sure you give people that ability, because even though you can only have 5,000 "friends," you can have an unlimited number of followers.

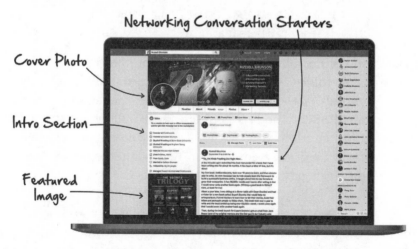

Figure 11.2:

If your profile page is set up correctly, it can convert people who want to know more about you into people on your lists.

Getting your profile set up correctly: There are three things that you can customize on your personal profile. You have to be careful because Facebook doesn't want your personal page to be for business, so none of these elements are meant to be a hard pitch for anything; instead it serves as a landing page where people can get to know you better and decide to be a friend or follower who will see your status updates in the future.

- **Your cover photo:** You can design and upload a cover photo that represents you and your brand. It's an image that your visitors will be able to see and know that they're in the right place. Do not put a CTA on your cover photo, as this screams that you are trying to sell something on your personal page.

- **Intro section (your business card):** In the intro section of your profile, you're able to tell a little bit about yourself.

- **Featured Image:** You can feature an image from a post you've made here. I have a picture of my three books. When someone clicks on that image, they are taken to a post where I have links to the three books in the description. This is the first way that I start filling my funnels from my personal profile.

What's on your mind? (conversations at your "home"): As you are "working your way in" and people are coming back to your "home" or profile page, they will see the recent conversations that you've started, and if a hook grabs them, it will pull them into your conversations and into your funnels. These conversation starters will also show up in the feeds of your friends and the people who follow you. Each post is an opportunity to hook someone, tell them a story, and get them to take some action.

If you've read the earlier chapter on Instagram, you will notice that the strategy here is very similar to how we post on our Instagram profile. If you remember Jenna's JK5 Method, we each picked five categories that represent our brand. My categories are family, funnels, faith, entrepreneurship, and personal development. Just like I rotate through these five categories as I'm posting images to my Instagram profile, I rotate through these same categories as I'm posting "what's on my mind." If all the personal posts are about business, oftentimes Facebook will shut you down for operating a personal page like a business page, so by diversifying what I post over those five categories, I am at less risk, and it also builds a connection with my followers outside of just my "work."

The big difference between my Instagram profile and my Facebook personal profile is that on Facebook, this is my home, so I'm okay with starting conversations with a goal to direct people into a funnel. Typically, Facebook will penalize personal posts (not show them to many people) that have a link in the status update, so I will typically make the post telling the story and then have the link to the CTA in the comments section. Here is an example of a post I made recently that follows this process:

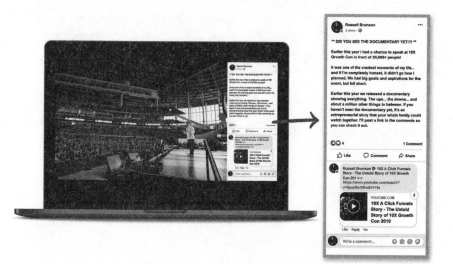

Figure 11.3:

To encourage Facebook to show my post to more people, I'll often post my CTA link in the first comment instead of in my actual post.

I try to make at least one update to my personal page each day. These updates are more than just an image and a caption; typically they are a longer form story, structured almost like a

Daily Seinfeld email where I have a hook, tell a story, and make an offer.

Each day, as I'm trying to figure out what to post, I ask myself, *What's the hook that will make people want to hear this story?* The hook could be a quick headline or a picture, but it should be something that will stop people scrolling through their newsfeed. After I place the hook, I tell the story, give the rant, or share the big "aha" that's been on my mind that day. Then after I tell the story, I figure out how that ties back into where I want to send someone. What's the offer I want to make to them? Sometimes the offer is as simple as wanting them to like my post, leave a comment, or tell me their story. Other times, the offer is for them to listen to a podcast episode or read a blog post. Still other times, I ask for the *big* offer, and I direct them to one of my front-end funnels.

My secret for figuring out what to post each day comes back to the JK5. I open my phone and look at the picture albums I set up to categorize all of my images. I look through the album for the category that I'm posting about that day, find an image that will work as a hook, tell the story behind the image, and then make my offer. You can also go Live on your personal profile and tell your story through video, but I personally like to save my Live videos for my Fan Page (so I can pay to boost them) or for my group where I'm using it as a way to "hang out" with my tribe.

As people come to your page from different sources, they'll first see your billboard (cover photo) and find out what you're all about, then they'll see your business card (the intro section) and finally they'll see your conversation starters (your posts). If one of these hooks grabs them, you've started a conversation on your wall with your dream customers. As people comment on your posts, be sure to spend some time replying to their comments. This one small act speaks volumes, and it helps to build relationships with your dream customers.

Your Fan Page Strategy (Buying Your Way In)

When Facebook first launched, it was structured so that each profile could only have 5,000 friends, and that limit remains to this day. Having this limit helped keep the integrity of Facebook as it was growing by keeping people's news feeds filled with the things and people they actually cared about, which helped cause a deeper addiction to the platform. The problem was that it made it hard for businesses and brands to really do business online, because their pool of potential customers was just 5,000 people. Other social networks didn't have this limitation, which caused people to mass create accounts to build up fake followings. Later, Facebook did create a way where people could follow your personal profile without being an actual "friend," which has made the strategy I shared earlier so much more powerful.

A few years later, on November 6, 2007, Facebook launched "Pages" (which I'll refer to through this book as "Fan Pages"), where a person or a brand could have followers or fans on that page.[30] There was no limit to the number of fans that someone could have. Adding Pages gave Facebook the ability to see the things people were interested in more closely, and this paved the way for Facebook's advertising platform that we came to love so much.

The first question I get from almost everyone I know who starts trying to drive traffic from Facebook is, "Do I need a personal page and a Fan Page, or can I use just one?" My answer always is that you need both. Each has a different role, and both are essential. Your personal profile is how you get free, earned traffic (working your way in), while your Fan Page is how you get the chance to buy traffic (buying your way in).

You should view your Fan Page more like your website. Julie Stoian, who has served as the ClickFunnels VP of Marketing, said:

> Think of your Facebook page as the Facebook version of your website. I treat this page very carefully. I only put the most curated and the best content on this page. It is the first impression for anyone who sees your paid ads. They will click on the profile of the brand running the ad, and

your Fan Page is what they will see. I treat this page almost like my YouTube profile, where, when people come to it, they will see the brand, but then they will hopefully start engaging with all of the videos and images and things that have been posted there. My test for if something should be on my Page is this: *Is this content good enough that I will spend at least $10–$20 to boost it? If you're not willing to pay for ads to that content, then do not post it on your Fan Page.*

Now, before I scare you away from posting anything on your Fan Page, I want to talk about the types of things that we do post there. The key is to post things that you believe will get high engagement from your fans. If your engagement is low, it will make all your posts across your Page go down, but if a piece of content you post has high engagement, then everything will go up. Often, I'll use my personal profile or my Instagram feed to start testing material and images and find the hooks and stories that people resonate with, and then I'll turn those things into more produced content on my Fan Page that I can boost with money.

There are four things that we post on our Facebook Fan Pages. Let me walk you through each one and the strategy behind how we use them.

Figure 11.4

We have a specific strategy for each area of the
platform, including our Facebook Fan Page.

Produced value videos: These are videos that have a good hook and story but *no offer.* The direct response marketer in me hates these videos, but the branding marketers loves them. For some reason, when you have a CTA, people will rarely share your videos. By not having a CTA, if people love the videos, they'll like, comment, and share, and that's how you get paid for this content. This increased engagement will boost everything else you do on your Fan Page. In Gary Vaynerchuk's book *Jab, Jab, Jab, Right Hook,*[31] he talks about the strategy of giving (jabbing) good content and building a relationship before you do the big ask (right hook). Because of that, we will try to do three to four content videos for everyone that is pushing a hard CTA.

Live value videos: These videos are almost the same as our "produced value videos" except that they aren't pre-produced. We go Live on the platform, and in real time we deliver the message. Facebook currently favors Live videos over published videos, so we do these often. There are also some powerful software tools that will let you take a produced video and stream it through their services so it's published as if it's live. I'll link to some of these services in the resources section here: TrafficSecrets.com/resources.

Live perfect webinars: These are the "right hooks" that will become your big paydays. If you've been providing value, now you have the opportunity to actually sell to your audience. In *Expert Secrets*, I shared my "Perfect Webinar" script, and I showed you Kaelin Poulin's "Perfect Webinar Hack," where Kaelin started using this script on her Facebook Lives to direct people into her front-end funnels. Jaime Cross from MIG Soap also modified this script into the "Five-Minute Perfect Webinar" that is a powerful and simple script to use on your Facebook Lives to drive people into your front-end funnels. You can print out these scripts for your own use by going to TrafficSecrets.com/resources.

Curated content from your other platforms (reruns): I'll take content that I'm posting on my other social networks that are getting high engagement and post it on my Fan Page. I don't link out to that other content; I'll actually repost it here natively. For instance, with my YouTube videos, I'll upload them to

YouTube, but I'll also upload them separately to Facebook. I look at this reposted content similarly to how we view reruns on TV. The videos are there, and we may watch and engage with them, but we're eagerly waiting for the new episode of our favorite show that is coming out soon.

After we post any of this content, we always do exactly what Julie suggested: I spend $10–$20 boosting that content. Sometimes the goal is to get engagement on the pitch-free content (with a goal to increase what happens when I post my Live perfect webinars). When there is a Live that pushes to a funnel, if I at least break even on my ad spend, I'll keep running the ads until I start losing money. Sometimes the Facebook Live video ad will be profitable, and we may keep running ads to it for months!

Your Groups Strategy (Your Hangout)

When I got started online, before there was Facebook, there were forums. I was a member of a dozen or so marketing forums that I would frequent each day to ask questions, get answers, and grow my personal brand. The owners of those forums were powerful. They had a huge congregation of people hanging out at the party that was happening at their house every day. The conversations that happened inside of these forums were the things that shaped our industry. I realized that if I wanted to have control over the direction of our market, I needed to be the one who ran the parties where everyone hung out. After all, the person throwing the party generally has the most influence in the group.

I decided right then that I needed to start my own forum. Back then, I had to get software to run a forum, servers to host the site, and about a dozen other things. It took me a few months, but I finally ended up launching a forum that grew pretty large. About that time is when Facebook launched their "groups." I was a little hesitant to create a new group, but because traffic on my old forum was drying up as people were shifting their habits to Facebook, we decided to give it a try.

We created the first "official" ClickFunnels group and invited our new customers into it. At first, we used it as a way to help take some of the responsibility of support off our shoulders and get the community to help serve each other. But then it started to grow. We told new members to come join our community to meet other funnel hackers and share their ideas, and then Facebook started to promote the group as well. Soon we had thousands of people a week joining without us spending a penny on advertising. As of the writing of this book, we have over 223,000 people in that group and Facebook adds over 1,200 new members per week! Our members currently average a total of over 317 posts a day (that's one every five minutes around the clock). There are over 9,414 comments and reactions per day (that's one every nine seconds and well over a quarter million each month). Some of our top posts can get 30,000–50,000 impressions each, which is all free organic traffic.

Facebook wants people to build groups, and as of this writing, they are rewarding people for doing it. I saw a commercial on TV the other day from Facebook promoting groups! Yes, they are actually buying commercials on TV to promote them. Can you see the irony there? One of the biggest advertising platforms in the world is trying to find more ways to get people building groups on their platform. For some reason, they want people building groups to increase the experience for their users, so this is where we're spending a lot of our time now.

Your group is your own personal party. It's a place on social media for your people to gather, hang out, and talk. I'm a big believer that most companies should have a group where the members of their community can network. It will become a huge source of traffic for you, help turn your warm audience into raving fans, and give you the ability to be an influence on the most important group in your marketplace.

I try to do a weekly "hangout" in my group where I can talk to our tribe and build a personal relationship with them. As of today, we have over 1,000 people per month that join ClickFunnels directly from this group, so the more I can jump in and build relationships with them, the better. I don't typically structure my hangouts; instead I jump in, tell a story, and take open questions from people in the group. At the end, I'll typically make a CTA for people to go get their free ClickFunnels trials, and then I'm done.

It's a really fun part of my week and it can help to endear your tribe back to you.

Your Messenger Strategy (Your Distribution Channel)

Facebook Messenger started as a simple way for us to chat with our friends who were also on Facebook, but in 2016, Facebook opened their "bot" platform.[32] Over the past few years, these bots made it possible for marketers like us to use Messenger in a similar way to email autoresponders. It gave publishers the ability to message subscribers directly with news and other information, and it also gave them the ability to set up basic chats between their subscriber and the Messenger app. Essentially, you can pre-write questions and answers to help solve your subscribers' problems or you can direct them somewhere else.

If you'd like to build lists, set up sequences, do broadcasts, and more, go to TrafficSecrets.com/resources to see an up-to-date list of some amazing companies that have built awesome Messenger integrations. I won't mention any specific ones in the book because companies come and go, but I'll update the list online so it always has the best Messenger integrations to work with.

Messenger has rules to protect it from being used as a platform where people are sending out spam, and because of that, if you're too aggressive, they can and will shut you down. So it's essential to use it in a way that enhances users' experience instead of in a way that annoys them. We rarely, if ever, send out more than one message per week. Most of our messages try to create engagement before a link is sent. A great way to do this is to send out quizzes or interactive conversations, basically anything that will keep engagement high and complaints low. If you do that, you'll be able to use Messenger without any issues.

Growing your Messenger list: There are three core ways that you can grow your Messenger list.

First, when people come to your Fan Page, you can have Messenger pop up to start a conversation that will add them to your Messenger lists.

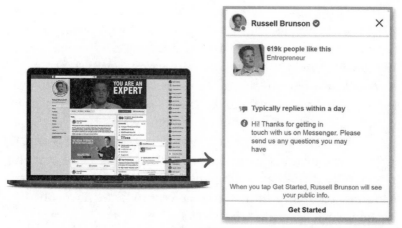

Figure 11.5

To grow your Messenger list, you can have Facebook automatically pop up a Messenger window in the lower right-hand corner. When they chat with you, they're automatically subscribed to your Messenger list.

Second, on your landing pages, you can have people select a box that will add them to your Messenger lists. Most of the Messenger chat-bot growth tools make it easy to add this to your landing pages.

Figure 11.6:

You can also grow your Messenger list by adding a Messenger checkbox to your opt-in forms. When they check the box, they'll be automatically subscribed to your Messenger list.

The third (and my favorite) way is to create a simple lead magnet and leverage your Fan Page to grow your Messenger list. Some of the Messenger growth tools make it easy to add people to your lists when they do a certain action. For instance, when people click a button on your post or comment with a certain keyword, you can add them directly to a specific Messenger list and it will send them a lead magnet right away.

Alison Prince showed me my new favorite model for how to do this. She is a member of my Inner Circle (my high-end coaching program), and she has a company teaching people how to start a business online selling e-commerce products. She will do a Facebook Live teaching "10 tips to . . ." or "seven tools that. . ."– type videos where she shares a list of cool things with people. Then she designs a really nice PDF with the things that she talks about on her Live. Throughout the Live, she'll show a printed copy of the lead magnet and tell people if they want a free copy, they just need to comment using a certain keyword and she'll send it to them through Messenger. Every time she goes live, she's adding hundreds of new people to her lists.

Publishing to your Messenger lists: Because my Messenger list is such a valuable asset, and because I don't own it (Facebook owns it and can shut it off at any time), I treat it very carefully. When someone first joins your list, you want to get them to interact with your Messenger bot because this helps to increase the engagement. Ultimately, this increases your ability to continue to send that person more messages in the future.

About once per week, we try to send out some type of conversation. Notice that I said "conversation" and not message. We don't just broadcast out a message for someone to go and visit a funnel. Instead, we'll ask them a question like, "Hey, are you still looking for ways to generate more leads online?" If they respond back with a yes, then I might say something like, "Cool. I have some new training that I think you're gonna LOVE, but I wanted to see if you'd rather have it as an audio file, a video, or a transcript." After three buttons pop up with these options, they can click one of the choices, which will take them to the next step in the bot's conversation.

Figure 11.7:

With Messenger, I can set up automatic conversations to reach my followers inside Facebook.

I personally like to use bots to guide people toward content on Facebook's platform (like a Facebook Live on my Fan Page) and have the actual selling happen off Messenger. That gives me an arm's distance from Messenger and selling anything directly through it. It also helps to boost my Facebook Live, which Facebook loves, and gives my subscribers value before I make them the offer.

Your Publishing Plan

We've covered a lot of things about publishing on Facebook. We talked about the core ways you publish inside Facebook with special focus on:

- Your personal page
- Your Fan Page
- Your groups
- Your Messenger lists

Each of these sections inside of the platform has a different strategy for how you publish. To make sure you hit each part of Facebook effectively to find and serve your dream customers, I have created an at-a-glance publishing plan so you can quickly see what content you should publish in each area, with your daily and weekly activities broken down into a simple, step-by-step process.

FACEBOOK PUBLISHING PLAN

DAILY: approx. 1 hr.		
Research & Network	10 min./day	Follow Dream 100: Like, comment, and send PMs.
	30 min./day	Write a value-filled post and answer questions in groups with a total audience of at least one million members.*
Facebook Personal Profile: 1 post/day	20 min./day	Choose a category from your JK5 and write a daily Seinfeld post about "What's on your mind?" (NOTE: These can be your daily Seinfeld emails.) Reply to comments.
Facebook Groups: 1/day	5 min./day	Create short, daily engagement posts that ask questions, give value, share tips, or tell stories. Reply to comments.
WEEKLY: approx. 45 min.		
Facebook Groups: 1 Live/week	25 min./week	Go Live in your group once a week. Tell stories, answer questions, and give a CTA if you like at the end. Reply to comments.
Facebook Messenger: 1/week	20 min./week	Choose from one of these three categories to send one message per week: interactive quiz, value-filled content, or interactive promo.
WHEN YOU HAVE CONTENT GOOD ENOUGH YOU'RE WILLING TO "BOOST" IT WITH MONEY		
Facebook Fan Page	n/a	Choose from one of these four categories when you post: produced value videos, live value videos, live perfect webinars, or curated content from your other platforms. Reply to comments.

Figure 11.8:

Use this publishing plan to see at a glance where you
should focus your efforts on Facebook.

STEP #4: WORK YOUR WAY IN

If you've done steps one through three and your personal profile is set up, then your house is now in order and you're ready to start being social and actually network. We do this by finding the groups in our marketplace that have already congregated our dream customers. First, I want you to focus on finding and joining the right groups. When you click on the group tab, Facebook will suggest groups that it thinks you'll like based on the influencers and brands that you're already following. You'll also be able to see the groups' names and how many members are in each group.

Similar to the strategy used for influencers and brands, your goal with groups is to get access to at least 1 million people through them. I look at the suggested groups, join the ones that have bigger member counts, and continue searching for more. After this initial exercise, you'll see new groups marketed to you through your Facebook feed, so I recommend continuing to join the groups that have already gathered your dream customers.

For example, if I'm a photographer and I type "photography" into the group search in Facebook, it will pull up dozens of groups I can join. In this case, there are over 507,000 people at four parties talking about photography. These are the parties that I'll be going to and networking at. Keep going to parties (i.e., joining groups) until your reach in these groups is over 1,000,000 people.

Figure 11.9:

**Join as many groups in your niche as you can until
you're able to reach over 1,000,000 people.**

Now, some people think that networking means going into these groups, spamming out links to your front-end funnels, and hoping that people will click on them and join your lists. This is not what I'm talking about. In most groups, this will get you kicked out almost immediately and will ruin your reputation in that market. Instead, every day I go into each of those groups and try to see what questions people are asking that I know the answer to. As soon as I can think of something awesome that I can share,

I write a value-filled post and post it in the group. No pitch . . . no ask . . . just value.

That is the secret to good networking. You are coming to serve, and if you do it consistently, people will see you, and they will follow you back to your home. But the secret is giving without withholding. This is the beginning of your value ladder, and the more value you give up front, the more people will want you.

After I make my post, I scroll through the other questions and try to comment or reply to at least three questions per group, and that's it. I spend 30 minutes total each day participating in these groups, providing value, and answering questions, and then I'm done. Consistency is the key. Keep providing value, and do not sell anything. Remember, your goal is to become the cool kid at the party, and if you provide value, everyone will want to come back to your house to hang out.

This strategy takes a little time, but if you are consistent and people see you showing up consistently, they will want to find out more. They'll click on your profile, and they will follow you. You'll be pulling people from these cold and warm groups and turning them into hot traffic that will start engaging in the conversations that you're posting on your own personal profile.

STEP #5: BUY YOUR WAY IN

There are a lot of companies who don't really want to get into the whole publishing game and want to focus only on paid ads instead. While I think that's very shortsighted, I do understand because it allows you to get ads up and running and to be able to test offers quickly. If you decide to start solely with paid ads, I would still recommend going back sometime soon and building the content foundation because doing so will create a more stable long-term foundation for your business.

As I discussed earlier, when new platforms come out, content creators are rewarded with free traffic to create adoption on the platform. Soon, though, the platforms transition to paid ads, and the content creators see less and less free traffic. Eventually, they have to pay for traffic, as this is where the platforms will make their money long-term. So even if you're getting traction with your content strategy, it's essential to master paid ads if you want to be relevant long-term to amplify the content, videos, and ads that you create.

All the paid ads happen on your Fan Page. This is where you can boost/pay to get your content shown to the followers of your Dream 100. Every video you post, every image you publish, and each post you write on your Fan Page can be promoted through Facebook's Ads Manager. You can also make "unpublished posts" that don't show up on your feed, but that you can start using to throw out hooks to grab the attention of your dream customers. Remember from Secret #9 that the more creative you can put out, the more success you will have. Use all these hooks to grab your dream customers from your prospecting pools, pull them into your retargeting buckets, and direct them to your funnels.

STEP #6: FILL YOUR FUNNEL

As you know, the last step of the framework is to take all this attention and use it to fill your funnels. At first, you do it by "working your way in." As you go out into Facebook's groups and start networking and providing value, you will be pushing people back to your personal profile (your home). On your personal profile, you will be rotating through the JK5 categories and making posts that can hook people when they show up on your page, as well as your friends and followers, and direct these people into your funnels.

To build an even stronger relationship with your friends and followers, you can invite them to come to your own social networking party (your group) where they can network with others and be part of your weekly "hangout" meetings. On your personal profile, they are only able to respond to posts you make, but here they can start their own conversations and get a sense of belonging inside your tribe.

After your social networking strategy is up and running, transition your focus to "buying your way in" with your Fan Page, where you will be producing and posting content that you feel good enough about spending $10–$20 to boost it. These will be seen by your existing audiences and help to build a stronger relationship with them, as well as directing them back into your funnels, but you will also be targeting the followers of your Dream 100 and the interests of your dream customers. This means that you are paying for these videos, posts, and ads to show up in their news feed.

Remember to study Secret #9 to know the best way to target your dream customers and pull them into your funnels. Your number-one goal is to transition the traffic that you are earning and buying into traffic that you own by taking them through one of your front-end funnels.

GOOGLE TRAFFIC SECRETS

The first time someone told me about Google, I was at a public library in 2001 in New Jersey, frustrated at how hard it was to find things online. The lady sitting next to me leaned over and said, "You should try www.Google.com. It's new, and every time I search on it, I'm always able to actually find what I'm looking for."

I shrugged and decided to give it a try. I slowly typed it in for the first time, letter by letter, and after the search bar loaded, I typed in the same keywords I had tried on a dozen other search engines. Within seconds, I found exactly what I was looking for! I'm assuming that your first experience was probably similar, and that's why we all kept going back.

STEP #1: UNDERSTAND THE HISTORY AND THE GOAL

It was 1996 at Stanford University when Larry Page and Sergey Brin started working on their first search engine called BackRub.[33] At the time, searching on the internet was just starting. Search engines like Excite, Yahoo!, Ask Jeeves, and more started to pop up. They each had different ways they indexed pages and showed their results.

Larry and Sergey had the idea that a better way to display search results was to look at the number of links coming back to a page (called backlinks) to estimate the value of that page. They theorized that the more backlinks pointed to a page, the more important the website must be, and therefore, the higher it would rank in the search engines. They wrote a mathematical algorithm that was based on that premise and created what are often called "spiders" to crawl the internet and count the number of backlinks pointing to every web page they could find, identifying the keyword phrases that are on the actual web page, and then ranking them for those keywords.

They found out quickly that their hypothesis was correct. This new algorithm made for a better searching experience for the end user, and it started to grow fast. The first year they hosted BackRub on Stanford's servers, but eventually, when they used up too much bandwidth, they had to move it. On September 15, 1997, they registered Google.com, and launched a dynasty based on a simple algorithm.

Google's algorithm made the so-called "cream of the World Wide Web" automatically rise to the top of the search results. In turn, the companies whose sites were indexed at the top of the search engines for certain keywords got flooded with so much traffic, so many visitors, and so many leads that many of them couldn't keep up with the business. Being ranked on the first page in Google for a major keyword could bring you hundreds of thousands (and in some cases millions) of dollars overnight! With that much money on the line for each ranked keyword, almost everyone who noticed what was happening wanted to be at the top, no matter the cost.

That's the funny thing about algorithms: they don't care who you are. They don't care who has the best product, the best customer support, or who will treat the customers the best. All they know is that if a page meets their certain criteria, they rank it higher than a page that doesn't meet their criteria. It's that simple. When you understand that, then the question quickly becomes, "What exactly is the algorithm looking for, and how do I tweak what I'm doing to beat the algorithm so I can be ranked at the top?"

Google's original algorithm was primarily based on backlinks. If you had 100 links on other people's websites all pointing to your page and your competitor had 101 links, your competitor would outrank you. As soon as people hacked the algorithm and figured out what made them win, they would do whatever they needed to rank them at the top.

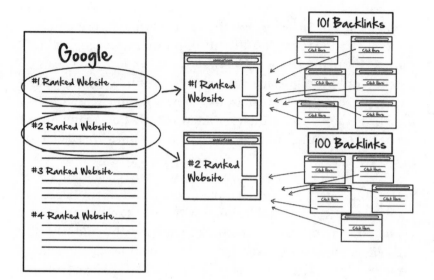

Figure 12.1:

Google's original algorithm ranked a website at the top
if it had the most backlinks for a certain search keyword.

I first discovered this when I was launching one of my first funnels ever. It was for my product teaching people how to make potato guns. I did some very basic keyword research and found that, at the time, there were about 18,000 people per month searching for the keyword phrase "potato gun." I was shocked that there were that many searches and no one was selling a product showing people how to make potato guns! So I made a DVD, set up my funnel, and tried to get traffic.

The first thing I did was type "potato gun" into Google, and I looked at the sites that were ranking on the first page. I had heard people say that the secret to being a good real estate investor was "location, location, location." I remember thinking that these 10 spots on page number one were the most prime real estate in the world for someone selling potato gun plans. Being ranked on that first page was the big secret!

I had to figure out how to get on that page, and the first step was figuring out the algorithm that decided which pages deserved to be at the top. Google was still in its infancy then, and as I started researching how to outrank my competitors, I learned that the only thing that mattered was backlinks. There were a few rudimentary tools that would show you how many links a page had, and within minutes, I knew exactly how many links I needed to be on the first page and how many links I needed to be in the top spot.

After that, it was on like Donkey Kong. I started doing everything in my power to get links. I would buy links from people. I found sites that would let me post links in their directories. I would post in forums and link back to my page. I would basically drop links on any and every page that would let me, including "Free for All," or FFA, pages (later nicknamed "link farms"), where you could submit as many links as you wanted. Within days, I saw my site move from the 100th page in Google to the 50th, to the 20th, and finally all the way to the second page! I was almost there! I was so close I could taste it. Within days, I would have my new potato gun storefront property listed on the most ideal real estate in the world: page one for my dream keyword.

And then it happened. It was my first of many experiences with a Google slap. Overnight, my page was gone, dropped from the search engines forever. I didn't know why. I didn't understand where it went, but as I went looking for answers, I saw that it wasn't just me.

In the big scheme of things, my potato gun keywords were tiny. While 18,000 people might seem like a lot when you're printing and shipping potato gun DVDs from your basement, it was tiny in relation to other keywords. Some keywords get hundreds of thousands or millions of visitors a month. Imagine being on page number one for "hotels" or "cars." These keywords can and do make hundreds of millions of dollars for those who can hold their spot at the top. But even the phrase "emergency plumber Boise Idaho" will grow a local company faster than anything else one could ever dream of.

So what was the Google slap? Well, each slap is different and is issued for different reasons, but the main reason always comes down to the battle between Google and the marketers. Google wants to show its visitors the best web page for every search. Marketers like us want our web page to be shown at the top. The battle between us and each platform is why the algorithms have to constantly change and evolve. That's why almost every book that has ever been written on getting online traffic is obsolete within months.

These slaps happen with Google, and they also occur with Facebook, Instagram, and YouTube. As soon as the platforms figure out the perfect algorithm that shows the best results, us marketers all start using our creative minds to figure out how to hack the algorithm so we can be in the number one spot or to make our videos go viral or get our posts, pictures, and images to get the most likes, shares, and views. With each keyword, image, or viral video potentially being worth millions of dollars, these platforms have created a scenario where the smartest people in the world are all focused on reverse engineering the algorithm for themselves, to get and keep their companies at the top.

That is why, in this book, I'm never going to tell you how to hack an exact algorithm. We never really know exactly what it is, even though we can get close by modeling what is currently having success. And it changes constantly. So instead of showing you how to hack an exact algorithm, I'll show you the history of each algorithm, as well as the changes that have taken place over time. After all, understanding the history and the changes make it easier to see the future and where things are going. I'll show you how to figure out what the algorithms are right now on each platform so you can play the game that is working today, in real time. The real secret to traffic isn't knowing exactly what the algorithm is before you get on each platform; the real secret is being able to look at each platform and quickly figure out what the algorithm is now.

Let me quickly take you through a history of each Google slap so you can understand the evolution of the algorithm and where it is today.

The Four Phases of Google

Phase #1—Popularity through backlinks: As you've just seen, the big breakthrough that made Google the best search engine in the world was that they ranked your web pages based on how many other pages were talking about you and linking back to you. Each link that someone else posted on a page that linked back to your website counted as a "vote" and pushed your page up through Google's rankings.

The game was fun. You would pick a keyword you wanted, find out how many backlinks the person who was ranked number one had, and then you only needed to get more backlinks than they had. For example, if the number-one spot had 100 backlinks, you needed at least 101 backlinks to replace them.

The problem is that it created a game that was easy to win if you were okay with spamming the search engines. People would hire huge teams of workers overseas to post their links on every website they could find. Eventually, software was also built that would allow you to post hundreds of links with the simple click of a few buttons. What started out as the perfect ranking algorithm quickly became a cesspool with the most spammed pages rising to the top. This didn't give Google's users a good customer experience, so they had to make changes.

Phase #2—Page rank and on-page optimization: To clean up this mess, Google started to look more closely at two things. The first was the actual quality of the links that were pointing back to you. They created something called "page rank" to give a quality score to every page.[34] This made it possible to assign a weight to every link that was pointing back to your website. No longer would 101 links beat out 100 links; instead, if you had fewer links coming from higher-quality pages, you could win, even with much fewer links. This solved a lot of problems for Google and cleaned up the results for a while, but inevitably it made people start focusing their spamming efforts on better sites. Pretty soon, a whole underground industry popped up where you could buy links on high page-rank sites.

Because garbage sites were rising to the top of the search engines, Google had its spiders look more closely at the actual content that was on the pages, not just how many links the web pages were getting.[35] Google rewarded people who structured their web page content in a way that gave people the best user experience. This created a whole new industry of specialists who became amazing at doing on-page optimization, essentially creating pages that Google loved to rank high. But, as happens with most good things, the marketers mastered the algorithm again. They created software that would find articles from other people's sites, scrape the articles, rewrite them (we used to call it "spinning" because it would take a percentage of the words in the article, look for other words in the thesaurus that had similar meanings, and replace the original words with the new, similar words so it looked like a new article), and display them in a way that would trick Google into ranking them high once again. Ultimately, it still gave end users a bad user experience. As good as Google's algorithm was, people kept finding ways to beat it.

Phase #3—The Google zoo: Panda, Penguin, Hummingbird:[36]
Starting in about 2011, the organic "Google slap" began, meaning Google made a bunch of huge algorithm changes designed to clean up their search results. Each update was given the name of an animal.

It started with Panda, which killed content farms and scraper sites that people had created to beat the algorithm. In 2012, Penguin went live, penalizing people who were buying links or obtaining them through networks that were designed to boost search rankings.

In 2013, Hummingbird figured out the intent behind a search rather than just the keyword itself, giving Google the artificial intelligence it needed to figure out what people were actually looking for. This was a huge update to Google's core algorithm, and it had only one goal: to make a better experience for those who were searching for something.

Phase #4—Mobilegeddon and Fred: For years, Google didn't implement any big updates. That is, until 2015, which has been called the year of mobile. It was the first time that mobile searches bypassed desktop searches on Google. This was also the year that Google launched their new updated algorithm that ranked you higher if your site was optimized for mobile. This update forced everyone to redesign their pages to create a better mobile experience for Google's mobile searchers.

Two years later, we were introduced to the update that was unofficially named Fred.[37] This update is the one that I think is most important for us all to understand, as it gives us the pattern to be successful with search in the future. Fred penalized sites that prioritized monetization over user experience. If your site had low user engagement, was thin in content, or had content heavily geared toward conversions, pop-ups, and aggressive advertising, you lost your rankings overnight.

So, why are Fred and all its predecessors so important? They help us to see Google's core goal: a better user experience. If we can align with Google's goals, they will send us an almost unlimited amount of traffic for free. Trying to spam the algorithms may give you short-term gains, but only until Google finds the loopholes and closes them. However, the real secret is understanding Google's intent and helping them to serve their searchers.

Why does Google care so much about their users' experience? Mostly because they still make the majority of their money from paid ads, and if people have a bad experience when they search, they won't come back. So if your goal is to try to figure out a way to deliver the best experience possible to their surfers, Google will reward you for that.

STEP #2: FIND YOUR DREAM 100 ON THIS PLATFORM

This is where the search engines start to become *really* fun for me. This process is similar to a treasure hunt, looking for the keywords and blogs that you can tap into to bring you thousands of visitors a day, sometimes overnight.

In Secret #2, we talked about two types of congregations. The first was "interest-based" congregations, such as influencers, brands, and other things that people are interested in. The second type of congregation we discussed was "search-based" congregations. Instead of targeting "interests," we would be targeting keywords and keyword phrases. For Google, we are going to be building out two Dream 100 lists. One list will be with the top bloggers in your market, and the second list will be a list of your Dream 100 keywords.

Your Dream 100 (bloggers): As I start looking at Google, before I put in the work of getting ranked in the search engines, I want to find the people who have already done the work, gotten ranked, and have readers who currently read their blogs. I will be utilizing these bloggers and their blogs in different ways, both buying my way into their traffic streams as well as working my way in. But for now, I just want to identify them and get them on my Dream 100 list.

Finding them can be as easy as going to Google and typing in your dream keywords and the word "blog" after it. You'll then see the top 10 listings in Google and which bloggers have made it to the top.

Some of the bloggers will have their own blogs that run on their own domain, while others will use popular blogging networks like Medium.com. You can go to Medium.com (and other blog networks) and search for bloggers in your market. Make this list and keep it handy, as we'll be leveraging these people soon.

Your Dream 100 (keywords): It's now finally time to dust off your "Dream 100" keywords that you wrote down in Secret #2 and focus on getting access to all the traffic that is on the first page in the search engines. Being ranked on page number one for one of your dream keywords is the equivalent of owning Boardwalk or Park Place in Monopoly. Owning one or more of these listings in this virtual real estate landscape can fill your funnels with traffic for years to come.

Make a list of the keyword phrases that you think your dream customers would be typing into Google if they were trying to find the result that your product or service offers. When I first did this exercise with ClickFunnels, the first 10 dream keyword phrases that I wrote down were:

- Sales funnels
- Digital marketing
- Internet marketing
- Online marketing
- Landing page
- Marketing automation
- Growth hacking
- Personal branding
- Website traffic
- Social media marketing

I figured that that my dream customers would be typing each of these phrases into Google to get the same result that my product could give them, and these became my dream keywords.

The next step was to find the long-tail keywords associated with each of my dream keywords. Often it can be really difficult to rank for a high-competition keyword, so I also wanted to see the long-tail keywords that would be easier to rank at first.

To do this, take your number-one dream keyword phrase and type it into Google. Google will suggest other keyword phrases in the search bar that people often search for when someone types in your dream keyword phrase. These are the other suggested phrases under your search results.

These keywords will become your "long-tail" keyword phrases. Write down your nine long-tail keyword phrases that are associated with each of your dream keywords that you would like to target. For example:

Dream Keyword: **Sales Funnels**

Long-Tail Keywords:

- Sales funnels definition
- Sales funnels software
- Sales funnels for real estate
- Sales funnels examples
- Sales funnels for artists
- Sales funnels templates
- Sales funnels explained
- Sales funnels 101
- Sales funnels for Shopify

You can also scroll down to the bottom of Google after you search for your dream keyword, and it will show you eight more keywords that are closely related to your search term.

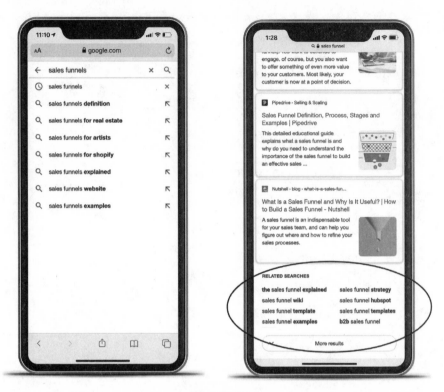

Figure 12.2:

When you type in your dream keyword, Google will suggest other popular,
long-tail keyword phrases (left). After searching for a specific result, Google will
also show you related searches at the bottom of their search results (right).

Keep looking until you find 10 solid keywords phrases to focus
on. If you do that with all 10 of your dream keywords, you will
end up with a list of 100 keywords.

This is the simplest way to build out your dream keyword list,
but there are some amazing software tools that can help take it to
the next level. Many of them will show you how many searches
each keyword gets each month, how competitive it is to try and
rank for these keywords, how much money you will pay per click
from the sponsored ads, and more. I have posted a list of all my
favorite keyword tools, as well as tutorial videos for my favorites,
at TrafficSecrets.com/resources.

STEP #3: IDENTIFY THE PUBLISHING STRATEGY AND CREATE YOUR PUBLISHING PLAN

Now that we have our dream keywords, we want to funnel hack the search engines to see what is already working for that keyword. To do that, all you have to do is type your keyword phrase into Google. Then scan the top 10 results and look for patterns of what type of posts are being ranked. I specifically look for what we call a "linkable asset," or what I call internally a "Letterman Top 10 List."

I call it that because I remember when I was teenager and my parents would sometimes watch *Late Show with David Letterman,* and while I didn't necessary like his show, there was one segment that I *loved,* and it was when he would do his famous Top 10 Lists, such as "Eminem's Top 10 Pieces of Advice For Kids" or "Top 10 Questions Justin Bieber Would Answer 'I Don't Know.'"[38] Then he would list out 10 funny things to go with each list.

A linkable asset works similar to Letterman's Top 10 Lists. They will usually be structured with a title like "25 SEO Tools to Instantly Improve Your Marketing in 2020" or "18 Things You Can Actually Eat on a Ketogenic Diet that You Assumed Were Bad for You."

These types of linkable assets are what Google loves for a few reasons. The first is that if you structure them correctly, people will love the content so much that they can't help but link back to it. Real, organic, quality links are what Google wants to reward you for, and writing a good article that people naturally want to link to is the secret to getting the right links. The second reason is these are the types of posts that readers on Google love. Because Google owns the Chrome browser and usually has their analytics code on most of your pages, they can see how long someone stays on your site, how long they scroll for, if they click on your links, and how many pages they visit inside of your site. The more time someone spends on your site, the more they scroll, and the more pages they click to are all signs that your end user is having a good experience. These types of articles with their "21 steps" or "205 resources," if written correctly, will get people to scroll through your page and spend a lot of time there, showing its value to Google.

As I'm scanning the organic results for my dream keywords, I'm looking to see if there are any Letterman Top 10 List–type articles being ranked. If there aren't, then I will work on creating my own linkable asset that I can post on my blog. If I do find one that is already ranking in the top 10 for my Dream 100, I will use the "skyscraper" technique that I learned from Brian Dean to build a taller skyscraper and outrank them in the search engines.

The skyscraper technique works after you have found content that has already generated a ton of links and is already ranking for your dream keywords, and then you model it to create your own bigger, better piece of content, i.e., a bigger skyscraper. I like to try to create at least one new skyscraper article per month.

On his blog, Brian describes the skyscraper technique as a way for *you* to have the content that everyone wants to talk about (and link to):[39]

> Have you ever walked by a really tall building and said to yourself: *Wow, that's amazing! I wonder how big the* eighth *tallest building in the world is.* Of course not. It's human nature to be attracted to the best. And what you're doing here is finding the tallest "skyscraper" in your space . . . and slapping 20 stories to the top of it.

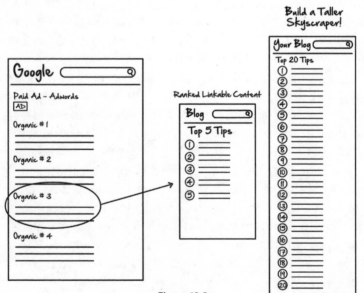

Figure 12.3:

To rank for your dream keyword, find an article that is ranked high in Google for that keyword and write a "taller skyscraper" article that Google will like better.

After you've found an article that is ranking for your dream keyword that you want to beat, the next step is to write a better piece of content. Here are four things that Brian recommended to do to your article to make your skyscraper taller:

- *Longer:* In some cases, publishing an article that's simply longer or includes more items will do the trick. For example, if you find a link magnet with a title of "50 Healthy Snack Ideas," publish a list of 150 (or even 500).

- *More up to date:* If you can take an out-of-date piece of content and spruce it up, you've got yourself a winner.

- *Better designed:* A visually stunning piece of content can typically generate a lot more links and social shares than something similar on an ugly page.

- *More thorough:* Most lists posts are made of a bland list of bullet points without any meaty content that people can actually use. But if you add a bit of depth for each item on your list, you have yourself a list post that's much more valuable.[40]

Important note: Brian recommends that you beat the existing content on all four levels.

In this longer new skyscraper, I will often use my dream keyword as well as my long-tail keywords throughout the article. Doing this with just one skyscraper article will often get me ranked for many, if not all, my related Dream 100 keyword phrases.

Getting quality links to your skyscraper: Publishing the longer, better skyscraper won't in and of itself get your site ranked onto page number one. After you've written the article, you need to promote it, and the way you promote an article is by getting a lot of the right links to it. Brian taught us to get the right links by looking at the links that are pointing to the linkable asset that we modeled. If people are already linking to that content, we know a few things.

- They have a website in the same niche that we're publishing.

- They're interested in the topic, because they have already linked to our competitor.

- They've already linked to an article on that topic, so it's not difficult for them to include a link to our longer, better, more updated article too.

You will need to email the people linking to your competitor and ask them to link back to you as well. You can contact them manually or you can use a shortcut to save you time. Go to TrafficSecrets.com/resources to find some tools that will scrape the contact information from everyone who is linking to your competitor.

In your email, you can let them know that you saw they linked to your competitor and that you'd love it if they'd link to your article as well since yours is similar but much more up to date and comprehensive. This strategy will help you to get the right links. Here's an example of an email that Brian sent out to 160 people who were linking to his competitor that got him great results:

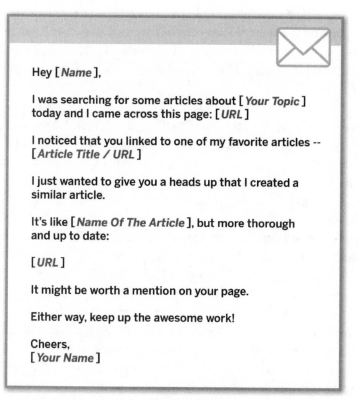

Hey [*Name*],

I was searching for some articles about [*Your Topic*] today and I came across this page: [*URL*]

I noticed that you linked to one of my favorite articles --
[*Article Title / URL*]

I just wanted to give you a heads up that I created a similar article.

It's like [*Name Of The Article*], but more thorough and up to date:

[*URL*]

It might be worth a mention on your page.

Either way, keep up the awesome work!

Cheers,
[*Your Name*]

Figure 12.4:

After you write your skyscraper article, you can email the website owners of anyone who has linked to your competitor's article and let them know you have created a newer, better article.

Brian said that he personalized and tweaked this template for each person he reached out to, and out of the 160 emails he sent out, he got 17 people to link back! That's an 11 percent success rate following the skyscraper method that helped him to get his article ranked.

The next way I work to get links back to my new article is by reverse engineering (funnel hacking) the backlinks that are going to the other nine organic listings on page number one for my dream keyword. I already found the people that are linking to my competitor's article and emailed them. I am now going to do the same thing to the people who are linking to the other nine pages that are ranked on page one. I send out a similar email to each of them asking if they'd be willing to link back to my linkable asset. By doing this, I am getting the same backlinks that are currently ranking the top 10 results for my dream keyword phrase all linking back to me.

There are lots of other ways to get links, all with varying degrees of what Google likes. "White hat" techniques are the ones that Google loves and rewards you for, whereas "black hat" techniques are just spammy ways to get links that trick Google. While you may get short-term gains with black-hat techniques, every one that I've ever used to beat Google has always caught up with me eventually. We now solely focus on doing what Google wants. I'll mention some other ways we get links in the "work your way in" section later, but Brian's skyscraper linking technique is one of the best and fastest ways to kick-start your link building.

These manual link requests will get the process started, and then I will stimulate traffic to the skyscraper pages by promoting my new article on my other social sites (Facebook and Instagram) and email lists. If you've followed the process we've discussed, your content will become a link magnet by organically getting the right types of links and continuing to rise in the search engines. This type of organic linking is what Google wants and rewards.

Your Publishing Plan

In this chapter, I've shown you how I look at marketing on Google. We've talked about some of the core ways to get organic traffic from Google. The following is a publishing plan that you and your team can use to systemize the ranking process.

GOOGLE PUBLISHING PLAN

WEEKLY: approx. 2 hrs.		
Network: As many as you can	30 min./week	Contact as many people as you can who linked to your competitor's skyscraper article. Ask them if they can also link to your article.
	1 hr./week	Find the other 9 website owners who are ranked for your specific keyword, and then find the people who are linking to them. Those links have gotten them onto page 1 for your dream keyword, so we want to get as many of those links as well. Each of the 9 could have another 10, 50, 100+ or more links, and you can contact each of them and try to get those links back to your skyscraper.
Guest Post: 1/week	30 min./week	Write one guest post on one of your Dream 100's blogs or websites each week and include one of your skyscraper article links.*
MONTHLY: approx. 2.25 hrs.		
Skyscraper Article: 1/mo.	2 hrs./mo.	Write one skyscraper article each month that is better than your competitor's article. Incorporate your dream keyword and two or three of your long tail keywords.
	10 min./mo.	Email your list with a link to your skyscraper article.
	5 min./mo.	Post on Facebook and Instagram with a link to your skyscraper article. Reply to comments.

Please note: The time requirements shown are variable. It may take you less or more time.

* This strategy will be discussed in the upcoming section: "Step #4: Work Your Way In."

Figure 12.5:

Use this publishing plan to see at a glance where
you should focus your efforts on Google.

STEP #4: WORK YOUR WAY IN

Working your way into the search engines has two amazing benefits. The first is that you can tap into the traffic streams of the bloggers that you put on your Dream 100 list earlier. The second is you can get some of the best quality links directly from these same bloggers who have quality sites in your market (the type of links that Google loves).

The way I work my way into the search engines is through "guest posting." That means I am looking for someone else who has a blog in my market and I am asking if I can make a "guest post" on their site. I'll email the blog owners and tell them that I had a few cool ideas for a post on their blog and ask them if any of them are of interest. If they say yes, then I write up the post, include a link to one or two of my skyscrapers, and have them post it. I give them good content, their readers will click on the links and I'll get traffic from that, the spiders will see the links to my skyscraper, and it will increase my rankings from there.

You can also work on becoming a writer or a columnist for high-traffic sites in your market. Some of the best SEO people I know are writers for *Forbes*, *Entrepreneur*, and other top-ranked sites. They are able to use their positions as writers on the sites to push traffic into their own funnels and post quality links to rank their skyscrapers.

I try to post at least one guest post per week on blogs in my market, as well as work toward becoming a contributing author for the sites that bring me the most traffic and quality links.

STEP #5: BUY YOUR WAY IN

When I first started to learn SEO, back before the Google slaps started, I got frustrated that I wasn't ranked number one for some of the highly competitive dream keywords that I wanted to rank for. One day I decided I wanted to be number one for the keyword "internet marketing." I set out on a journey to rank organically for that keyword, and after eight long months I finally ended up getting to page number one! I think I topped out at the number four spot on page one before I got slapped during one of the algorithm updates.

But about a month into that long journey, I got frustrated and I looked at each of the people who were already ranked number one for my dream keywords. I started to notice that a lot of those sites were articles and weren't actually selling any products. They had some banner ads on them, but they didn't have a product like mine to sell.

I started emailing a bunch of them, knowing how hard I was working to try to get that ranking, wondering why they would put in that much effort to rank when they didn't have an actual product to sell. I got emails back from about a half dozen of them, and I found out something very interesting. Most of them were SEO guys who were really good at ranking pages but had no idea how to create products. So instead they would get a page ranked on page one, and then they would either sell ads on their page or link to other products as an affiliate. As soon as they told me that, I had the big idea.

What if while I was waiting to get my site ranked on page one, I started getting traffic immediately from all the people who were currently ranked number one? My goal in the short-term wasn't to outrank them; it was to get ads for my funnels on their pages.

I started to negotiate deals with them, and within days I was prominently displayed at the top of some of the sites that were already ranked for my dream keywords. Getting on these pages turned on a faucet of traffic over night!

I quickly started to realize how much more valuable a click to your funnels is from one of these pages than even the same from the Google homepage. Just think, a phrase like "internet marketing" could have thousands of people searching for it per day on Google. However, the people who do the following three-step process are actually more valuable to you:

1) Type a phrase into Google

2) Click on one of the results

3) Click on the link to your funnel from this other page

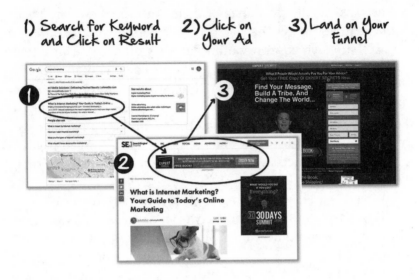

1) Search for Keyword and Click on Result

2) Click on Your Ad

3) Land on Your Funnel

Figure 12.6:

People who follow this three-step process of searching for your keyword, clicking on one of the results, clicking on your paid ad *inside* that result, and landing on your funnel are more valuable to you because they're warmer traffic.

The first click on Google is typically from the "browsers" but the second click comes from the people who are the most serious: the buyers. Because they've made two clicks to get to you, they are so much more likely to convert when they do get to your page. Tons of the clicks that hit Google's homepage will be wasted on people who aren't serious, and if you're paying for these clicks, it can be very expensive. However, the people who have to click two clicks to get to you are the ones who are most serious and will be worth the most money to you long-term.

When I look at my Dream 100 websites, I try to quickly weed out the ones that don't have any advertising on them already. Instead, I'm looking for sites that have AdSense ads, banner ads, affiliate links to other products, and email newsletter subscription boxes. Then I start contacting the owners of these websites to find out my advertising options.

- **If they have an email newsletter,** I ask them if I can purchase a solo ad to their email list (more on this in Secret #17).

- **If they have banner ads on their website,** I ask them how much it costs to purchase a banner ad.

- **If they have Google AdSense on their site,** then I add their site to my list to target later with Google Display Network or GDN (more on this in Secret #9).

- **If they have an article on that page,** then I try to see if I can get them to add a link back to one of my pages in their article.

Getting your links to your funnels on the pages that are already ranked for your dream keywords is one of the fastest ways to get super qualified traffic into your funnels.

STEP #6: FILL YOUR FUNNEL

Are you able to see now how you can get access to the traffic that is coming from the search engines? We focus on creating blog posts that are linkable assets that will act as link magnets that you can get ranked on page one for your dream keywords. While we're waiting for these pages to rise in the search engines, we do guest posting on the blogs in our market to get both instant traffic from their readers and more links pointing back to our linkable assets.

We then go to the pages that are already ranked on page one for our dream keywords, and we work to buy ads on these pages so we can plug our funnels into the existing streams of traffic that are going to these pages.

The last step is buying ads on Google's paid search platforms. There are two main ways that you can get paid traffic from Google. The first is the paid ads on the search engine results pages (the ads that show up above and below the organic results for your dream keywords) and the second is from AdSense ads that other people have put on their pages. You get access to these ads through the GDN.

I won't be showing the actual tactics behind how to run Google Ads as they are always changing, but the strategy behind how you run Google Ads in Secret #9 is the same. First you create prospecting ads as hooks to capture your dream customers and pull them into your funnels. For those that don't immediately convert, we move them into our retargeting buckets and move them from engaged, to landed, and then to owned. After we own the traffic, we use our follow-up funnels to ascend them up our value ladder.

YOUTUBE TRAFFIC SECRETS

There is something special about YouTube that I don't think many people understand. YouTube is the only platform where you can create something and post it online where it will actually grow exponentially over time.

When you post a video on Facebook Live, it will show up in the newsfeed of your dream customers for a few days, and then it's gone forever. You can extend the life of that video by paying for ads to boost it, but eventually it will fall to the bottom of your feed, never to be seen again. And although Facebook Live is like a good talk show for current events, the art you create has a limited life span. The same is true with Instagram, where eventually your pictures will fall to the bottom of your feed and your Stories will expire. Some platforms have more longevity and last longer, but they all perform progressively worse over time.

Every platform, that is, *except* for YouTube. As soon as artists create videos and post them on YouTube, their viewership can start to grow and continue to grow forever. I have videos that I published five years ago that still get hundreds of views a day. Other videos that we published more recently received an initial viewer surge (we can often get thousands of views per day simply because it's a new video), but the numbers of new views continue to rise day after day. YouTube's algorithms are built to keep people on YouTube, so they try to recommend videos that are most likely to keep their viewers engaged as long as possible.

This gives us creators a reason to spend more time producing amazing videos that will serve us and our audiences for the rest of our lives and beyond. And when you understand a few key things about how YouTube's algorithms work, it will help you set up your videos for long-term success.

Six years ago, I got a call from a guy named Joe Marfoglio, who asked me if he could become an affiliate for a new product I had just launched. It was a course we had created helping people to overcome pornography addiction. Excited to get someone else besides myself driving traffic to our new product, I said yes. He told me that he was going to create a few videos and post them on YouTube, driving traffic through his affiliate link to our product.

I gave him permission and didn't think much more about it at the time. Within a few months, Joe was driving more sales by himself than all my marketing efforts combined. Confused, I asked him what he was doing, and he told me that he had just posted two videos on YouTube and that was it. I asked him if I could see the videos and he sent me the links.

One was a short, 2-minute-and-47-second video he had created, and the other was the sales video that I had created to sell the product. Both these videos were getting thousands of views a day. As I was writing this chapter, I went back to find these two videos and was shocked to see that the first video had received 1.2 million views and the longer video had over 815,000 views!

Figure 13.1:

In six years, this video has received over 815,000 views, and because it's on YouTube, it gets more views every day.

Despite the fact that we stopped selling that product a few years ago, these videos continue to drive traffic every day. I had Joe pull the stats, and that month alone, more than six years after he posted them, the videos had 10,361 views and were able to generate 553 clicks back to our funnel. That is the power of creating videos with YouTube.

STEP #1: UNDERSTAND THE HISTORY AND THE GOAL

Did you know that YouTube is the world's second largest search engine (behind Google), and it's also the second most trafficked website (also behind Google)?[41] Oh, yeah, and in case you didn't know, it's also owned by Google. It was created in 2005 by three PayPal employees (Chad Hurley, Steve Chen, and Jawed Karim) above a pizzeria in San Mateo, California.[42] In less than two years after YouTube started, Google purchased it for $1.65 billion.

Right now, over 1.9 billion people log into YouTube every month, over 400 hours of video are uploaded to YouTube every minute, and over one billion hours of videos are watched on YouTube every day.

YouTube is interesting because it functions similar to a social platform. You create content, try to get people to engage with that content and build up subscribers just like other social networks.

YouTube also functions as a search engine, which is why, unlike social networks, your videos continue to grow over time. If you learn how to optimize your videos the way that YouTube would like you to, they will reward you by ranking you for your dream keywords inside of YouTube, and often they'll even post those videos inside the search results of Google.

STEP #2: FIND YOUR DREAM 100 ON THIS PLATFORM

Six months after we had launched ClickFunnels, we were trying to figure out new ways to get more people to create accounts. We hadn't used YouTube yet as a traffic strategy, so I called up Joe Marfoglio (my friend who ranked the videos for our pornography anti-addiction product a few years earlier) and asked him if he could help. During our initial call, he got excited and had me jump on a videoconference where I could see his computer screen. He opened up YouTube, and I watched as he showed me one of the most powerful marketing tactics I had ever witnessed.

First, he typed in the names of some of the people who were on my Dream 100 list—people who we had been targeting on Facebook to see if they were also publishing on YouTube. Many of them didn't have YouTube channels, but others had really big channels with hundreds of thousands of subscribers. As I looked at each of the videos on their channels, Joe said, "You know you can buy ads that will be shown in front of any of those videos, right? As soon as anyone goes to watch a video on their channel, the first thing they will see are your ads."

At the time I had no idea that was possible, and almost instantly my mind wondered about the possibilities. "Wait, I can buy ads on each of their videos and use it to bring people into my funnels?"

"Exactly," Joe said. "You are leveraging their name, their credibility, and their content to drive people into your funnels."

He then went to the YouTube search bar and asked me what keywords I thought my dream customers would be searching for. I asked him to try the keyword "internet marketing," and within a few seconds I saw dozens of videos that were already ranked for that term. Joe explained how we could easily create videos and get them ranked for these dream keywords, just like we did for the pornography anti-addiction video. Joe said, "We can put in the work once, and these videos will serve you for the rest of your life. Heck, they'll keep driving traffic to your funnels even after you're dead!"

Laughing, I asked him, "While we're waiting for these videos to get ranked at the top, could I buy ads on all the other videos now?" He smiled and politely told me yes.

Within just a few minutes, I started to see why I was going to love YouTube so much. After I got off that call, I immediately did exactly what I'm going to tell you to do now. You need to build out two Dream 100 lists: one list with the names of the people, brands, and influencers that you would like to target, and a second list with the keyword phrases that you would like to create videos for. I'll go into more detail on how we find the right keywords in the publishing section later in this chapter.

STEP #3: IDENTIFY THE PUBLISHING STRATEGY AND CREATE YOUR PUBLISHING PLAN

Just like Google, YouTube has an algorithm that decides which videos to rank to increase their users' experience. To prevent people from ranking videos that ruin the experience for end users, the algorithm is constantly being updated and changed. The way to win at YouTube is to figure out ways to create and post videos that are in alignment with how they want videos to be posted. That's why it's so important to closely watch your Dream 100 and see what things they're doing that YouTube is rewarding them for. If they change how they like descriptions, tags, or linking, you'll see the changes in the videos that are getting a lot of views, and then you can change your strategy to match theirs. Most of the things that I will be showing you in this publishing section are things that I learned from Joe Marfoglio as he's consulted us at ClickFunnels with our YouTube strategy.

Set Up Your Channel

Before we start creating any videos, we need to make sure the channel is set up so that when potential subscribers come, they'll turn into actual subscribers.

Name of your channel: For your channel name, you should focus more on branding than keywords. Your channel name will show up everywhere in searches, suggested searches, related channel suggestions, and on your videos when you leave comments. You want people to be able to see your name and brand and get a sense of what your channel is about. You'll notice that my channel name is Russell Brunson—ClickFunnels. I do this because I want people to recognize my name as well as my main brand when they see my channel name come up.

"About Us" page: This page is important for two reasons. First, it lets people know more about you when they're checking you out before they subscribe. Second, the information you write here will show up in the search results for your channel and will be a big key to people finding and subscribing to your channel.

Header image: When people come to your channel page, the first thing they'll see is your header. Your header should be simple and speak clearly to your target audience so that they know the value they'll get from your channel. Those who see mine will know quickly what I do and how I can help them.

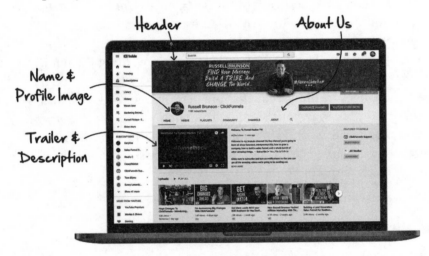

Figure 13.2:

When people see your YouTube channel, you want them to immediately know who you are and what you're about.

Profile image: Many people mistakenly put their logos here. Instead, use a picture of yourself because it will dramatically increase engagement.

Channel trailer and description: When people first come to your channel page, they'll see an actual trailer for your channel as well as a brief description about your channel. It is only shown to new visitors who aren't subscribers yet, so this video is speaking specifically to them.

Here are Joe's script guidelines for an engaging channel trailer:

Introduce yourself and welcome your viewer to your channel. You want the viewer to feel like you are talking to them and that you understand them.

Go briefly into your backstory and explain why you have the authority to be creating the content you make on YouTube.

Pitch your value statement. Leave no doubt in your viewer's mind what this channel is about. Talk about the channel, what it is about, and why it matters.

Share your posting schedule so they know when to expect new content.

End the video with a really strong CTA. This means you need to tell the viewer what you want them to do. Tell them to subscribe to your channel and turn on notifications so they don't miss any of your new videos.

Make sure this video is no more than 60–120 seconds long. Any longer than that and you will lose your potential viewer.

Figure 13.3:

Create a short channel trailer by following this simple script: introduction, backstory, value statement, posting schedule, and CTA.

When shooting this video, don't get overwhelmed or bogged down with details about the camera and the equipment. If you're just starting out, you don't need to buy anything fancy. I still use my iPhone for the majority of my videos.

Identify Your Dream Keywords that You Want to Make Videos For

The first step is to find all the long-tail keywords around your dream keyword that you can make videos for. If you have a brand-new channel and try to rank for a keyword like "how to make money online," it's going to be extremely difficult to outrank some of the bigger channels. But Joe has a strategy that has proven successful in the past to get you tons of views, traction, and subscribers:

> This is a tactic I learned from my good friend Jeremy Vest. He calls this tactic "finding your channel's focus phrase." You can think of it like trying to find your channel's "how to shave." What does that mean? A lot of you have probably seen a video or heard about the Dollar Shave Club. They made an incredible video that went viral everywhere on Facebook, Twitter, and YouTube with millions upon millions of views, and that launched their company into the stratosphere. But did you know another razor company was dominating YouTube and raking in millions of views from their hyper-targeted market and they did it without any viral or hype videos?
>
> That company was Gillette. What they found was that the most influential keyword in their space was "how to shave." They centered their channel around that keyword. Now, if Gillette just wanted to rank for "how to shave," they wouldn't get a ton of traction. It would have been really hard, right out of the gate, to rank for that keyword. Instead, they took "how to shave" as the root keyword. Then, they looked through suggested search terms and added words to the back of it. Gillette created hundreds of videos with that root keyword, such as, "how to shave

your head," "how to shave your back," "how to shave your beard," "how to shave your legs," and so on. Gillette made video after video with the root word "how to shave." These videos have collectively received millions of views across their channel.

The dream keyword "ABC Hack": Here's a trick to find hundreds of keywords you can choose from. If my root keyword is fairly broad, like "how to make money," you can type in the same words in the YouTube search bar followed by a space and the letter *a*.

The suggested search results will show you: "How to make money . . ."

- As a beginner
- As a kid
- At home
- At school

Then you can replace the *a* with *b*, and the suggested search results will show you: "How to make money . . ."

- Blogging
- By investing
- By posting ads

Then move on to *c* and *d* and so on. You will want to get at least 50 of these "how to make money" keywords to use as keyword titles in your videos.

Create Your First Video

Now that you've done all the research, set up your channel, and made a list of keywords to target, now it's time to start creating videos. As I'm creating videos, there are two types of video that I focus on.

The first are called "discoverable videos." These are videos based on keyword phrases that I publish as hooks to rank for these keywords with a goal of grabbing people's attention, pulling them into my channel, and turning them into subscribers. How you structure these videos is very important because if one of them takes off and gets 100K views, you want to be able to make sure that you are able to create subscribers and leads from all of these viewers.

Here is the script that Joe created that I use for every discoverable video we create:

Figure 13.4:

To create a discoverable video, simply follow this five-step script outline: hook, trailer, intro, story/content, and offer.

- **Hook:** Create a 15-second concise introduction. This is where you're going to hook people using the same keywords that they're searching for. You'll tell them the value of your video and present a hook for them to look forward to so they continue watching.

- **Trailer:** Place your quick branded intro or "trailer," which should be no more than four to five seconds maximum. Do not put a 30- or 60-second branded intro here. You'll lose the majority of your viewers right there.

- **Intro:** Talk to your viewer about who you are and why they should listen to you for the next 15–30 seconds. Share a little bit about your story so that you make a connection with that new visitor. Don't assume that they know who you are.

- **Story/Content:** Share content and story for the next 7 to 12 minutes. Here is where you deliver the value from the hook you mentioned earlier.

- **Offer:** Add your CTA. As a discoverable video, the offer will normally be to get people to like, comment, subscribe, or turn on the notifications.

Use this show formula as an outline to write out your video script. Once you have an outline and a tight script, take out your cell phone or camera, look right into the lens, and film yourself recording that video. The goal of these videos is to hook people who are searching and direct them back to your "home" to become subscribers. Typically, I'm not selling on these videos, outside of selling the subscription to my channel.

The second type of video I create is called "video webinars," which are usually less keyword focused, as they are created to build a stronger relationship with my current subscribers. These videos are the ones that I'm posting for my existing followers, at my home. These are the videos that I use to sell things. I'll still try to find keywords to rank them for, but oftentimes I am trying to create or teach something that may not fit inside of a certain keyword phrase. I use the Perfect Webinar script, or the Perfect Webinar Hack, or the Perfect Five-Minute Webinar (all from *Expert Secrets*, and you can print the scripts at TrafficSecrets.com/ resources) with a goal of moving them from traffic that I've earned into traffic that I own.

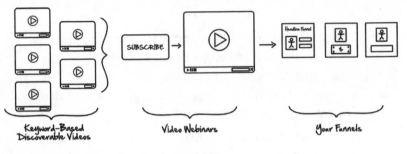

Figure 13.5:

To create a video webinar, you can still follow the five-step script
from earlier, but instead of asking your subscribers to like, comment,
or subscribe, you'll encourage them to get a lead magnet.

Upload Your Video and Set It Live

After I've created the video, there are six things that we currently
do for each video we upload to make sure we're aligned with
YouTube's algorithm.

Look at YouTube as a TV show: YouTube very much sees itself like
a TV station. Unlike Facebook Live where you can go live anytime
you want, YouTube wants you to create a show, schedule it, and
publish it on a consistent schedule. For example, you may publish
your videos every Thursday at 7:00 P.M. EST, or every Tuesday and
Thursday at 7:00 A.M. EST. Create a schedule for yourself that you
know you can keep up with, and be consistent as you stick to that
publishing schedule.

Find the keyword for your new video: Make sure you have
identified the keyword phrases you want to use for your new
video. Earlier we walked you through how to find these phrases,
and now we're ready to use them.

Write your video title: Your title should have two elements: it
must contain your keyword phrase, and it also needs a strong hook
that works in tandem with your thumbnail to "sell the click." For

example, if I were trying to create a video that would rank for "potato gun," some possible titles might be:

"Potato Gun—The 17 steps to build your gun in under an hour"

or

"How to build your Potato Gun with stuff you can find at Home Depot for under $30"

Create your thumbnail "hook": This is the visual hook that will grab people when they're watching someone else's video to convince them to watch your video next. Make sure it looks good when it's shrunken down tiny. The best practices that usually get the most clicks are using large faces/images, bright colors, and as few words as possible. It needs to pop off the page. Look at your Dream 100's video thumbnails to get an idea of how they're grabbing attention with their thumbnails.

Figure 13.6:

When creating thumbnails, be sure to have clear hooks with
an image of your face to get more clicks.

Write your description: Ideally, these will be between 150–300 words. The first two sentences should contain your keyword and CTA because this portion is "above the fold," i.e., the portion that everyone sees before they scroll down. You will also want to add your subscribe link and a link to your front-end funnels, as well as links to other related videos and playlists you have on YouTube. To optimize your search results, I recommend adding up to three hashtags.

Add tags: While still helpful for search ranking, tags mean less than they used to. Keep your tags highly relevant to your main keyword: the more closely related to the topic, the better. If you branch out, you'll only confuse the algorithm.

Figure 13.7:

Just as important as the video itself is the content *about* the video, such as the keywords, title, description, and tags.

Those are the core things that we're looking at when posting each video. Again, these specific things may change, so that's why it's so essential to closely watch your Dream 100 to see what things are being rewarded in YouTube and then make changes as needed.

After your video is posted, you want to get people watching it as soon as possible. I'll usually encourage the traffic that I own, such as my email lists, fans, and followers, to watch the new video. Because these are your best fans, they'll likely watch more of the video, like more, comment more, and share more—all those things that will show the algorithm that your video is good. After your initial surge of traffic to the video, YouTube will start posting it in the side bar of videos that are related, and they will often rank it for the keywords that you are targeting.

YouTube's algorithm will then watch and see how your video performs. The better it does, the more they'll reward it. Here are the three things we've noticed that have the biggest impact on your video's success:

Click-Through Rate (CTR): How many people who see your thumbnail actually click on it? The benchmarks we want for CTR are:

4 percent—Acceptable

6 percent—Good

9 percent—We should throw a party!

Initial retention: The first minute of retention is very important. You need to hook people fast and keep them watching. Watch the videos from your Dream 100 to get ideas on how they hook people past the first minute. Try to keep minute one retention above 70 percent.

Overall retention: As for your overall video retention, how long is the actual video being watched? We look at how many people make it to the end of the video. The benchmarks for video retention are:

35 percent—Acceptable

40 percent—Good

50 percent—Party time! (You'll get a lot more reach if your account averages this or better)

The "Binge-Watching" YouTube Hack

One of the best things you can do for your channel is to get people to binge-watch your videos. When YouTube sees people going from one video in your channel to another, and another, not only will it boost your views on those videos, it will lift the entire channel.

One secret is instead of putting up a longer, 30- or 60-plus minute video, create a YouTube playlist and break up your long videos into smaller 5–10 minute videos that are part of a series inside of that playlist. Then when someone watches the first video on the playlist, it automatically directs them to video two in the series, and when that video ends, it directs them into video three, and so on. This gets people watching a half dozen or more videos on your channel in a row and boosts all your rankings across your channel!

It's very simple to set up a playlist in YouTube, add your videos, and promote the new "series" to the traffic you own. Think of the ripple effect that promoting a new playlist to binge-watch will create.

- It's a huge value add to your own list and will build a better relationship with your viewers.

- It gets your hottest subscribers watching your newest videos, which should give you higher initial and overall retention than a cold viewer who finds you on YouTube.

- You're likely to get more likes and comments from these viewers, especially if you ask them to engage in these ways in the emails and messages you send to them promoting this new series.

- Most of them will move through each video in the playlist because they're excited to see your new series, which will make these videos rank higher, which will also boost your entire channel.

This becomes such a big win-win-win for you, your viewers, and YouTube that we try to build launching a new playlist that viewers can binge-watch into our publishing plan at least once per month.

Your Publishing Plan

In this chapter, you've seen how you can create videos on YouTube that will rank for your dream keywords on both Google and YouTube. Each week you should be launching new discoverable videos to target your dream keywords, and each month launching a playlist where you can teach your subscribers, boost your rankings, and give them something awesome to watch. I'm including a YouTube publishing plan so you can see how to weave it into your daily and weekly processes.

YOUTUBE PUBLISHING PLAN

WEEKLY: approx. 2 hrs.		
Research	30 min./week	Watch the videos of your Dream 100 to determine what hooks, titles, descriptions, hashtags, and tags they're using to serve your audience.
Your Channel: 1-2 videos/week	1-1.5 hrs./week	Publish one to two videos each week at the exact same time every week. Be consistent. Reply to comments.
	10 min./week	Email your list with a link to your video.
	5 min./week	Post on Facebook and Instagram with a link to your video. Reply to comments.
MONTHLY: approx. 1 hr.		
Playlist: 1/mo.	30 min./mo.	Curate one new playlist per month that your subscribers can binge watch.
Your Channel: 1 collab/mo.	30 min./mo.	Collaborate with other YouTube influencers once per month. You can do a video together, post one of their videos on your channel, or have them post one of your videos on their channel, and then afterward link to each other in the video description.*

Please note: The time requirements shown are variable. It may take you less or more time.

* This strategy will be discussed in the upcoming section: "Step #4: Work Your Way In."

Figure 13.8:

Use this publishing plan to see, at a glance, where you should focus your efforts on YouTube.

STEP #4: WORK YOUR WAY IN

The core way we work our way in to YouTube is by following the publishing plan we just laid out. Every day, we're picking new keywords we want to rank for, and then we go and create videos to target these keywords. If you are consistent in publishing these videos, you will continue to show up in the search results for more keyword phrases, more people will subscribe to your channel, and your videos will keep growing.

Similar to Instagram, you can also do collabs with other channels where you can make a video with another influencer and have them post it to their channel with links pointing back to you. Sometimes we will do a swap with collabs where I will post a video on my channel linking to them, and then they will post one linking back to us, but it doesn't always have to be a one-for-one swap. Often, I'll have someone post a video for me on their channel in exchange for featuring them on my podcast. That way they get exposure on my primary show, and I get exposure on theirs. There are lots of ways to make collabs work; you just need to be creative and figure out how to make it a win-win for both of you.

STEP #5: BUY YOUR WAY IN

One of my favorite YouTube shortcuts is to find videos that are getting a lot of views, but where the creators of the videos don't really understand how to make money from their views. For example, a few years ago I purchased a website called Vygone.com. I went on YouTube and found that there was a customer who had bought the product and had made a video using it. At the time, the video was getting hundreds of views per day, yet there were no links or a description or anything.

I called her up and asked her if I could pay her to put a link in the description back to my new website. She agreed, and almost five years later, this video still sends me hundreds of clicks each month.

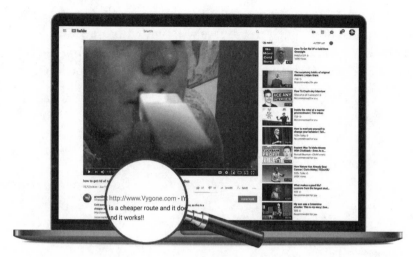

Figure 13.9:

After noticing that someone else's video about my new company, Vygone, was getting a lot of views, I paid the video owner so I could place my funnel's link inside her video description.

There are plenty of other ways to buy your way in; you just need to use your creativity. You could pay people to create a video and post it on their channel for you. You could even pay them to let you put a playlist with a video series on their channel. The ideas and opportunities are endless!

STEP #6: FILL YOUR FUNNEL

Every video you post on YouTube will extend your reach, and if you take the time to optimize them correctly, the videos will continue to drive traffic to you for the rest of your life. It all starts with consistently publishing keyword-based discoverable videos to get you a spot on the organic listings, as well as the Google search results. We use paid ads to place our ads on top of the other videos that are ranked for our dream keywords and the videos of our Dream 100.

We will use the same paid ads strategy on these videos that you learned about in Secret #9: we will put out prospecting ads to hook our dream clients, move them into the retargeting buckets where we will turn them into traffic that we own, and then we will ascend them up our value ladder.

AFTER THE SLAPS AND THE SNAPS

So what happens if you're reading this book, and Facebook has recently been shut down by the government for controlling too big of a monopoly or a new social platform is getting traction and you want to figure out how to get in early before it's too late? As you know, my goal with this book is not to give you a fish, but it is to teach you how to fish. In my 15 years online, I've watched as dozens of networks and hundreds of ads sources have come and gone. With all this change, we've not only survived, but we've thrived. The reason we've been able to weather the storms and get in front of the traffic trends is because of the principles you've been learning in this book.

Even though we talked about it during the introduction of this section and you've seen it conceptually over the last few chapters, in this chapter I want to give you the exact blueprint we use as we look at every new traffic opportunity. For this example, I am going to apply the Fill Your Funnel framework to grow and monetize my podcast. To do that, I need to apply this framework to the Apple podcast directory. As I break down how to dominate the podcast network, notice how we use the same framework in order to have success.

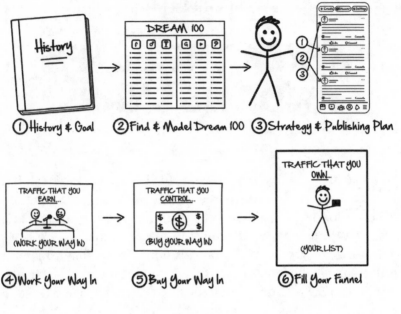

Figure 14.1:

In this section, we'll use the Fill Your Funnel framework
to show how it relates to podcasting.

STEP #1: UNDERSTAND THE HISTORY AND THE GOAL

Each show type and platform has its own positives and negatives, but of all the platforms, podcasting is my personal favorite. It's actually harder to grow subscribers on your podcast than on any of the other platforms, but I believe the subscribers you do get are way more valuable. When people listen to your podcast, they are plugging you into their ears during a part of their day when you usually get to have their sole attention, such as when they're driving, working out in the gym, or lying in bed thinking. During these most intimate moments, you have the ability to tell stories, break false beliefs, and really serve people in a manner that I don't think you can do with any other type of media.

Podcasting tends to attract a more affluent audience and people who have a higher net worth. In fact, a recent survey showed that podcast listeners are 45 percent more likely to have a net household income of over $250,000 per year.[43] That tells me a few things. First, if you want to increase your own personal net income, you should be listening to podcasts instead of radio. Second, your dream customers, the cream of the crop, are those on your list who also listen to podcasts.

When someone comes into my world (i.e., joins my list), one of the first things I try to get them to do is to subscribe to my *Marketing Secrets* podcast. If I can take them off whatever platform they found me, have them leave their inbox, and have them plug me into their ears, I'll be able to have more of an influence than anything else I could possibly do.

STEP #2: FIND YOUR DREAM 100 ON THIS PLATFORM

Podcasting is one of the easiest platforms to find your Dream 100 on, because almost every podcast is published in the Apple podcast directory, so you don't have to look far. Most people will also include their podcast in other directories like Stitcher, iHeartRadio, and Spotify, but because it's rare that a podcast would be listed on one of those directories and not on Apple, I do all my searches on Apple.

Apple's ranking algorithm for podcasts is currently based on three things. First (and most important) is the number of new subscribers. The more new subscribers you get, the higher your podcast will rank. That is the number-one factor and trumps the other two, so much so that my main goal is to get people to go and subscribe. We do contests, give away prizes, and talk about it in every show episode. The other two ranking factors are number of downloads and the number of new comments. Both of those are important, but not nearly as important as the number of new subscribers. If you focus on that, then the comments and the downloads will follow.

To find your Dream 100, Apple will show you 200 of their "top" podcasts for each category, and this gives you a huge list to use for your Dream 100. Even those that aren't listed in the top 200 can still have thousands of downloads per episode. I also recommend searching for other keywords to find shows that for some reason have a lot of downloads and legacy subscribers but aren't getting new subscribers, and therefore aren't showing up high in the rankings. They can have huge faithful followings even though they aren't ranked in the top 200.

Get to know your Dream 100 personally and they will become your strategic board on how to get and keep your podcast ranked. Share with them your wins and what's working for you, and they'll be more likely to share their wins with you as well. When the platforms have ups and downs, it's very useful to be able to talk to others in your same market on the same platform who are testing the algorithms and trying to figure them out as well.

STEP #3: IDENTIFY THE PUBLISHING STRATEGY AND CREATE YOUR PUBLISHING PLAN

The strategy with podcasting is pretty simple compared to other platforms: you just have to decide which type of podcast you want to host. My guess is that if you listen to a lot of podcasts, then you probably have your own favorite format. Some people love interview-style shows, others would rather use the time to just share their own thoughts, yet still others like to do a blend of both. I don't think it really matters which format you want to do, as long as you pick something that you can be consistent with.

When I first launched my original *Marketing in Your Car* podcast, I did it because I knew that every day I was going to be in my car for 10 minutes. Therefore, I knew I could commit to recording at least three episodes a week on my phone. If it wasn't something simple, I knew I wouldn't be consistent. I have other friends who love interview-style shows, and thus needed to build out their own little studio in their house. After they had the studio, they knew that they would be consistent. Whatever type of podcast you choose, make sure you set up your environment for success.

As with most things in life, consistency is the key to having success with a podcast. Podcasts have a compounding effect. Each episode that you publish will hook new fans, who will then go backward and binge-listen to your show from the beginning. Because of that, each episode's audience will be bigger than the last, and each show will indirectly promote your past shows. For example, all the episodes I published when no one was listening six years ago still get hundreds of listens per day from the people who are finding out about my show today.

Your Publishing Plan

As with all the other publishing plans, you can follow them to a T, or you can change them to make them work for you. With podcasting, you'll want to make sure you choose a consistent publishing schedule. Your listeners will come to anticipate when your upcoming shows will be released, so help build that trust by publishing your show on the same day(s) each week.

PODCASTING PUBLISHING PLAN

WEEKLY: approx. 3 hrs.		
Research	30 min./week	Listen to the podcasts of your Dream 100 to determine what style of podcast they're doing and how they're talking to your audience.
Your Podcast: 2 episodes/week	1 hr./week	Publish two episodes each week at the exact same time every week. Be consistent.
	10 min./week	Email your list with a link to your podcast episode.
	5 min./week	Post on Facebook and Instagram with a link to your podcast episode. Reply to comments.
Other Podcasts: 2 interviews/week	1 hr./week	Get interviewed on two other podcasts each week. Be consistent.*
	10 min./week	Email your list with a link to your podcast interview.
	5 min./week	Post on Facebook and Instagram with a link to your podcast interview. Reply to comments.

Please note: The time requirements shown are variable. It may take you less or more time.

* This strategy will be discussed in the upcoming section: "Step #4: Work Your Way In."

Figure 14.2:

Use this publishing plan to see at a glance where you should focus your efforts on podcasting.

STEP #4: WORK YOUR WAY IN

The one thing that's a little harder with podcasting than any other platform is there isn't a really simple way to promote and build a podcast, at least not for most people. You can't just put out a good episode and hope that people share it organically like all the other social channels, and most people don't go into Apple Podcasts daily searching for new stuff. The average podcast listener subscribes to six shows, and that's it. Usually, they start listening to a show based on a recommendation from a friend. If they like the experience, they'll search for a few other related shows. They will "max out" their available listening time with a few new shows, which will become the shows they consume from that point in time moving forward. Typically, the only way they will add a new show is if it's recommended by a friend or if they hear about it on another podcast.

This is why many people who have tried podcasting stop because it's so hard to get the initial traction and long-term growth. For those that understand the principles you've learned so far in this book, though, it's actually really easy.

Our strategy to grow our podcast following: build our Dream 100 list of podcasts that our dream customers were already listening to, and then go and work our way in. We messaged every podcast that we could find in our industry and asked them if I could be interviewed on their podcast. When I was interviewed, I was asked the question that almost every podcast host asks: "For those who have enjoyed this episode, how can they learn more about you?" And my answer was always the same: "I have my new podcast called *Marketing Secrets*, and if you go to MarketingSecrets. com or search for me here in Apple Podcasts, you can subscribe and get my best marketing secrets twice a week!"

And just like we thought, the podcast listeners who heard the interview and connected with me came in droves. They loved podcasts, they loved to rate and review podcasts, they shared their favorite podcasts with their friends, and they did all the things that we had been trying to educate our non-podcasts listeners to do without any coaching.

Recently I watched with fascination as the very famous podcaster Jordan Harbinger (who had one of the biggest podcasts in the world called *The Art of Charm* that was getting over 4 million monthly downloads) got into a fight with his business partner and eventually got kicked out of his own show.[44] I felt so bad, knowing how much work he must have spent over the past few years growing a podcast to that size and then losing it all. Then one day I was listening to my favorite podcast, *Mixergy*. On it, Andrew Warner interviewed Jordan about his podcast, how he grew it initially, and how he lost it.

Then at the end of the show, Andrew asked him what listeners should do if they wanted to follow Jordan after the show. Jordan suggested they should subscribe to his new show called *The Jordan Harbinger Show*.

Right then, I realized that he was doing the exact same thing that I had been doing. He understood that all his faithful future followers were already listening to podcasts, and he just had to go out there and convince them that he was worth listening to. Then I started to watch as Jordan hit the podcast circuit and was on show after show after show. In just a matter of months, Jordan's new show had passed over 3 million downloads.

STEP #5: BUY YOUR WAY IN

This next section almost didn't make it into the book because I was too blind to see it until last week. My second favorite podcast is called *Business Wars*. Last week, at the end of one of their episodes, they took me to a mini episode that they had just published. It started with the show host's voice saying that they had a very special episode that the Business Wars team wanted to share from a guy named Jordan Harbinger![45] Then they told their whole audience that they were going to play a few highlights from Jordan's show that they thought everyone would like. Finally, they encouraged everyone who was listening to go and subscribe to Jordan's podcast if they wanted more information!

As you can probably guess, I started to freak out, jumping around, as I realized for the first time that you could buy ads in other people's podcasts to promote your podcast! We are now buying ads as well as full episodes on the podcasts that our dream customers are listening to.

STEP #6: FILL YOUR FUNNEL

Now that you have your podcast and you know how to grow your following, I want to spend a little time talking about how you can leverage your podcast and other people's podcasts to fill your funnel. Even if you don't have your own podcast show, you can still leverage this powerful platform to get traffic.

The strategies to promote your funnels are the same as how we grow the show. Every time I have a new book launch, a new webinar, or a new funnel that I quickly want to get a lot of traffic for, one of the best ways to do so is to hit up the podcast circuit. You can message hosts and see if they can get you on their show. Once you're on, when they ask you the magic question about how people can learn more about you, simply tell them to get a copy of your book, register for your webinar, or get your free lead magnet. Then give them the URL of your funnel.

You can also purchase podcast ads to promote your podcast or any of your other funnels. Recently, we ran a few tests for paid ads on John Lee Dumas's *Entrepreneur on Fire* podcast. They did so well that we ended up buying an entire year's worth of ads from him! We're also going back to the shows that I did interviews on that had the biggest impact on sales, and buying ads from them. Lastly, we're buying ads on *Mixergy* and other podcasts that I love.

Some podcasts run their ad department in house, where you can contact the show directly. They'll usually have a media kit that will show you information such as the demographics of the show and how many downloads they get per episode. Many podcasters work with agencies to sell their ads. Most agencies will sponsor many different shows and they can open the doors to many other podcasts that you may not have known even existed.

A NOTE ABOUT OTHER PLATFORMS

I desperately wanted to write chapters in this book about some of the other platforms that were market leaders at one time, like Twitter, Snapchat, and LinkedIn. There is still so much opportunity on all these platforms, and some of them may come back and beat out the ones that I did show in this book.

I also had a desire to talk about some of the newer platforms that I think are going to be huge, like Twitch or TikTok, or even a platform such as Pinterest that many ClickFunnels users get the majority of their traffic from. But I knew that if I tried to write a chapter on every exciting platform, this book would be over 2,000 pages long. In addition, it would have felt more like me trying to give people "fish" than teaching them how to fish, because these platforms have only existed during a quick snapshot in time.

I picked Facebook, Instagram, Google, and YouTube so you could see the strategy behind how we attack each network as they come out. With that knowledge, you now have a process you can follow for any new network you decide to jump into and a process for how to recover during the next Google slap or Zanos snap.

CONVERSATION DOMINATION

Before we go further, I do want to give you one word of warning. Many people think that they have to be on *all* platforms to be successful. That is not true. In fact, the majority of the times, the opposite is true. Often, people will try to publish and buy ads on all the platforms and never get great at publishing on any of them, or their ad dollar is spread so thin across all of them that they never actually get any traction.

For each business, there should be *one* primary channel that you focus on. It will likely be the same platform that you've already created your show on during Secret #7. This will also probably be the same platform that you spend most of your own personal time on, because you've been a consumer of media on that platform, so it will be easier for you to see how to become a producer of media on it as well. Right now, all your focus, from your Dream 100 to paying for ads, should be on that one platform.

I can already hear some of you saying, "But, Russell, you're publishing on every platform. I see your podcast, your YouTube videos, your blogs, your Facebook Lives, and your Instagram Stories. You're not practicing what you preach."

I want you to understand that while I do publish on all these platforms now, I didn't at first. If I had, I never would have become "Russell Brunson," whatever that means. Five years ago when we first launched ClickFunnels, we picked one platform and doubled down on it, and for us, that was Facebook. We focused on building our Dream 100 there, understanding the strategy and creating our publishing plan. We then worked hard to "work our way in" and "buy our way in" to each person in our Dream 100. It was a long hard process that helped us to build a company that did over $100 million in sales *before* we started publishing on platform number two. About that time, we decided to take this little podcast that I had been publishing for a while and start working on it. We had to find our Dream 100, figure out the strategy, work our way in, buy our way in, and create a publishing plan. As you can tell, the pattern repeats itself.

And then we repeated the process with Instagram, and later our blog. Each new channel required a new Dream 100, new strategies, and a new team. Had we done them all at once, we would have crumbled under the weight of it all. So for those of you who are reading this section now, know that for you, if you were sitting in front of me right now, I'd have you pick one platform, build your show on it, get to work on your Dream 100, and then only focus on that for at least the next 12 months of your life.

The other thing I often hear is: "But, Russell, I'm just going to record a video, and then I'll post the video to YouTube, rip the audio for my podcast, and transcribe the audio for my blog post. I'll just create the content once, and then I'll post it everywhere." While the concept is very sexy, and there are many people selling this as the best way to be everywhere at all times, by doing it you are missing the understanding that each platform has its own unique language. Usually content that works really well on one platform will fail when copied to another one.

People on Facebook want to hear your personal stories, talk about current events, and watch you go live. People who listen to podcasts are used to listening to longer-form interviews. People who read blogs are looking for longer-form content that is usually structured in a list with lots of examples and details. People on Instagram want images and to see behind the scenes of your journey and your life. Lastly, people on YouTube are looking for keyword-driven how-tos and entertainment. If you just rip your keyword-heavy YouTube video and put the audio on your podcast, it will seem strange to someone who listens to podcasts, and really weird when someone reads it as a status update on your Facebook wall.

Instead, focus on one platform until you've mastered it, which means that you'll know your Dream 100, your content strategy will be systemized and happening on autopilot, and you'll have a process in place to work your way in and the people in place to start buying your way in. After that is completed, then you can and should add in the next layer. Eventually, you'll want to be omnipresent on each platform. Personally, what I really want is for someone to pick up their phone, and no matter which app they open, the first person they see will be me. But if you make that jump too quickly, it will more than likely cripple you before you have a chance to really build your following.

THE PROCESS TO ACHIEVE CONVERSATION DOMINATION

I've seen people try to be omnipresent on every platform, and they usually try to do it in one of three ways.

First, they publish a primary show and then publish that same information in different formats to every network. You can get some success with this, but your efforts will be watered down, at best. The second way is publishing completely unique content on each platform. While this is possible, it usually requires building a huge team of people to accomplish it, and it will take a ton of your own personal time. For a few years, this is what I did with my team. But after a while I got tired of producing so much stuff all the time, until one day I had an idea.

What if we created a master show that we streamed on Facebook and Instagram Live that was scripted out to have all the individual assets we needed for each core platform? Then we could prepare all week for the show and stream it live, where our team would have all the assets they needed to make unique content that fit the native language for each platform. And that's when the *Marketing Secrets Live* show was born.

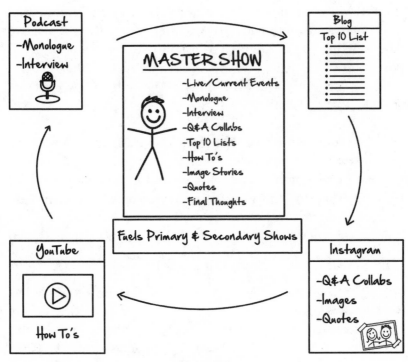

Figure 15.1:

To create content for my entire team to repurpose,
I go live once a week to create a master show.

I look at this show as if it's a talk show like *The Tonight Show*. I like to go live, because the energy when you go live versus a pre-recorded video always comes off better. I'll start the show and spend a few minutes waiting for people to jump on the live feed, talk about a few current events, and then I begin the official show.

Monologue: I start with my monologue, similar to how most talk shows start, where the host gets up, tells some stories, and tries to connect with the audience. My monologue is structured very similar to how I do my *Marketing Secrets* podcast. When the monologue is over, this piece of content will become a future episode on the podcast.

Interview: I will typically interview someone on the show, either in the office or over the phone. This interview matches the native language that people are used to listening to on a podcast, so in post-production we'll turn this interview into another podcast episode. The monologue and interview become the two podcast episodes that I post every week.

Q & A Collabs: Before we start the live show, I send a few of my Dream 100 a question by video on my phone, where I ask them to respond to the question and send a question back to me. I show their question live and give them my response, and then I ask them my question and show their video response. After the show is done, we post the edited video on IGTV and tag them, and then they will post it to their IGTV and tag me back.

Top 10 List: I pull a "David Letterman" and share a top list. The list I am sharing is going to become my skyscraper article for my blog. I may share the "21 Best Things You Can Post on Twitter to Get More Followers," or "My 13 Favorite Squeeze Pages for 2020." I show an image of each item and talk briefly about it, and when the segment is done, my team will take it and quickly use my explanations to write the skyscraper post in my voice and start the link-building process.

How-Tos: I look at the keywords that I want to rank for on YouTube and do a segment showing two to three different ways to do things. Every how-to will become a YouTube video targeting a specific keyword phrase that we will post and then rank.

Image Stories: I go through my JK5 categories and show at least one image per category and tell the story behind it. That gives my team a better understanding about the image's meaning when they are writing the captions and trying to get people to engage with it.

Quotes: I like to start wrapping up the show by sharing my favorite quotes and explaining why they are my favorites. That way if my team turns them into quote cards, they will have good explanations that they can use from my own words to post in the captions.

Final Thoughts: This is one piece that I don't repost anywhere. I just remember seeing Jerry Springer do it on his show back in the day (yes, I used to watch Jerry Springer, please don't judge me), and it was the thing that would get me to watch the full show.[46] I want to keep something special for our live viewers to keep them engaged until the end.

When the show is over, we quickly record all the information that my team will need to bridge together the content for each platform. For example, I will record quick introductions for the two podcast episodes with "Hey, everyone, this is Russell Brunson and welcome to the Marketing Secrets podcast. In this episode, I am going to interview _____ about _____. Be sure to listen to the end to find out his number-one secret about _____."

I will also record intros like this for the YouTube videos, setting up the "how-to" they are about to watch by saying something like, "Hey, this is Russell Brunson and I want to welcome you to my channel. Today, I'm going to show you guys how to _____, but before I do, be sure to subscribe to my channel and turn on the notifications so you don't miss my next amazing video that is coming out soon. Now let's jump into the video."

I may also record a quick outro for these videos that says something like, "Thanks again for watching this video. Be sure to like the video, and post in the comments telling me about the last time you [something related to the video]."

By creating this show once per week, my team has all the customized content that they need for each platform.

PUBLISHING AND DREAM 100 ON EACH PLATFORM

Can you see how you can use this master show and leverage it to create the content for your primary show as well as all your secondary shows? Even with that plan, I wouldn't try to launch on all five platforms at one time. Go about it slowly and methodically. As you decide to branch into each new platform, follow the steps in the Fill Your Funnel framework:

- Step #1: Understand the history and the goal of the new platform

- Step #2: Find and model your Dream 100

- Step #3: Identify the publishing strategy and create your publishing plan

- Step #4: Work your way in

- Step #5: Buy your way in

- Step #6: Fill your funnel

YOUR DISTRIBUTION CHANNELS AND TRAFFIC THAT YOU OWN

The last and arguably most important step in your strategy is the promotion of your primary show and secondary, supporting content. Publishing on each platform will give you limited distribution to your fans and followers, but in order to help stimulate growth of whatever show you have just published (and the more you can push eyeballs to the new episode), the more each platform will reward you for that work.

Outside of your friends, fans, subscribers, and followers on each platform, we have a few other distribution channels that we've been working on building.

Email: Email is the traffic that we own, and it's one of our core distribution channels. After people have moved through your Soap

Opera Sequences, they should be on your daily Seinfeld broadcast list. This list is the one that you will promote your new show on as soon as it's ready to direct a huge surge of new people to your content and help stimulate its growth. Typically these are the people who have the best relationship with you, so having them viewing, liking, commenting, and sharing early after you launch the show will tell the algorithm of any network that this content is good and should be rewarded with more organic growth.

Messenger: While you're renting your Messenger list from Facebook, and they could take it away if they don't like how you're publishing to it, it is still the most powerful channel today. The open rates and click-through rates are second to none. Using your Messenger list to promote your new content is one of the fastest ways to boost your new episode.

Desktop Push: If you've been building a list with desktop push notifications, it's another great way to promote your content when it goes live.

Make sure the part of your content launch strategy is to use your own distribution channels to promote your content on each platform as it goes live. This will always give it the best chance of getting an organic lift free from the platforms as well as getting it ready for the paid ads that you want to run toward it. Having views, comments, and likes before the paid ads get turned on will make each dollar you spend more effective.

Here is a breakdown of how we run our conversation domination publishing plan that allows us to be in front of everyone on each channel they subscribe to. To help you prepare for your own show, please go to TrafficSecrets.com/resources to print off a fill-in-the-blank outline for your own use.

CONVERSATION DOMINATION

WEEKLY: approx. 7 hrs.		
Preparation: once/week	2 hrs./week	Prepare for the show. • Decide the theme for your show and what you'll say in the monologue. • Set up interview with Dream 100. • Collect videos of your Dream 100 asking questions. • Write a list based on your theme. • Choose 2-3 keywords you want to rank for on YouTube. • Choose the image(s) you want to share from Instagram. • Choose the quote(s) you want to share. • Decide on your final thoughts.
Go Live: once/week	1 hr./week	Go Live each week on Facebook & Instagram with the following outline: • Monologue (becomes 1 podcast episode) • Interview (becomes 1 podcast episode) • Q&A Collabs (become IGTV episodes) • Top 10 List (becomes 1 skyscraper article for blog) • How To's (become YouTube videos) • Image Stories (become description "words" for your image posts) • Quotes (become quote cards + description "words" for your posts) • Final Thoughts (not published)
Publishing: throughout week	4 hrs./week	Team uses assets from the show to post on all the platforms.

Please note: The time requirements shown are variable. It may take you less or more time.

Figure 15.2

Use this publishing plan to see at a glance where you should focus your efforts in order to achieve conversation domination.

GROWTH HACKING

Welcome to the third section of this book! I'm so excited to have you here. So far, you've learned who your dream customers are, where they're congregating, how to get your hooks in front of them, and how to turn all your traffic into traffic that you own. In Section Two, we talked about the framework we use to get traffic from any advertising platforms to get unlimited traffic into your funnels. We also showed you how to create publishing plans so you could consistently show up in front of your dream customers. Now, we finally get to move into growth hacking.

What is growth hacking, though? I'm smiling to myself, because when I got started online 15 years ago, we didn't have Facebook. The Google slap had crippled most of our companies, so we had to figure out other ways to get traffic into our funnels. We tried and tested everything. Some things were super "black hat," and while they weren't anything bad, they were frowned on by companies like Google. For instance, we would set up cloaked pages that would trick the search engine's spiders into thinking our pages were perfectly optimized for search. However, when real people (who didn't come from a search engine spider's IP address) would show up, they would see a completely different squeeze page that was optimized for conversion. We built link farms to get our pages ranked at all costs. We figured out ways to get emails past spam filters and delivered into our subscribers' inboxes.

But it wasn't just black-hat techniques that we played with; we also spent countless hours working on getting free PR that would push people from TV, radio, and top online news sites into our funnels. We tried everything we could think of: black hat, white hat, and about a thousand shades of gray in between.

For us, it was a battle of life or death. If we didn't figure out how to get eyeballs to our pages, we didn't eat. All the tricks and hacks that we tried were looked down on by "real" businesses. Some called us spammers, while others were harsher and called us scammers. We didn't know what to call it, so we just called it "internet marketing."

Those are the days that I'll never forget. It was the Wild West, and we were there early, way before our time. I played on this playground for almost a decade before what we did was considered cool. When I first heard the term "growth hacking," some writers had published articles talking about some of the fast-growth startup companies like Dropbox, Uber, PayPal, and Airbnb.

Once people shared their amazing growth-hacking techniques for quickly growing their companies, I started to laugh out loud. Every "hack" they shared was a basic technique we had been doing for over a decade! Many of these hacks were the same things that others used to shame us for, but they had now become cool. Because of ClickFunnels's rapid growth, many people have told me we are a unicorn because we have such a unique growth strategy, which is that we don't grow through funding; we grow by hacking.

In this last section, I'll share with you the most powerful white-hat growth-hacking techniques that we still use to this day. Even though these appear to be new growth hacks to many, we've been mastering them for the past 15 years. In truth, our success comes from going backward, diving deep into the playbook that we wrote before the term *growth hacking* was even cool. Have fun with these hacks, as they're incredibly powerful and will give you an advantage against anyone who wants to compete against you.

THE FUNNEL HUB

When I first started playing this internet marketing game, there were two competing teams: "branding" and "direct response." I was a kid who wanted to play, but I wasn't sure whose team I should join.

The people on the branding team made some really good points. They believed that marketing should focus heavily on clean design, connection with your audience, and creating a feeling that enticed people to come back to buy from you over and over.

The direct response team had some very solid counter arguments that made a lot of sense to me too. They focused their marketing efforts on getting conversions, creating processes where you could track every advertising dollar you spend, and working toward getting an immediate, positive ROI.

In the end, though, because I didn't have a ton of money to build a brand and was financing everything out of my own pocket, I agreed more with the direct response marketers and joined their team. I became obsessed with conversion. I created pages, wrote copy, and ran ads that could out-convert anyone. People would come, they would buy, and then they would leave; those who bought usually never returned. However, as long as the money I spent on ads was less than the money I made, I was winning the game.

But then Google changed. The PPC (pay per click) slap came, and my ads disappeared overnight. The realization that all my cash flow had dried up scared me enough to try almost anything to get traffic into my funnels. It started me on a journey to search for any trick or hack I could try that anyone had reported was working.

From the dozens of things we were trying, one seemed really promising. At that time, the search engines valued backlinks that came from news and PR websites. Writing and submitting a press release was an easy way to get an awesome link that would help rank your website, and, if your press release was good, you could actually get picked up by real press.

How cool would that be? I thought. *One of my products could be on TV!*

I was in. I bought the courses to learn the strategies, Dream 100'd all the PR sites I could find, built a list, and wrote and submitted press releases. Some were free and others were paid, but 100 percent of the press releases I submitted were rejected.

I didn't know what I was doing wrong. It wasn't that some of them were rejected; all of them were rejected. I started contacting the sites' editors to find out why they all said no. It took a while to get through the gatekeepers, but after getting inside, they all told me a similar version of the same story: "At the end of the press release, you link your website, but there's nothing there."

"What do you mean 'there's nothing there'? That's the squeeze page for my funnel. It's one of the highest converting pages I've ever created," I responded.

"I don't understand what it is. It's definitely not a website and looks like some type of scam," they replied.

Scam? That page had made me more money than any website that their other press releases had linked to. In the end, though, they didn't care. They were used to seeing traditional websites. For me to be a legitimate business in their eyes, I needed a legitimate website.

I began to funnel hack the websites that the other press releases were linking to. While most of them had beautiful brands, none of them was structured for conversion. The direct-response marketing legends whom I learned from would have openly mocked me for even looking at these beautiful, low-converting websites. I hated everything about these websites, but at that point, I would have done almost anything to figure out how to win the game and get their traffic. If it meant I needed to build a brand, I was going to do it.

I dusted off some of the old branding books that I had buried at the back of my bookshelf to see what I could learn. At first, the thought of creating anything that wasn't focused on optimization and ROI made my skin crawl. However, I knew that if I wanted to get access to other people's traffic, I would have to play their game.

A few days into my study, I realized that by picking the direct response team, I had thrown the branding baby out with the bathwater. Direct response gave me the ability to bring in customers profitably, but branding was what would get them to come back again and again. *DotCom Secrets* is based on my foundation in direct response, and *Expert Secrets* is focused on what I learned in my journey of branding and storytelling. I now believe that having both branding and direct response blended together is essential in today's world, even more so than when I first started experimenting.

To get the approval from the PR agencies, I decided to create a new website I could link to instead of replacing my funnels. This new website would be used as a type of brand hub, where people could learn more about me, my company, our products, and how we could help them. It looked more like the traditional website that people were used to seeing, so my hope was the press would be more willing to link to it. Once you clicked into this brand hub, the links inside directed people into our front-end funnels.

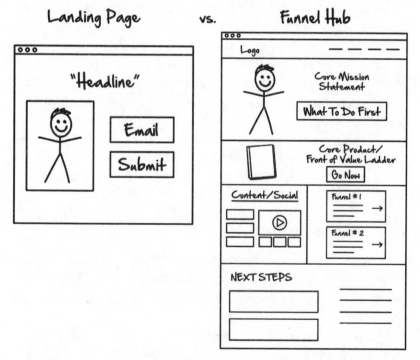

Figure 16.1:

To get your funnel (left) accepted by PR agencies, you can create a funnel hub (right) that has more content on it, yet it still drives people into your funnels.

At the time, it wasn't very sophisticated, but it worked. I resubmitted my press releases and they started getting accepted. After hundreds of press releases had been accepted, my links increased, my hub moved up in SEO ranking, and traffic started to flow. Because I had this site, it gave me more credibility and I was able to get more traditional media to pick us up.

THE BIRTH OF THE FUNNEL HUB

I wish that I could say that over the past 15 years I put a huge focus on the brand hub site that I had created, but unfortunately, I didn't. While I leveraged it to get traditional media, I never really understood its full potential.

Recently, two of my Inner Circle members, Mike Schmidt and AJ Rivera, wanted my opinion on something they had created called the "Funnel Hub." I trust them both a lot, so I blocked out some time to hear what they had to say. Within about three minutes of them talking, I knew that they had figured out the evolution of what I had tried to do 10 years earlier with my brand hub site. They had thought it through at such a deep level that I had them build a funnel hub for me as well, which I continue to use to this day.

In this chapter, I'll be quoting from the conversation I had with Mike and AJ to help you understand why a funnel hub should be a core part of your traffic strategy.

The Shadow Funnel

Mike and AJ showed me some stats on a few of the funnels that we drive a lot of paid ads to. He had talked to my traffic team previously, so he had an idea of about how much money we were spending.

"Between these four funnels, you guys spent $485,927 last month alone in ads on Facebook, Google, YouTube, and Instagram to sell your products," they stated.

"Yes, and we were profitable on every one of those dollars. All four of those funnels broke even immediately, and we usually pull a profit, so technically it didn't cost me $485,000. I made money and got a ton of new customers into my value ladder."

"We know," they said, "You're the king of funnels. We're not here to talk to you about that. We're actually here to talk to you about the shadow sales funnel. The $485,000 that you spent sending people into your core funnels created a huge shadow funnel that you're not monetizing. In fact, many of your competitors are building their companies on the back of your hard work, and it's not costing them anything."

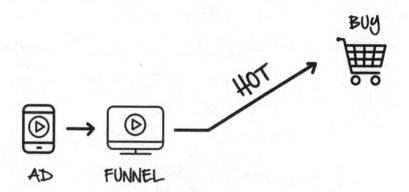

Figure 16.2:

When we create a funnel, we assume most people will simply buy our product after seeing it.

"What? I'm confused. What's a shadow funnel?"

"The shadow funnel is the traffic that's created in the wake of all the traffic that you're sending to your funnels. For example, when someone sees an ad for any of your products, you're capturing the percentage of people that buy immediately. However, there's actually a bigger percentage of people who see your ad, and, regardless if they click through or not, don't buy. Instead, they might open a new tab and search for you in Google. This is the beginning of the shadow funnel.

"Other times, they might hear a friend talk about you, hear you mentioned in social or traditional media, hear you on a podcast, or hear one of your fans or followers talking about your work. In any case, there are an unlimited number of ways that this earned traffic and paid traffic that had not immediately converted falls into your shadow funnel. Right now, you're just letting it fall by the wayside and hoping that somehow they'll find you again in the future."

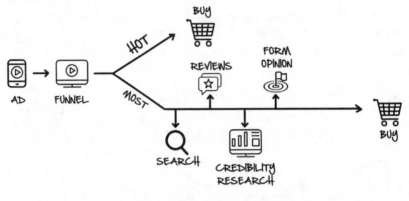

Figure 16.3:

What actually happens is most people need convincing before they buy, so they go through a "shadow funnel," researching for more information about you and your products.

I was getting sick to my stomach thinking about how much traffic this might have actually been for me.

Mike and AJ continued, "First, they'll type in your name, then your company's name, and finally the product's name. They're looking for ratings, reviews, and anything they can find to prove your credibility. They'll visit your blogs and social media accounts, including your Facebook, Instagram, and Twitter profiles. They'll join your lists, read your emails, and listen to your podcasts. From this research, they'll start to form an opinion of your company. At this point, the ad that started them on this journey is long gone, and when they're ready to move forward toward your value ladder, they'll actively search for information on where to start."

Then they showed me the number 251,680.

"What's this?" I asked.

"That's how many people worldwide in the past 12 months have searched for 'Russell Brunson,'" they said. "That's the shadow funnel, and that's just your name. That doesn't include your company or product names, and as you continue to get more momentum, your shadow funnel will grow. Many people try to rank for their dream keywords, but they typically forget about their own branded names.

BRANDED TERMS	NON-BRANDED TERMS
✔ Russell Brunson	✗ Digital Marketing
✔ Expert Secrets	✗ Sales Funnel Courses
✔ ClickFunnels	✗ Funnel Conversion Techniques
✔ DotCom Secrets	✗ Sales Funnel Coach
✔ One Funnel Away Challenge	✗ Sales Funnel Builder
✔ Russell Brunson reviews	✗ Funnel optimization techniques
✔ Is Russell Brunson legit	✗ Funnel expert
✔ Russell Brunson scam	✗ How to build a funnel
✔ Russell Brunson case studies	✗ Funnel examples

Figure 16.4:

As I was busy trying to rank for non-branded keywords, I didn't realize that over 250,000 people were searching for brand keywords like my name. Because I hadn't set up funnels for these branded terms, I was losing out on tons of traffic.

"When they search for your name, they land on random pages or funnels, and you have no control over this user experience. They might land on a page that is in the middle of your value ladder, and they won't be ready for it. Or, even worse, they might see pages from your competitors trying to leverage the hard work and the money that you have been spending! You need to take control of the shadow funnels that you've created and control what people are finding when they search."

YOUR FUNNEL HUB

After Mike and AJ scared me with their shadow funnel discussion, they started to talk to me more about the funnel hub.

"From the outside," they said, "it looks kind of like a website, but the strategy is completely different. Its goal is to organize all the funnels and offers in your value ladder in one place. When people start searching for you, it'll let you control what they find when they search; inevitably, it will help you ascend people up your value ladder. It's a central hub that organizes all of your funnels and offers and gives you the look and feel of a more traditional website to help build your credibility and magnify your authority."

They probably could tell I was loving everything they said, because at that point, they smiled. "You know what else? In *Expert Secrets*, you told us to create a lot of things as we were designing our tribe. Things like:

- Who is your Attractive Character?

- What is your future-based cause?

- What is your customer manifesto?

- What does your value ladder look like?

- What do you stand for, and what do you stand against?

"We always had those on a Google Doc, and we kind of knew what they were, but our followers never knew. The funnel hub is the place where we gather all these things together so people who are looking for us can quickly understand who we are and how we can serve them."

Then they said, "You're publishing on so many platforms— your blog, podcast, YouTube channel, Facebook pages, and Instagram accounts. Your funnel hub can become your brand stream to organize all your media in one place. This way, your followers can find all your published content from all your platforms in one place."

HOW TO CREATE YOUR FUNNEL HUB

As you can probably tell in this part of the story, I was sold on creating my funnel hub. You can see my active funnel hub at MarketingSecrets.com. I now build a funnel hub for each core company that I create.

Because most funnel hubs have a blog built into them, as well as pulling in multiple types of RSS feeds and other types of media, we typically do not build them on ClickFunnels (although you could if you weren't going to blog). We built ours in WordPress, which, in addition to being the most popular content management platform in the world, is free.

Here is the basic layout of a funnel hub.

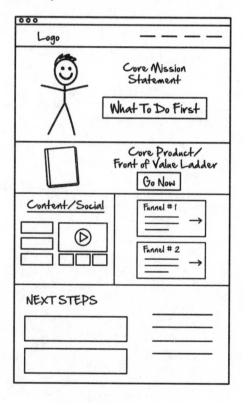

Figure 16.5:

To build your funnel hub, you can add features such as a blog, RSS feed, social posts, and front-end funnels.

Leveraging the funnel hub to take advantage of all your shadow traffic, earned media, traditional press, and word-of-mouth advertising can be huge. It's simple to set up when you get started, and, as your brand grows, your funnel hub will then be ready to capture all the traffic.

OTHER PEOPLE'S DISTRIBUTION CHANNELS

I'm going to share a little secret with you. I have a lot of entrepreneur friends who watch *Shark Tank* (as they should), and they believe for some reason that each shark has the Midas touch where any business they touch will magically turn into gold. You can see this belief in every pitch given inside the Shark Tank. Entrepreneurs are willing to give up huge percentages of their companies with the hope that one of the sharks touching their company alone will cause it to explode.

I love *Shark Tank*. In fact, I've watched pretty much every episode of *Shark Tank* and its overseas sister show, *Dragons' Den*. (Yes, I've watched all the Canadian and U.K. versions as well.) I even ripped copies of Japan's version, The *Tigers of Money*, but I couldn't understand a word anyone said. Regardless, I'm a shark, dragon, and tiger nerd, and I watch closely the types of deals that each shark takes. For this example, I'm going to focus on the U.S. version of *Shark Tank* and some of the sharks you're probably more familiar with.

Daymond John: He built up the famous brand FUBU and spent his youth building a distribution channel to sell clothing and other similar items to retail.[47]

Lori Greiner: She's created over 700 retail products and built up a distribution channel to sell products on TV through QVC, as well as infomercials. She has also built strong distribution channels with most major retailers.[48]

Mark Cuban: He built up and sold Broadcast.com for $5.6 billion. He also spent decades building online and offline media distribution channels, which included his purchase of the Landmark Theaters in 2003.[49]

I could go on and on with all the other sharks, but I'll stop with just these three to illustrate my point. As you watch the entrepreneurs pitch the sharks, notice which deals each of the sharks bite on. Rarely is it a matter of them picking any business knowing that their Midas touch will magically make it successful. On the contrary, they pick businesses based on whether or not they can plug them into their pre-built distribution channels.

Think about it. With every clothing deal that you see, yes, the sharks will talk about it, but if Lori can't see it on TV, or if Mark doesn't have an influencer with their own followers (distribution channel) that he can instantly plug it into, they'll find a way to say no. But when Daymond sees a clothing deal, he knows that in just one phone call, he can plug that product into his existing distribution channel and will get paid from that connection for the rest of his life.

The same thing happens when someone pitches a product that would be a good fit for Lori's distribution channel. Notice how her eyes light up when she can "see this product on TV" or "picture this at Bed Bath & Beyond." She owns a distribution channel, and if the product is a good fit, she plugs it in.

The same is true with Mark and every other shark or dragon who has ever been on the show. They each have built and mastered one distribution channel, and they're looking for products they can plug into it. That's the big secret.

People often ask me which types of businesses I invest in or which partnerships I do, and my choices are 100 percent based on the distribution channels that I know and understand. If I don't know where someone should buy their traffic, or which lists they should rent, or who could get their site ranked, or who could make their video go viral, I'll never touch the project. I only take on projects that I know will work with 100 percent certainty, and which I know will work because I already have a distribution channel in place for them.

I shared this because you need to understand that each of your Dream 100 has a distribution channel; that's why they're on your Dream 100 list. Each person has the Midas touch, and it's your job to figure out how you can plug your products into their distribution channels.

DISTRIBUTION CHANNEL #1: EMAIL SOLO ADS

We spent the whole first section of this book focusing on how you can build up your own distribution channel by converting traffic that you earn and buy into traffic that you own (your own list). There are hundreds of people in almost every market who have already built up their own email lists, and one of the easiest ways to quickly increase your traffic is to buy ads in their email lists.

When I'm looking for email lists to buy ads in, I'm traditionally looking for a solo publisher, someone who has already created their own brand and list, where I can pay them to send out an email talking about my products or services. You can also reach out to bigger brands that you can pay to send out ads in their newsletters.

The solo publishers are likely already on your Dream 100, and it can be a simple process to ask them if they are willing to sell a solo ad in their newsletter. The ones who've had experience with this will typically say yes and have some sort of base pricing. Bigger brands will usually have an online media kit that lists their prices if you want to buy an ad in their lists or on their websites.

You can also find a lot of advertising opportunities in email newsletters by searching on Google. I'll often type in "[my niche] email advertising" or "[my niche] online media kit," and I can usually find publishers that will sell me a place in their email lists. I always join their lists for a few weeks before I buy any ad so I can see how they treat their list. If they only send tons of promotions, then I figure they beat up their list pretty badly and they're probably not the type of list I want to rent. However, if they send out good stuff and have a good relationship with their list, then I'll contact them for a media kit. Not all clicks are equal. Fewer clicks from a newsletter where someone has a good relationship with the publisher will always be better than more clicks from someone who has a bad relationship with their audience.

I wish I could give you a set pricing that you'll typically pay, but it almost always ends up in a negotiation, so keep in mind that their rates are usually negotiable. They say, "suckers pay rate card," and I tend to believe this is true. Publishers will usually try to have you pay based on how many people are on their list because that larger number serves them, but I would prefer to pay based on how many clicks their emails typically get. To find out that number, I'll usually ask to see a report of the last 5–10 emails they sent out and how many clicks each email got. Then I reverse engineer the process by saying to myself, *If I were to get that many clicks, then based on my normal landing page conversion rates, I should make "x" amount of money.* This process helps me know approximately how much I'm willing to spend to pay for that ad, and I try to negotiate toward that number.

After you negotiate the ad cost, you'll create the email, send it to the publisher, and then they'll send out the email for you. If they want to send you their email list and have you send the email out, then run away fast. This is a scam and not something you should ever do. They should be emailing their list from their servers with your creative that you gave them. I like to have the email come from the publisher endorsing the landing page that I want to send the reader to.

The best part about email ads is you get results really fast. When someone sends the email, you'll get the majority of all your clicks within 12 hours, the rest of your clicks within 36–48 hours, and then the clicks usually stop. I like to use email campaigns to test landing pages because I can run split tests really fast.

The worst part about email ads is you can waste a lot of money fast *if* you're not ready. I may spend $5,000 on an email drop, where the traffic will all come and go fast, but if I spend that same

$5,000 on Facebook, I may be able to run traffic more slowly for a few weeks. So be aware of that as you are running email ads.

Lastly, solo publishers will often try to sell you "sponsorship ads," which are smaller ads embedded inside their emails. I'm not a huge fan of these, and I've had a really hard time getting them to be profitable. For me, if I can't buy a solo ad, meaning the entire email is my message, then I usually won't do it.

DISTRIBUTION CHANNELS #2 AND #3: FACEBOOK MESSENGER AND DESKTOP PUSH

As of today, I don't know many people selling ads in their Messenger lists, but I do think that this market will start to grow. Usually, the messages that are sent through Messenger need to be a little more stealthy because Facebook doesn't like you sending out straight promotions. Because Messenger doesn't allow you to send blatant promotions to your subscribers, the open and click-through rates are second to none. I recommend finding people in your Dream 100 who are actively building up Messenger lists and asking them if you can buy ads to their lists.

The same is true with desktop push notifications. This is a newer type of list that is getting a lot of traction right now. We're starting to build up a Dream 100 list of people in our market who are building up these lists so we can purchase broadcasts from them.

OTHER DISTRIBUTION CHANNELS

There are tons of different distribution channels out there that you will start identifying as you keep your eyes open. Recently, we started going to all our Dream 100 and buying postcard and direct mail campaigns to their buyer lists. Sometimes it's harder to get them to block out the time to send an email, but most of them aren't sending anything to their customers in the mail. We've been setting up deals with them where they send their customers' shipping addresses to a secure mailing house (so we never actually get access to their addresses) while we send a pre-approved mailing piece to that mailing house. The mailing house will then print our letter or postcard and then send it to the customer lists of our partners.

Some of my friends have built up big text message lists, so we're buying text blasts from them. Others run big Facebook groups, so we're paying to post a sponsored post in their groups. Others have big groups on LinkedIn, so we're paying the group owners to send messages to their followers for us. And still others have large forums, so we're buying promotions to their customers' user base and banner ads on their sites.

Most of the blogs in our market sell ads on their sites. Some have big Google AdSense blocks, and we'll test ads initially using GDN to see if the ads convert well. If they do, I'll go directly to the blog or website owners and try to pay them to replace that AdSense block with my banner ads. I've even paid people for their website exit pop-ups so I can tap into the traffic that is leaving their websites.

There's an unlimited number of ways to do this. The key is to keep your eyes open for streams of traffic and distribution channels that people own; then figure out how to buy ads in them. Each new distribution channel you plug into will give you a raise. Every day when I come into the office, the first thing I ask myself before I get out of my car is, "How can I give myself a raise today?" Immediately, my mind will start looking for distribution channels in my market that I can tap into. Sometimes I'll remember a website, a blog, or an email list that I've been on forever that I forgot about. When your mind is looking for these opportunities, somehow they start jumping out at you.

When you don't have access to Facebook or Google ads (like we didn't for so long), the number-one way to get traffic is searching for these distribution channels and using them to build up your own lists. It's a guerilla technique that works no matter what is happening in the networks, and you can immediately start plugging this technique into your daily routine.

INTEGRATION MARKETING

My first mentor, Mark Joyner, whom I introduced you to earlier in this book, wrote a book called *Integration Marketing* about a decade ago. It shifted my mind-set from just finding distribution channels and buying ads in them to figuring out ways that we could integrate into the actual sales processes of our Dream 100.

For example, let's say I find a partner who is getting 1,000 new leads into their funnels every day. Instead of just buying an ad one time to that list, what if my email was sent to every new lead on their email list on day three? That way, I set up the deal once, but I get the benefit of that integration every day. Now, every day 1,000 new people get my message. I'm now integrated into my partner's sales process, and as they grow their company, mine grows as well!

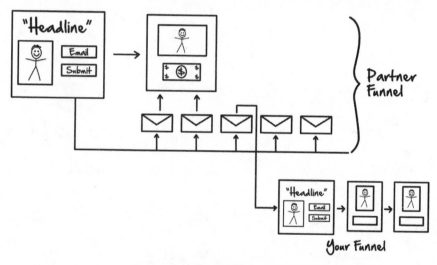

Figure 17.1:

When you integrate your funnel into other people's funnels or
email campaigns, you get the benefit of having additional streams
of traffic for as long as they are in business.

Integration marketing works beyond just email. We've set up deals where we integrate a pop-up on people's blogs so every reader the blog gets can potentially join my list. We've set up other deals where we have people add an exit pop-up to their website, so that when people leave their site, a big percentage are sent over to our funnels! There are so many fun and creative things you can do. Your imagination is your only limitation.

As soon as I became aware of this concept, I started looking for these integration opportunities everywhere. I looked for products that people would need immediately before they started using ClickFunnels, things like domain hosting, graphic design, and business licenses. Then I figured out a way to set up a partnership with each company. For instance, after a person buys their domain, gets a logo design, or gets their business set up, they're introduced to us. We set up many of these deals years ago, and because we're integrated into our partners' distribution channels, tons of customers are driven to us every day without us having to do anything again.

YOUR AFFILIATE ARMY

I want to take you back in time to November 2003.

My wife had just closed her eyes, and I had finished a homework assignment on my laptop in bed. Before I shut down the laptop for the night, though, I decided to do one last search to hopefully give me some direction on my side hustle. My wife had been working to support us both, and we wanted her to be able to retire from her job and for us to start a family. I had spent the last year trying to figure out how to play the "business" game, but, no matter what, everything I had tried had led me to a dead end.

I'm still not sure exactly what I typed into Google. All I know is that after a few clicks, I ended up at the front page of an underground marketing forum that was filled with thousands of people who were making money online. I created a free account and instantly got access to a community of people who were doing exactly what I had dreamed of doing. I had no idea that anything like this existed online!

I started scrolling through the posts and saw people discussing the newest Google algorithm changes, what things they were testing, what worked, and what didn't. I was eavesdropping on the conversations of internet millionaires who were sharing everything so freely and had no idea I was there!

For hours, I devoured every post and wrote down every resource. I realized that the answer to every question I ever had was there, and these people were the ones who were discovering what was working and were sharing it in real time. I had found my people . . . my tribe! As the clock changed from 10 P.M. to 11 P.M. to 12 A.M. to 1 A.M., every hour seemed like a few seconds. I was so excited, but my body and eyes were so tired.

I've got to read just one more post, I thought. *Just one more.* Afraid that perhaps I was in a dream and if I woke up, I might lose access to this exclusive club, I kept scrolling and reading. That's when I looked over and realized it was 2:47 A.M. Wrestling practice started at 6:00 A.M. *Do I go to sleep now and get a few hours of sleep?* I knew the answer was yes. I needed to sleep, or I was going to really struggle to make it through tomorrow.

I went to close my laptop, but then I saw it. The question. The golden question! The one that I had been asking in my head over and over again for the past few months.

What's the best way to get traffic to a website?

I wanted to click on it, but I didn't know if I had the energy to go down that rabbit hole, at least not then. I looked at the question for at least 30 seconds and decided I had to know. I clicked on the title, and it brought me immediately inside of an intense conversation with everyone talking about why their way to drive traffic was the best.

Some said SEO, but then all the SEO guys started to fight over which method of SEO was the most effective: cloaking, doorway pages, link spam, log spam, and about two dozen other things I had never heard of. Then the PPC guys came out as well. Each had a different strategy that one-upped the person who posted before them. Others talked about email marketing, safelists, or buying solo ads.

My heart raced faster and faster, and every new idea seemed better than the last. And then it happened. The owner of the forum—probably the wealthiest guy who was there—made a comment. It wasn't long—just eight words that stopped everyone in their tracks—the ultimate mic drop. These eight words changed my life.

I rely on my own network of affiliates.

At first it didn't really make sense to me. I read it again and again. Knowing that he was one of the best marketers in the group, I knew there was something to it and that I needed to figure it out.

Then it hit me! He had an affiliate program that had hundreds of affiliates who sold his products for him. Because he gave them a commission after they made a sale, he had no risk; he only paid them if they actually made a sale!

I looked at his response again: *I rely on my own network of affiliates.* I saw his brilliance. Instead of relying on his own efforts to do SEO or PPC, he could have dozens of others ranking pages for him and running ads selling his products. Instead of relying on his own email list, what if he found 10 or 20 or 100 affiliates who each had lists of tens of thousands of people? Instead of his message getting sent to thousands of people, he could reach millions.

The amount of leverage you get when you build an affiliate program and rely on the efforts of other people is huge. It's kind of like building a team and hiring people to do these tasks for you, except when they're an affiliate, you don't pay them for the work. Instead, you pay them commissions based on the sale. They have the risk, and you both share the rewards!

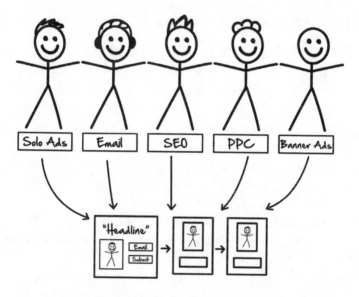

Figure 18.1:

You don't have to be good at everything. You can get an army of affiliates to promote your products and services with their preferred method of traffic.

That was the epiphany I was looking for. Instead of becoming the best person in the world at driving traffic, I needed to create an opportunity for the top affiliates to make money by promoting my products and services. Then I could focus my efforts on recruiting, training, and paying them.

Throughout this book, we've spent a lot of time talking about the Dream 100, and this is where it starts. If you've been building out your Dream 100 within each platform, you have your potential army of affiliates ready. This chapter will then focus on five steps:

1. Recruit your army of affiliates

2. Make them affiliates

3. Give your affiliates a reason to promote

4. Train your affiliates to become super affiliates

5. Compensate your affiliates

STEP #1: RECRUIT YOUR ARMY OF AFFILIATES

If you've been following the Dream 100 process, then you've already created lists of your potential affiliates. If you've been digging your well before you've been thirsty, then you've been building relationships with them. If you haven't yet, I'd recommend going back and starting that process as soon as possible. Every Dream 100 person has their own distribution channel. Some have an email list, others have a following on Facebook or Instagram, others have a podcast with a lot of subscribers, and some have more than one of those channels.

We've talked about working your way into their audiences as well as buying your way in. Asking your Dream 100 to be an affiliate is blending both of these things together. You have to work your way in to build relationships and to get people to say yes to promoting, but then you have to pay your way in for each sale they make. When someone is an affiliate, though, it takes the risk off you. You're no longer buying ads and hoping they convert. Instead, your Dream 100 is promoting you, and you only pay them after they've made the sale.

So how do you turn your Dream 100 into an army of affiliates? The first thing you have to do is ask them to be an affiliate, even though asking is oftentimes the hardest part. If you've been digging your well with your Dream 100, and if you have a relationship with them, you should know the projects and ideas that they are working on. In return, they should also know what things you're working on.

Tim Ferriss, author of *The 4-Hour Workweek*, spent over a year getting to know some of the most influential bloggers in the world *at the same time* he was writing his book.[50] He started digging his well before he was thirsty. When they asked him what he did, he would tell them that he was writing a book. After he finished the book and was ready to launch it, he sent out over 1,000 pre-release copies to the bloggers he had met. He also asked them to write a review about the book on launch day. Most of these people loved his book, so on launch day, a huge percentage of them wrote blog posts about it to their followers. Tim's army of affiliates helped to send his book into bestseller status overnight.

Every time we have a big launch coming out, we let our affiliates know the launch date, and we ask them to block it out on their calendar. In a typical launch, I may ask 100 people to promote. Thirty people will usually say yes, yet just 15 or so of them will actually promote. It's just a numbers game, and often it doesn't fit into their promotional schedule at the time. Don't take it personally; just know that the more people you ask, the more likely you'll get the yeses you need to have a good launch.

One strategy we often use (that was pioneered by Chet Holmes and made famous by Dana Derricks) is to send out packages to our Dream 100 telling them about the promotions we have coming up. Each package could be worth thousands, and in some cases, one yes could be worth millions from the right partner. Because of this, we spend a lot of money sending out cool stuff in the mail to recruit affiliates. The key is getting their attention and giving them a reason to promote.

As you're recruiting affiliates to sell your product, it is important to understand that there are different types of affiliates, each with a different motivation. Some are only concerned by how much money they make and want a high-converting funnel, while others are more concerned with whether or not the product is a good fit for their audience. For me, I don't care what their motivation is. I just want to serve their customers, so I want to make sure they're happy at all costs. Since one yes from one of them could bring hundreds of your dream customers, it's worth putting in a lot of effort to build these relationships.

STEP #2: MAKE THEM YOUR AFFILIATES

After your Dream 100 has said they want to be an affiliate, you have to make it official by getting them to join your affiliate program. Inside ClickFunnels there is an affiliate platform called Backpack that you can use to add an affiliate program to any funnel inside of your ClickFunnels account. You just need to turn it on for a funnel, and it will create a page where your Dream 100 can sign up to become an affiliate. Within the software, it will provide tracking links for your funnel, track their sales, and pay their commissions. We've created an extensive training inside ClickFunnels on how to set up your affiliate program. Go to TrafficSecrets.com/resources to find it.

Often, your best affiliates will be your customers. I always like to let my customers know that they can actually make money by referring their friends. You can put links to your affiliate sign-up page on your funnels, on your thank-you pages, and in your emails. That way, you are helping them to earn commissions on the products they already love and helping them to spread your message.

STEP #3: GIVE YOUR AFFILIATES A REASON TO PROMOTE

Once someone is an affiliate, you need to give them a reason to promote. They could promote millions of products, so you need to explain why they should promote your products, and, more importantly, why they should promote you now. Usually, we're able to get affiliates to promote based on one of three things:

- A new launch
- Their turn on a rolling launch

- Something special or new

A new launch: Launching a new product is one of the easiest ways to get affiliates to promote because you can tell them about the new project that you've been working on, send them copies of the product in the mail, and let them experience what you're going to be selling. We usually roll out two to three new front-end products each year that we ask affiliates to promote. We set a launch date and start recruiting affiliates 60–90 days before each launch. We send out Dream 100 packages, call them on the phone, send emails, and do whatever else we need to do to have them block out our launch dates on their calendars. The earlier you can ask them to dedicate time to your launch, the better, so they can make sure they don't have any other promotional conflicts.

As we get closer to the launch date, we'll typically put everyone who has agreed to promote into a special Facebook group where we can communicate with them about everything that's happening in the launch. This helps to build a community of affiliates and create a fun competitive environment where we share leaderboards and give people multiple reasons to promote during the launch.

The rolling launch: A rolling launch is similar to a new launch, but instead of everyone promoting on one single launch date, you let people each have their own turn to do a launch to their lists. This is how we initially launched ClickFunnels. Once I knew my webinar converted, instead of having everyone promote it at once, I set up special webinars for each affiliate. I would do two to three of these a week for a few months. This rolling launch gave us the ability to work with each affiliate to find a time in their own promotional calendar that would work.

The longevity of a rolling launch is a lot longer. For a typical product launch, there is an opening day and a close cart day, and affiliates who couldn't promote during that time missed out. Also, a huge launch can often lead to too many new customers too fast, which might clog up your customer support. A rolling launch gives you the ability to onboard new customers at a much easier pace.

Something special or new: Often I'm recruiting affiliates who don't want to be part of a product launch. They may be SEO marketers, or they may be really good at PPC, or they may want a higher commission because they're so good. There could be dozens of different reasons, but my goal is to be able to serve their customers, so I'll work with them individually to see what is best for them. I may set up a special landing page, a different offer, a higher commission, or whatever else they need that will give them a good reason to promote for me.

STEP #4: TRAIN YOUR AFFILIATES TO BECOME SUPER AFFILIATES

As you'll soon find, the better the affiliate is, the lazier they often are; and the worse the affiliate is, the more training they'll need. Both of these became problems for us. New affiliates didn't know what to do or how to promote us; the good affiliates knew how to do it but wouldn't promote unless we made the process very simple for them. (Good affiliates make a lot of money and have a lot of people begging for their attention.) In both cases, nothing would happen. To solve this problem, we created affiliate training centers that had two goals:

- Show new affiliates how to promote our products. We trained them how to run ads, track their sales, and more.

- Offer copy-and-paste ads that our super affiliates could grab and quickly edit. We gave them sample email ads, banner ads, copy for Facebook posts, and more.

With Backpack (inside of ClickFunnels), you can create an affiliate center. The affiliate center is one of the most powerful tools you can have in your traffic arsenal because it's easy to create an affiliate center for each of your funnels.

Figure 18.2:

Your affiliate center is a place to give your affiliates as many assets and as much training as possible for them to be successful.

STEP #5: COMPENSATE YOUR AFFILIATES

"How much should I pay my affiliates?" This is the question I get the most, and one that I get hit with the most resistance toward when I tell people my philosophies. While most people are always asking how little they can pay their affiliates, I want to figure out ways that I can pay them the most possible. The more you're able to pay your affiliates, the more likely they are to promote you. They're your commission-based sales team, and affiliates who are good have unlimited opportunities to sell anything they want. They don't need you; you need them.

When we first launched ClickFunnels, I noticed that most of the other software companies were paying their affiliates 20–30 percent commission on their sales. We launched immediately with a 40 percent commission for our affiliates, and because of that, we were able to recruit most of their top affiliates. They stopped promoting the other software products and started promoting ours.

At the time, I started watching how many top network marketing programs bought cars for their top recruiters. After reviewing our own affiliate program at ClickFunnels, I realized that if one of our affiliates brought in 100 ClickFunnels members at $100 per month, then 5 percent of those commissions ($500) would equal enough to cover the lease payment on a dream car. So we added a bonus in our affiliate program: we would pay any affiliate an extra $500 each month to pay for their dream car if they had more than 100 people signed up under them and $1,000 per month toward their dream car if they signed up 200 people.

These few things alone helped us to get some of the top affiliates in the world to start promoting us. I didn't want to stop there, though; I wanted to figure out how to pay them more. Shortly after we launched the ClickFunnels affiliate program, we started launching new front-end funnels that our affiliates could promote. The first one was the *DotCom Secrets* book, where people could pay $7.95 shipping to get a copy of the book, and then we would upsell the audio book and other related courses. We set it up so affiliates would earn 50 percent of all sales that came from that funnel, and when they upgraded to ClickFunnels later, we would also pay them their 40 percent recurring commission on those sales.

We did this for the first three weeks of the book launch, and then we started looking at our stats. We noticed that for each person who bought the book, we were making about $20 in sales from the upsells. It was also costing us about $20 to give away the book for free from our own Facebook Ads. (If you remember, we were okay with that because it was a break-even funnel. And we were okay with losing money as long as we could push them back into ClickFunnels.)

Then we had an idea. Instead of paying people a percentage of sales in that book funnel, what if we gave them a flat CPA of $20 for every book they sold? We wouldn't make any money, and in some cases, we could lose some money, but it would incentivize our affiliates to promote harder. So that's what we did the last week of the launch. We paid $20 for every free book our affiliates gave away, and our army of affiliates sold tens of thousands of copies of that book! We broke even, our affiliates got paid, and from that promotion alone we got thousands of new ClickFunnels members for free!

As you can see, there are two core ways you can pay affiliates. The first is to pay out a percentage of the sale, and the second is to pay them a flat CPA for every sale they make.

My rule is that I try to pay out 50 percent of the profit I make in my funnel. For instance, if I have a digital product or a course, I assume my fulfillment costs will be about 20 percent of the sale, so I split the remaining 80 percent with the affiliate who brought in the sale. If I'm selling a physical product and my costs of goods sold are 60 percent, then I only have 40 percent profit, and I'll split that with the affiliate right down the middle. If I have a front-end funnel, then I'll usually give 100 percent (or more) to the affiliate to really motivate them to fill the front of my value ladder with my dream customers.

There have even been times that we've paid $80 or more on a free book, because we knew that within a few weeks of sale, we would be profitable. I recommend staying at or below 100 percent commissions on any front-end offer until you've mastered your numbers and know the actual lifetime value of your customers and are okay to float the money for a few months while the customers are going through your follow-up funnels.

Building a successful affiliate program has brought us more traffic, leads, and sales than any other marketing technique. If you pay your dues with your Dream 100, recruit them to be an affiliate, treat them well, and always figure out more ways to make them money, they will keep your funnels filled with your dream customers. If I turned off all other traffic techniques that we've been using and only use this one, I'd still have an army of people buying Facebook Ads for me, sending out emails for me, ranking websites, and buying ads. Make this a priority and it will serve you for the rest of your life.

COLD TRAFFIC

Thus far, I've focused on two types of traffic: warm traffic (the fans and followers and lists of your Dream 100) and hot traffic (your own list). For most companies, this is all that you will ever need to focus on. I strongly believe that you can build most companies to multiple eight figures a year just by focusing on warm traffic and then turning it into hot traffic. If you want to scale beyond that, though, you'll have to master one other type of traffic: cold traffic.

In *DotCom Secrets*, I called this "traffic temperature," and it's a concept that I started to understand after first hearing this amazing quote from the late Eugene Schwartz:

> If your prospect is aware of your product and has realized it can satisfy his desire, your headline starts with the product.
>
> If he is not aware of your product, but only of the desire itself, your headline starts with the desire.
>
> If he is not yet aware of what he really seeks, but is concerned with the general problem, your headline starts with the problem and crystallizes it into a specific need.[51]

Figure 19.1:

Prospects are at different stages in their awareness of the problem, solution, and product based on the temperature of the traffic.

To me, it meant that traffic that was cold needed to be spoken to differently than traffic that was warm or hot because they weren't even aware that a solution existed, let alone that there was a product to solve their problem.

Most of the landing pages, offers, and ads that you've created up to this point are for people who are solution aware or product aware. They know they have a problem, they've tried a bunch of solutions, and you're presenting them with a new opportunity that will get the results that they want. Because they are already aware of the potential solutions, have done some research, and have probably tried a bunch of your competitors, when you have a chance to hook them and tell them your story, they already have a context for the problem you're trying to solve for them.

For example, in my market, many of my customers have a problem: they want to make more money. To solve that problem, they could try any number of solutions: they could set up an e-commerce store, sell things on eBay, learn SEO, master Facebook Ads, or do about a hundred other things. They're aware of all the possible solutions, so I have to show them that my solution (funnels) is a new opportunity that trumps all the others. If they're product aware, they've probably heard of all my competitors, so I have to convince them that my product is superior, and then they will buy it from me.

Cold traffic, on the other hand, often isn't even aware they have a problem. If you remember the three core markets, cold traffic is a group of people that are at the 3 Core Desires level. All they know is that their health, wealth, or relationship isn't good; they don't have any understanding yet of anything beyond that. They haven't been congregated into groups yet, so no one is helping them. If they are aware they have a problem, they're still at the beginning of their journey and have no idea what to do or where to turn. Anything presented to them at this point has to be filled with a lot of education to get them ready for what you have to offer.

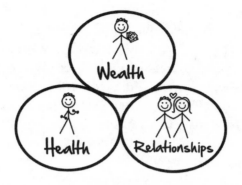

Figure 19.2:

Often, cold traffic is only aware that their core desire
(such as health, wealth, or relationships) isn't good.

Getting something to work in cold traffic will seem difficult, but it's actually as simple as changing your language patterns. To illustrate this, I'll share a test we use to see if something will work well with super cold traffic. Imagine I walk into the food court at the mall and see 300 people sitting at tables, eating lunch and minding their own business, completely unaware of what I'm doing. If I stood on top of a chair and shouted from the top of my lungs, "Hey! Who here would like to grow their companies using sales funnels?", what do you think would happen? You guessed it: they'd probably look at the crazy guy on the chair for a second and instantly go back to eating. Chances are almost no one would raise their hands. But if I pulled up that same chair and I changed what I yelled at the top of my lungs to "Who here wants a money-making website?" I bet half the food court would raise their hands.

Interestingly enough, the solution to both these problems is that they need a funnel, but to the people who are more unaware, my language doesn't make sense to them. The difference in talking to hot, warm, and cold traffic is the language that you use. "Funnels" don't make sense to the masses, so I have to change my language to "money-making website" to match what they would understand. After I have their hands raised, I can educate them on a certain type of website called a funnel, and I can help them to become solution aware. Finally, after they've warmed up, they'll be more willing to make a purchasing decision.

If you create a funnel that converts really well to warm traffic (the followers of your Dream 100) and your hot traffic (your own lists), it might not convert well to cold traffic. You see, no matter how much cold traffic you get, you'll probably go broke before you even get a single customer. You have to create a different type of funnel that speaks to where they are and then warms them up. Let me show you how it works.

STEP #1: CREATE YOUR "COLD TRAFFIC CUSTOMER AVATAR"

The first step in this process is to create a new "cold traffic customer avatar." This avatar will be similar to your current dream customer avatar, but cold traffic is much earlier in their journey. They are six months to a year (or more) before they became your dream customer. They know they have pain in the three core desires that you serve (health, wealth, or relationships), but they haven't started moving toward a solution yet. These people can become your dream customers, but right now they are only *problem* aware. They are unhappy because they know there is a problem, but they're not yet aware of the solutions that are possible and they're definitely not aware of any products that will solve their problems. They only know what the problem is and the results they want.

To identify this cold traffic customer avatar for myself, I had to look deep into my own past. For most of you, if you've followed a traditional entrepreneurial journey, this avatar will mostly likely be you five to ten years ago. Think about it: most entrepreneurs have struggled with the desire of health, wealth, or relationships and went on a journey to get themselves out of pain. During this journey, they fell in love with their own process of change, and they became obsessed with helping others out of the same pain that they once had. This is how most entrepreneurs find their mission.

If that's true for you, you need to look back in time to where you were struggling with that same problem that your cold market clients are experiencing right now. For me, I have to think back almost 30 years ago to 12-year-old Rusty (yes, that's what my parents and all of my friends called me back then). For some reason, as a 12-year-old, I had one desire: I wanted money. I'm not sure why. I had a great childhood and nothing was lacking, but for some reason my core desire was for wealth.

This desire caused my problem: I didn't have any money. And how did I try to solve this problem? Well, it started with me ordering Don Lapre's course on classified ads from a late-night infomercial. (I shared this story at length in *DotCom Secrets*.) It was the first vehicle (submarket) that I learned about, and I was hooked. I saved up my money to try to buy classified ads.

Shortly after I was introduced to one of the submarkets (making money with classified ads), I started to become aware of a lot of them. One day I was at the grocery store, saw a magazine called *Small Business Opportunities*, and begged my mom to buy a copy for me.

Inside of the magazine were dozens of ways to make money (lots of submarkets), and each had a way to request an information kit to learn more. I called every 1-800 number, requested every kit, and within weeks started getting hundreds of letters and packages in the mail, each offering a new way to help me achieve the result I thought I wanted.

One kit showed how to get rich selling gold chains at the mall. The next showed how to get rich painting glow-in-the-dark stars on people's bedroom ceilings. Others showed how to get rich in real estate, the stock markets, or commodities trading. Because I was only aware of my problem, each message pitched me on the potential solutions for my problem (i.e., different ways to make money).

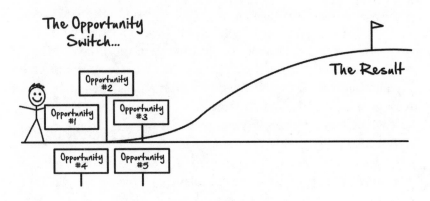

Figure 19.3:

**There are many different opportunities all leading to
the same result (making money).**

Every day when I came home from school, my parents would have a pile of "Rusty's junk mail" that I would grab and take into my room. I opened every letter, read every sales pitch, and tried to understand which ones would help me get the result I thought I wanted. Some of the pitches I would just throw away, and others would keep me up at night as I tried to figure out how I could convince my parents to give me money to order their opportunity. Still others were so good that I would mow lawns and do chores or anything else possible to get enough money to purchase their information.

Later on in life, it would take me a while to remember what it felt like reading all those sales pitches, but after I put myself back in those moments, my 12-year-old self became my customer avatar for cold traffic. Now every time we create an ad, pick our targeting, design our landing page, and make an offer for cold traffic, I try to go back in time and look through the lens of 12-year-old me.

Is this ad something that would make Rusty click, or would I keep on scrolling? Is this offer something that would cause Rusty to beg his parents for their credit card, or better yet, force him to earn money because he had to have it? Or was this something that he would have just thrown in the trash?

So my question for you is this: What is your version of 12-year-old Rusty? What were the things that would have grabbed your attention at the beginning of your journey? What words and phrases would you have used back then to explain what it is you're doing now? If I had seen words like "funnel" or "traffic" back then, I would have kept flipping through the magazine. Instead, they had used words that described the problem I had and the result I was trying to get in a way that I understood, and *that's* why they were successful.

STEP #2: CREATE A BRIDGE

Marketing is all about creating bridges from what someone wants and desires to the solution that you provide. In *DotCom Secrets*, I shared this image showing the seven phases of a funnel, where phase one is the traffic temperature and then phase two is the pre-frame bridge.

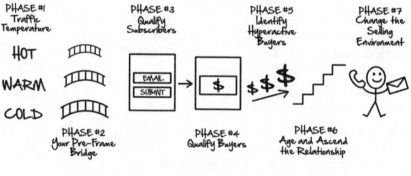

Figure 19.4:

The warmer the traffic, the smaller the pre-frame bridge needs to be.

As you can see, the warmer the traffic, the smaller the pre-frame bridge needs to be. If your audience knows, trusts, and loves you (the hottest traffic), then your bridge could be as simple as telling them you have something cool that you think they should buy. At our last Funnel Hacking LIVE event, we had 4,500 funnel hackers in the audience—by far my hottest traffic—and I asked them, "If I told you to buy something right now, how many of you would trust me enough to just walk to the back of the room without knowing what it was, but you'd do it because you believed me?" Over 60 percent of the room shot their hands up in agreement.

That is the power of hot traffic and the reason why the game becomes easier and easier as you focus your efforts on tapping into your Dream 100's hot traffic (your warm traffic) and converting it into traffic that you own. The traffic that you own becomes your hot traffic. Can you see now why I stressed the goal of converting warm traffic that you can earn and control into traffic that you own so much?

As you move down the warm traffic bridge, it takes a little longer to bridge the gap between what people already know and believe and what you have to offer. Sometimes that bridge is an email from your Dream 100 endorsing you. Other times it's a presell content video that people watch on Facebook or YouTube warming them up to you and providing value before you direct them into your funnels. And other times, the funnel alone is structured to be the actual pre-frame bridge that warms them up.

The last and longest bridge is the cold traffic bridge. But how long does it need to be? It all depends on how cold the targeted customers are. The first time I tried to grow past our Dream 100's customers and figure out cold traffic, I took a segment of my customer list and ran some intense data analysis on who our existing customers were. If you want a company to do this for your customer lists, go to TrafficSecrets.com/resources to find an up-to-date list of companies that you can hire.

When we got back the data, we found a lot of interesting trends, but one that really stuck out was that a huge percentage of our customers at the time were conservative Republicans. The report even referenced a few of the websites that this group spent a lot of time on.

Excited to find a new segment that I had never targeted, I went to these websites (as well as other similar sites) and found that most of them had online media kits that allowed me to buy ads in their email newsletter as well as banner ads on their websites. I put in an order to send an email out to 2.3 million people that would direct them into our funnel that converted warm traffic. I was doing the math in my head, and based on what I knew at the time (how big their list was, how many clicks I should get, and how my warm traffic funnel normally converted), I figured this email alone would make me a few hundred thousand dollars.

Once the publisher sent the email, I watched as hundreds of thousands of clicks came to my funnel. That excitement quickly turned to horror, however, as these people almost immediately bounced off and didn't buy. When the campaign ended, we had made about a dozen sales, and I had lost over $30,000 from the ad. I was defeated, and I swore I'd never look at cold traffic again.

Then something interesting happened. I had joined these email lists before I paid for the ad because I wanted to see my email when it hit, and each day afterward I started seeing how other people who were marketing to these lists were doing it. I started clicking on their ads, and slowly I started to funnel hack them. The links didn't take me immediately to a funnel, which didn't make sense to me. Instead, the links took me to a page that looked similar to the site that I had just been on. It looked less like a funnel and more like an article. I read the article, and, within a few minutes, I saw something I hadn't before. This article was speaking a very different language than I was. It was speaking directly toward the conservative Republicans it was targeting, using their language, and telling stories about things that they believed in and cared about. Then, within those stories, it started to bridge the gap between what the conservative Republicans believed and what the advertiser was offering.

Toward the end of these articles was a link to join a newsletter that would give you more information. I clicked on the link and joined that newsletter. I noticed that for most of these cold traffic bridges, they didn't sell anything to me for a while. I got newsletter number one in their follow-up funnel, which continued to bridge concepts and beliefs with me through stories. Within a few messages, they started to transition and push me into their front-end funnels. At this point, even I was ready to buy.

They didn't take people directly from a cold ad into a warm funnel. Instead, they took them through a warming-up process to prepare them for the warm funnel. After I saw that, I was ready for round two!

So we spent time trying to figure out:

- What language patterns (words and phrases) should I use to explain what I'm trying to warm people up for?

- What false beliefs do people have that would keep them from buying when they did see my funnel?

- What stories did I have that could bridge the gaps and break their false beliefs?

- What content pieces did we need to create to tell these stories?

We then wrote an article landing page which would become our cold traffic pre-frame bridge. When we bought our next solo ad to the list, we sent all the traffic to this article page. From the article page, we directed them to a lead funnel that captured their email address, and then we built a follow-up funnel that led them to different posts on our blog, videos on YouTube, and other places where we had strategically placed content to warm them up. Eventually, we introduced them to our front-end offer after we had warmed them up.

The results? We were able to finally get cold traffic to work! Typically with warm traffic, we try to break even immediately during the first funnel we direct them toward, but with cold traffic, it takes longer because it's a much longer bridge. With some sources, we're able to break even within a week, but others take two to three months or longer. That's why it's so essential that if and when you break outside your Dream 100, you already have a solid value ladder in place with follow-up funnels and sequences that convert. If you're able to get your offers to convert to cold traffic, then you can buy ads almost anywhere, including buying ads in colder email lists and banner ads on most websites.

In order for most companies to scale past nine figures per year, you'll need to master cold traffic. To begin with, though, I'd still focus all your efforts on warm traffic and the Dream 100. I always tell people that there is a huge pile of cash sitting in front of you, waiting for you to go and grab it. Don't step over it while trying to go after bigger piles of cash somewhere else. Stop and grab the big pile of cash (your hot and warm traffic) first, and then after you have it all, you can start looking more at the cold traffic channels.

OTHER GROWTH HACKS

To conclude, I'm going to share some other fun ways to get traffic into your funnels. I could keep adding more chapters with more ideas, but at some point, this book would become too big to consume. Instead, I'll use this chapter to help stimulate more fun ideas and growth hacks that you and your team can use to start brainstorming other ways to get traffic into your funnels.

My close friend and fellow early marketing pioneer Mike Filsaime pioneered a concept over a decade ago that he called "butterfly marketing."[52] Basically, he believes that tiny changes in your marketing can produce huge results. It is cause-and-effect applied to marketing online.

I had heard people talk about the butterfly effect when I was in school. I still remember my teacher talking about how something as small as a butterfly flapping its wings in a certain location could cause a tiny, almost imperceptible change in the environment that, when combined with other changes in the weather system, could be indirectly responsible for a hurricane forming on the other side of the world. But how do butterflies relate back to digital marketing? Mike argues that there are a lot of little things you can do inside of your sales funnels that, while seemingly small and insignificant, could have a massive impact after virally compounding over time.

Mike spent a lot of time trying to figure out which things you could plug into your sales funnel that would get the people who came to your funnels to refer other people for free (word-of-mouth marketing). To make something truly viral, you had to get past a referral point that Mark Joyner calls "copulation rate," or the rate that your viral marketing is growing.

In other words, if you referred 100 people into your funnel and relied 100 percent on viral marketing from that point forward, and if these 100 people each referred less than one person, then your growth would quickly die. If they each referred exactly one person, then your viral growth would flatline. However, as soon as each person you referred brought in more than one person, then you would have something that would be truly viral.

Figure 20.1:

To have something go viral, you need each person to refer more than one person.

Now, getting to a true copulation rate is very hard, and it's impossible to sustain forever because eventually you would have everyone in the world. Eventually, you hit a saturation point and the viral growth will slow down and eventually stop.

I've only had one funnel that hit a true copulation rate of greater than one. It was a front-end funnel we built to recruit people into a new network marketing company that we were helping to launch. This funnel required people to sign a nondisclosure agreement (NDA), and then they got five invite codes to invite others into the funnel. After they referred five people, they would then be given five more invite codes.

We modeled this based on how Google initially launched Gmail. They gave each Gmail user the ability to invite a limited number of people onto the platform. Invites became so valuable that people were selling them on eBay for over $100 each![53]

Our viral front-end funnel signed up over 1.6 million people in just six short weeks. During these six weeks, we averaged three new sign-ups for every one person who joined the site, and I had a chance to see true viral growth. Unfortunately, the company this funnel was promoting didn't have everything ready for the launch, and they had to delay three or four times, pushing the launch out to over nine months later. People got bored and the viral growth slowed to a stop.

Now, most of us are probably not going to have the chance to have a site that has true viral growth, and that's okay. There are still plenty of things that you can do inside your funnels to promote true viral, "refer a friend" style growth, where you can turn your traffic into more traffic. I'll share with you a few ideas from companies that you know that may give you ideas of things you can weave into your funnels.

Dropbox: When users signed up for an account with Dropbox, in their upsell flow Dropbox offered to give the new member more free storage if they linked their Twitter and Facebook accounts and shared information about Dropbox on those accounts. This helped Dropbox grow to over 500 million members worldwide![54]

Facebook: When people first created their Facebook accounts, they were encouraged to add all their contacts so Facebook could see if these people were already on the site and connect you to them. Then Facebook took all the people who weren't on the site and sent emails inviting them to join Facebook from the new member.[55]

Hotmail: In the early years of Hotmail, Hotmail added a signature line to every email that went out that said "PS: I love you. Get your free email at Hotmail.com." That little hack helped them to get to 12 million users in just 18 months.[56]

I had heard stories of some of these famous growth-hacking companies, so as we launched ClickFunnels, we started to weave some of these concepts into our sign-up flow. Here are a few of the things that we tested that were successful.

ClickFunnels + Dropbox's growth hack: After someone created their ClickFunnels account, we gave them a limited account that only had the ability to create up to 20 funnels. Then we gave them an affiliate link with an opportunity to double their funnels from 20 to 40 when they referred a new user to ClickFunnels. This helped our members to bring in more members.

ClickFunnels + Facebook's growth hack: We didn't have the capability to have people import their friends and then send them emails, so we had to be creative to figure out how we could model this growth hack. At the time, we were sending a lot of traffic to webinars that would teach people about ClickFunnels. On the webinar, we would present people with an offer to create their free 14-day trial account. We had an idea to plug in a "tell-a-friend" script in the page after someone registered for the webinar. Once they referred five friends to the webinar they'd just signed up for, they could get a free copy of one of our best-selling products. We found that the majority of our visitors would refer their friends just so they could get a free copy of the product. Typically, we'd get about 20 percent or more of our sign-ups for each webinar from those sign-up referrals. That extra 20 percent was free traffic we didn't even have to pay for.

ClickFunnels + Hotmail's growth hack: As we were launching ClickFunnels, we knew that people would eventually create millions of pages online. To capitalize on this, we attached a badge on the bottom of each page that says "This Page Made with ClickFunnels." The badge was coded with the page owner's affiliate link, which took the viewer to ClickFunnels. Because we made every ClickFunnels member an affiliate when they signed up, every ClickFunnels user had the ability to make affiliate commissions when other people clicked on that badge and signed up for ClickFunnels. We gave people the ability to turn the badge off, but by default it was turned on. Over the past five years that we've had the badge on our members' pages, we've added over 10,000 members and currently make over $1,000,000 per month in recurring revenue (over $12 million per year) from that one growth hack.

Each of these growth hacks that we have implemented into our funnels have been tiny little changes that produced huge results. We've had others that we've tested that didn't have a big enough impact to report here, but I wanted to tell you the stories of the more successful ones so that you'll start noticing them as you're going through other people's sales processes. As a funnel hacker, you should be closely watching the sign-up processes through this growth-hacking lens. See the creative things people are doing that you can model inside your funnels, and then test the ones that you like.

This is a marketing game of hunting for buried treasure. Just think, that one tiny badge we placed on our members' pages, almost as an afterthought, pays us over $12 million per year. Each of these little butterflies, growth hacks, or whatever you want to call them, has the ability to change the metrics of your company forever. Start looking at marketing and traffic as a game, and keep your eyes open for the next million-dollar hack that's right in front of your face!

CONCLUSION

TYING IT ALL BACK TOGETHER

I know that this book hasn't been light reading. Unlike most books on traffic that focus on one platform or one strategy, I didn't want to just give you a tactic that only worked today and maybe not tomorrow. I wanted to give you a framework that you could use to get traffic from any platform, today, tomorrow, and forever. My goal wasn't to give you a fish; my goal was to teach you how to fish, and I hope I did just that.

This book is the final book in my Secrets trilogy. For some of you, this will have been the first book of mine that you've read because traffic was the thing you felt you were missing most in your company. Traffic is just one part of the equation, though. If the traffic you're sending into your funnels from the strategies in this book isn't working, then you typically either have a funnel strategy problem (that can be diagnosed and cured with the information inside *DotCom Secrets*) or you have a conversion problem (which can be solved by mastering the concepts inside *Expert Secrets*). Using these three books together will help you to have a more holistic approach to your online digital marketing strategy.

Now that you've finished the book, you're probably asking yourself, "What should I do next?" This book was created to be like a playbook that you don't just read once, but one that you can reference over and over again. Each concept builds on the one before it, and after you master it in one platform, you can layer on another platform as you work toward complete conversation domination.

For right now, though, this is what I recommend you do while these ideas and concepts are still at the top of your mind:

- Decide on who you really want to serve. If you really want to fill your funnels with your dream customers, you have to know and understand them better than they understand themselves.

- Pick the platform you want to publish on first. This will probably be the platform that you personally spend the most time on now, because you'll understand how to communicate in the unique language of that platform the best.

- Build your Dream 100 list of the people who have already congregated your dream customers on this platform.

- Start digging your well with your Dream 100. Figure out ways to serve them and start working your way in.

- At the same time, learn the tactics of how you can buy your way in on that platform.

This is where you should start and focus 100 percent of your energy until your funnel has hit the Two Comma Club, meaning it's made at least $1 million. At that point, layer on a second platform and then a third. With every dollar you make online, reinvest a big percentage of your profits back into advertising. Finally, don't stop. Traffic is the lifeblood of any company, and consistent lead flow is the secret to a healthy business.

Every day, look at ways that you can give yourself a raise. Ask yourself: "How can I get more traffic?" "Who can I connect with on my Dream 100 today?" "What new integration opportunities are there?" "Are there new people whom I can add to my Dream 100?" "How can I get them to become an affiliate?" "What can I do to incentivize them to promote?" "How can I get them to promote more often?"

All these questions stem from my primary question of "How can I give myself a raise every day?" Ask that question, and flip through the pages of *DotCom Secrets, Expert Secrets,* and this book to find your answers. These playbooks weren't created based on ideas but rather on battle-tested principles that I discovered after spending over 15 years in the trenches. These are the ideas that stuck and that work consistently.

I hope that you can use these secrets to find more of your dream customers and serve them at your highest level. They are waiting for you to find them so you can change their lives. If you focus on that, your business will become a catalyst of change for people in their lives, and that's the real purpose behind business.

Thank you for allowing me to serve you through these pages and this series. It's truly been an honor, and I can't wait to see what you do with the frameworks that you've learned. Come hit me up on any of the social media platforms, say hi, and please share with me how these "secrets" have changed your life.

Thanks,
Russell Brunson

P.S. Don't forget, you're just one funnel away . . .

ENDNOTES

Foreword

1. Costner, Kevin. *Field of Dreams*. DVD. Directed by Phil Alden Robinson. Los Angeles: Gordon Company, 1989.

Introduction

2. Downey, Jr., Robert. *Avengers: Infinity War*. DVD. Directed by Anthony Russo and Joe Russo. Los Angeles: Marvel Studios, 2018.

SECTION ONE

Secret #1

3. Collier, Robert. *The Robert Collier Letter Book*. Robert Collier Publishing Inc., 1989.

4. Newman, Lily Hay. "America's First TV Ad Cost $9 for 9 Seconds." *Slate*. July 1, 2016, https://slate.com/business/2016/07/the-first-legal-tv-commercial -aired-on-july-1-1941-for-bulova-watch-co-watch-it.html.

Secret #2

5. Holmes, Chet. *The Ultimate Sales Machine*. Penguin Publishing Group, 2008.

6. Bilyeu, Tom. August 4, 2016. "Tom Bilyeu on Building a Unicorn." Podcast audio. *Foundr*. https://foundr.com/tom-bilyeu-quest-nutrition.

7. Derricks, Dana. *Dream 100*. Self-published. https://www.dream100book.com.

8. Tiku, Nitasha. "What's *Not* Included in Facebook's 'Download Your Data.'" *Wired* online. April 23, 2018, https://www.wired.com/story/ whats-not-included-in-facebooks-download-your-data.

Secret #4

9. Mackay, Harvey. *Dig Your Well Before You're Thirsty*. The Crown Publishing Group, 1999.

Secret #5

10. Blau, John. "eBay Buys Skype for $2.6 Billion." *PCWorld*. September 12, 2005, https://www.pcworld.com/article/122516/article.html.

11. Rusli, Evelyn M. "Facebook Buys Instagram for $1 Billion." *The New York Times* online. April 9, 2012, https://dealbook.nytimes.com/2012/04/09/ facebook-buys-instagram-for-1-billion.

Secret #6

12. Frey, David. "Follow-Up Marketing: How to Win More Sales with Less Effort." *Business Know-How*. January 11, 2017, https://www.businessknowhow.com/ marketing/less_effort.htm.

13. Litman, Mike. Presentation at Big Seminar, Atlanta, GA, 2005. http://www .generatorsoftware.com/transcription/bigsem5/MLitman.doc.

14. Kennedy, Dan. "The Most Important Question You Should Ask When Advertising." *Dan Kennedy's Magnetic Marketing.* February 26, 2013, https://nobsinnercircle.com/blog/advertising/the-most-important-question-you-should-ask-when-advertising.

Secret #7

15. Spiegel, Danny. "Today in TV History: Bill Clinton and His Sax Visit Arsenio." *TV Insider* online. June 3, 2015, https://www.tvinsider.com/2979/rerun-bill-clinton-on-arsenio-hall.

16. *Celebrity Apprentice*, "Walking Papers, Parts 1 and 2," NBC, April 1, 2012.

17. Vaynerchuk, Gary. Presentation at Traffic & Conversion Summit, San Diego, CA, 2016.

18. Durmonski, Ivaylo, Lisa Parmley, Mohit Pawar, and Prashant Pillai. "Endure Long Enough to Get Noticed." *Nathan Barry.* February 18, 2019, https://nathanbarry.com/endure.

19. Vaynerchuk, Gary. "Document, Don't Create: Creating Content That Builds Your Personal Brand." *GaryVaynerchuk.com.* December 2, 2016, https://www.garyvaynerchuk.com/creating-content-that-builds-your-personal-brand.

20. Barrymore, Drew, and David Arquette. *Never Been Kissed.* DVD. Directed by Raja Gosnell. Los Angeles: Fox 2000 Pictures, 1999.

SECTION TWO

Secret #10

21. Wikipedia contributors. "Timeline of Instagram." *Wikipedia, The Free Encyclopedia.* Accessed September 27, 2019, https://en.wikipedia.org/w/index.php?title=Timeline_of_Instagram&oldid=916307088.

22. Smith, Kit. "49 Incredible Instagram Statistics You Need to Know." *Brandwatch.* May 7, 2019. https://www.brandwatch.com/blog/instagram-stats.

23. Hartmans, Avery and Rob Price. "Instagram Just Reached 1 Billion Users." *Business Insider* online. June 20, 2018, https://www.businessinsider.com/instagram-monthly-active-users-1-billion-2018-6.

24. Rusli, Evelyn. "Facebook Buys Instagram for $1 Billion." *The New York Times* online. April 9, 2012, https://dealbook.nytimes.com/2012/04/09/facebook-buys-instagram-for-1-billion.

25. Shinal, John. "Mark Zuckerburg Couldn't Buy Snapchat Years Ago, And Now He's Close to Destroying The Company." *CNBC* online. July 12, 2017, https://www.cnbc.com/2017/07/12/how-mark-zuckerberg-has-used-instagram-to-crush-evan-spiegels-snap.html.

Secret #11

26. "Then and Now: A History of Social Networking Sites." *CBS News* online. Accessed September 26, 2019, https://www.cbsnews.com/pictures/then-and-now-a-history-of-social-networking-sites.

27. Patrizio, Andy. "ICQ, The Original Instant Messenger, Turns 20." *Network World.* November 18, 2016, https://www.networkworld.com/article/3142451/icq-the-original-instant-messenger-turns-20.html.

28. Noyes, Dan. "Top 20 Valuable Facebook Statistics - Updated September 2019." *Zephoria Digital Marketing*. Accessed September 26, 2019, https://zephoria.com/top-15-valuable-facebook-statistics.

29. Tiku, Nitasha. "What's *Not* Included in Facebook's 'Download Your Data.'" *Wired* online. April 23, 2018, https://www.wired.com/story/whats-not-included-in-facebooks-download-your-data.

30. "Facebook Unveils Facebook Ads." *Facebook Newsroom*. November 6, 2007, https://newsroom.fb.com/news/2007/11/facebook-unveils-facebook-ads.

31. Vaynerchuk, Gary. *Jab, Jab, Jab, Right Hook*. HarperCollins Publishing, 2013.

32. Constine, Josh. "Facebook Launches Messenger Platform with Chatbots." *TechCrunch*. April 12, 2016, https://techcrunch.com/2016/04/12/agents-on-messenger.

Secret #12

33. McAlone, Nathan. "The True Story Behind Google's Hilarious First Name: BackRub." *Business Insider* online. October 6, 2015, https://www.businessinsider.com/the-true-story-behind-googles-first-name-backrub-2015-10.

34. Soulo, Tim. "Google PageRank Is NOT Dead: Why It Still Matters." *SEO* (Blog). August 6, 2019, https://ahrefs.com/blog/google-pagerank.

35. "On-Page Ranking Factors." *MOZ*. Accessed September 26, 2019, https://moz.com/learn/seo/on-page-factors.

36. "Panda, Penguin and Hummingbird: Google Algorithm Zoo Explained." *Avocado SEO*. November 11, 2016, https://avocadoseo.com/panda-penguin-hummingbird-google-algorithm-zoo-explained.

37. Schachinger, Kristine. "Everything You Need to Know About the Google 'Fred' Update." *Search Engine Journal*. December 19, 2019, https://www.searchenginejournal.com/google-algorithm-history/fred-update.

38. *Late Show with David Letterman*. CBS, 1993–2015.

39. Dean, Brian. "Link Building Case Study: How I Increased My Search Traffic by 110% in 14 Days." *Backlinko*. September 2, 2016, https://backlinko.com/skyscraper-technique.

40. Dean, Brian. "Skyscraper Technique: SEO Strategy Checklist." *Backlinko*. https://backlinko.com/wp-content/uploads/2015/10/Backlinko_SkyscraperTechniqueChecklist.pdf.

Secret #13

41. Chi, Clifford. "51 YouTube Stats Every Video Marketer Should Know In 2019." *HubSpot*. February 12, 2019, https://blog.hubspot.com/marketing/youtube-stats.

42. Wikipedia contributors. "History of YouTube." *Wikipedia, The Free Encyclopedia*. Accessed September 27, 2019, https://en.wikipedia.org/w/index.php?title=History_of_YouTube&oldid=916710807.

Secret #14

43. "Podcast Statistics (2019) – Newest Available Data Infographic." *Music Oomph*. Accessed September 26, 2019, https://musicoomph.com/podcast-statistics.

44. Harbinger, Jordan. March 14, 2018. "Jordan Harbinger Tells Me How He Booked Guests Like Shaq and Other Podcasting Techniques." Podcast audio. *Mixergy*. https://mixergy.com/interviews/the-jordan-harbinger-show-with-jordan-harbinger.

45. Harbinger, Jordan. August 15, 2019. "Introducing The Jordan Harbinger Show." Podcast audio. *Business Wars*. https://www.stitcher.com/podcast/business-wars/e/63233619.

Secret #15

46. *The Jerry Springer Show*. NBC, 1991–2018.

SECTION THREE

Secret #17

47. "Daymond John." *The Shark Group*. Accessed September 26, 2019, https://www.thesharkgroup.com/speaking/daymond-john.

48. "Lori Greiner." LoriGreiner.com. Accessed September 26, 2019, http://www.lorigreiner.com/meet-lori.html.

49. "Mark's Bio." Mark Cuban Companies. Accessed September 26, 2019, http://markcubancompanies.com/about.html.

Secret #18

50. Ferriss, Tim. The 4-Hour Workweek. Potter/Ten Speed/Harmony/Rodale, 2009.

Secret #19

51. Schwartz, Eugene M. Breakthrough Advertising. Boardroom Reports Inc., 1984.

Secret #20

52. Filsaime, Mike. Butterfly Marketing Manuscript 3.0. CreateSpace, 2011.

53. "Gmail Invites Auctioned on eBay." Geek.com. May 3, 2004, https://www.geek.com/news/gmail-invites-auctioned-on-ebay-556690.

54. Drew and Arash. "Celebrating Half a Billion Users." Dropbox. March 7, 2016, https://blog.dropbox.com/topics/company/500-million.

55. Strickland, Jonathan. "How Facebook Works." HowStuffWorks. Accessed September 26, 2019. https://computer.howstuffworks.com/internet/social-networking/networks/facebook.htm.

56. "PS: I Love You. Get Your Free Email at Hotmail." TechCrunch online. October 19, 2009, https://techcrunch.com/2009/10/18/ps-i-love-you-get-your-free-email-at-hotmail.

ACKNOWLEDGMENTS

It was August 17, 2004, and I was on a family vacation at a little lake with my young bride. It was at a time before smartphones were created and the internet hadn't made it to the lake yet. I felt very disconnected from the world. It was really nice.

I had just started my little business a few months earlier and I was still trying to figure out what I was even doing. Curious if anyone had emailed me or tried to buy something from me during this trip, I decided I needed to get online and check my email.

Late one afternoon, I took a drive to find somewhere that I could access the internet. I drove around the small town and finally found a library that was about to close. There was a sign outside that said they had access to the internet, so I jumped out of my car and snuck in a few minutes before they asked everyone to leave.

I walked over to one of the computers and logged in to check my email. As I was waiting for it to load, I started to get nervous, hoping that I hadn't missed anything important. When the inbox loaded, I saw about a dozen new messages.

Most were ads, none were from customers, and then I saw one email that stood out. The subject line said *WE DID IT!* and the message was from a guy named John Reese, one of the early internet marketing pioneers that I was following.

We did what? I wondered as I opened the email.

Inside, the email stated, *We broke the record we had set out to accomplish.* I wasn't sure what record he was talking about, so I continued to read.

We set out a goal to make 1 million dollars in a day, with the launch of my new product called Traffic Secrets. We spent the last few months creating this launch campaign, and today it went live. In just 18 short hours, we passed our goal of a million dollar in sales!

I was shocked. I sat back in my chair and I read that sentence over and over. A man, someone who was just a few years older than me, had made more money in a day than I thought was possible for me to make in my lifetime. If he could do that . . . then what could I do? What was actually possible?

Then I looked at the name of his product: Traffic Secrets. About that same moment, the people at the library asked us all to leave because they were closing the doors. After leaving the library, and for the rest of the week, all I could hear in my head were the words "traffic secrets." If he knows how to get enough traffic to his website to make a million dollars in a day, I had to know his secrets. I knew that traffic was the key that I didn't have yet, and it was the missing ingredient that I needed in my business if I wanted it to be successful.

That started a journey that I have been on now for over 15 years: to learn how to get traffic (i.e., people) into my website and funnels. During this process, I've had a chance to learn from so many people, I could never name them all.

People like Mark Joyner, who taught me the power of an email list and the strategies for how to grow them; Chet Holmes, who introduced me to the concept of the Dream 100 that became the framework for how we get traffic today; Dan Kennedy and Jay Abraham, who taught me the foundation of direct response marketing; and, of course, John Reese, who was the first to teach me all his traffic secrets on multiple platforms.

Since I started this journey, I've had some amazing partners who have taken these ideas and run with them in different departments of our company. Brent Coppieters and later Dave Woodward helped to find, recruit, and train our affiliate army that drives more traffic into our funnels than all other sources combined. John Parkes, who jumped in to learn Facebook Ads for us a few years ago and eventually built a huge media buying team with people running paid ads for us on Google, YouTube, Pinterest, Twitter, Snapchat, and more, as well as organic traffic on all the major platforms. They are testing and innovating these strategies on a scale that few people have ever even dreamed up.

Each tactic, every strategy, came from conversations I had with other amazing entrepreneurs and marketers. It would be impossible to remember where every idea came from, but I've tried throughout this book to give credit to the original person I learned each concept from to the best of my memory.

I also want to thank everyone who helped me to write this book. I don't think people would believe the countless hours that go into a project like this until you embark on one yourself. I want to give a special thanks to Joy Anderson, who helped to edit the book, made sure my thoughts and ideas were clear, kept us on schedule, worked with the designers, and helped take this book across the finish line. Thank you for all the extra time you put in to help make this a masterpiece.

I have one last special acknowledgment that I want to make. During the Expert Secrets book launch, I had decided that I was not going to write another book. Literally a few hours later, I got an email from John Reese asking me if I would like to purchase the brand and the domain name TrafficSecrets.com. My heart jumped, and instantly I knew that this was the final book in the series. It was the last essential set of secrets and frameworks that I needed to arm my entrepreneurs with if they were going to have long-term success with their companies.

I quickly told John yes, and a few days later the domain was in my account and I started to work on this project. I want to thank John for allowing me to keep the Traffic Secrets legacy alive. If he wouldn't have created belief in me 15 years ago that all of this was possible, there is no way I'd be here in this position now sharing these secrets with you.

ABOUT THE AUTHOR

Russell Brunson started his first online company while he was wrestling in college. Within a year of graduation, he had sold over a million dollars of his own products and services from his basement. Over the past 15 years, he has built a following of over a million entrepreneurs, sold hundreds of thousands of copies of his books *DotCom Secrets* and *Expert Secrets*, popularized the concept of sales funnels, and co-founded the software company ClickFunnels, which helps tens of thousands of entrepreneurs quickly get their message out to the marketplace. He lives in Idaho with his family, and you can visit him online at RussellBrunson.com.

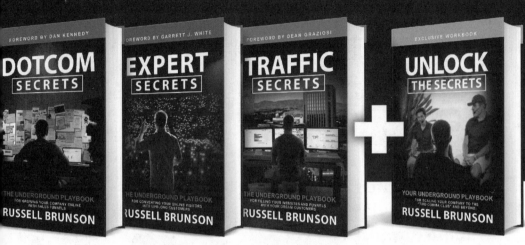

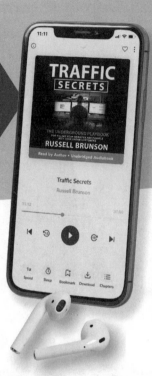

MARKETING SECRETS

Have You Liked The Secrets That You've Learned About In This Book?

*If So, Then **Subscribe** To My FREE Podcast Called "Marketing Secrets" Where I Share My Best Marketing Secrets Twice A Week.*

You Can Subscribe For FREE and get exclusive content, interviews and the most cutting edge secrets and ideas at:

MarketingSecrets.com

Listen on **Google** Podcasts

Listen on **Apple Podcasts**

AVAILABLE ON **STITCHER**

Listen on **Spotify**